THE
PRE-DREADNOUGHT
REVOLUTION

[signature] November 2013

THE
PRE-DREADNOUGHT REVOLUTION

DEVELOPING THE
BULWARKS OF SEA POWER

WARREN BERRY

For Ffion and Seren

Cover illustrations. Front, top: Canopus class pre-Dreadnought *Goliath*. (National Museum of the Royal Navy); *bottom*: The masted turret ship *Neptune* firing her starboard guns whilst in line-ahead formation with other British battleships. (National Museum of the Royal Navy). *Back*: The foredeck of HMS *Queen Elizabeth*. (Author's collection)

First published 2013

The History Press
The Mill, Brimscombe Port
Stroud, Gloucestershire, GL5 2QG
www.thehistorypress.co.uk

© Warren Berry, 2013

The right of Warren Berry to be identified as the Author
of this work has been asserted in accordance with the
Copyright, Designs and Patents Act 1988.

British Library Cataloguing in Publication Data.
A catalogue record for this book is available from the British Library.

ISBN 978 0 7524 5794 9

Typesetting and origination by The History Press
Printed in Great Britain

CONTENTS

ACKNOWLEDGEMENTS

This book is based on a dissertation the author prepared for the award of a Master of Arts degree in naval history at Exeter University in 2002, and much of the textual primary and secondary information used then has been incorporated into this present volume, although in some instances enlarged by further research. The advice and assistance provided by Exeter University staff where that earlier volume is concerned is still fully appreciated, as is the help given by the Librarian and staff of the Naval Library at Portsmouth and the Curator and Curatorial staff of the National Maritime Museum's documents section, together with staff at Bath, Bristol, and Trowbridge reference libraries.

Where all the textual information used in this book is concerned, detailed and specific reference to individual sources has been made in the appropriate section, and a comprehensive bibliography has also been included. In the case of photographic illustrations, most have been used with the kind permission of the Curator of Photographs at the National Museum of the Royal Navy at Portsmouth. The small numbers of photographic images not so owned are from the author's collection.

A number of drawings have been included in the various appendices provided, and these in most instances have been sourced from nineteenth and early twentieth century publications that are long out of print. Very few drawings exactly like these appear to exist in later publications, and because of this it was felt that in celebration of what are in essence illustrations of contemporary engineering design and function, and in deference to their originators, who used them to illustrate certain concepts and aspects they were describing at the time, these drawings could be usefully included in this volume. By so doing it was hoped that readers would be assisted in appreciating more readily some of the descriptive narrative included in the book, and notes and source information for all these drawings are mentioned as appropriate in the section on sources.

Finally my special thanks go to my wife for her ongoing encouragement and practical assistance in a number of areas, including those associated with numerous textual issues and the organisation and presentation of many of the images I have used.

It should be noted also that where copyright might have been unintentionally infringed, the author will be happy to acknowledge associated sources and copyright ownership in future editions of the book.

SAILING SHIPS AND SEA POWER

In 1814, after more than twenty long years, the wars that Great Britain and other European nations had fought, firstly with Revolutionary and then with Napoleonic France, came to an end. Where Britain was concerned its navy had been a major participant in those wars as indeed it had been in the associated war with America that had taken place in 1812, and which had resulted in that country winning its independence. During the French wars the officers and men of Britain's navy had built a reputation for their ability to exert command of the sea when this proved necessary, and to fully protect their island nation from any other naval forces that might be directed against it. This enviable position had for the most part been made possible by the stoutness and sea-keeping ability of the British ships, and by sound seamanship and a tradition of victory based on the navy's disciplined fighting ability using the smooth-bore cast-iron guns that formed the armament of the wooden hulled ships in the nation's sailing battle fleet. The apparently unassailable position that Britain thus found herself in was clearly of advantage militarily but, in addition, the resulting control of many of the world's shipping routes meant that the ability to freely trade with her colonies, as well as other countries, rapidly increased both Britain's wealth and her standing as a world trading power.

At the end of hostilities with France the British battle fleet consisted of some 218 line-of-battle ships and around 560 frigates and smaller vessels.[1] In practice though, some of these ships had either been in continuous commission for a long time or had been hastily built during the war years, and were now in need of major repairs. Irrespective of this Britain's six naval dockyards were unable to provide on-demand refitting and repair facilities to the extent that was required, and big backlogs of such work often occurred. There were numerous reasons for this, including poor accessibility to many of the dockyards from the sea, a lack of suitable dry docks and building slipways, a general shortage of storage and undercover working space, and highly labour intensive work processes that were very traditional and often unresponsive to new ideas and technologies. The effect of this was high costs, and repair work that had to be carried out over an extended period, with the result that only a proportion of the fleet could effectively be kept in service at any one time.

But with the ending of the Napoleonic wars the position rapidly changed, for although warships were still required to control trade routes, counter piracy, hunt down slavers, and protect British interests throughout the world, the need for a large and costly battle fleet in the post-war navy no longer existed. The British economy had been sorely affected by the extended war years, which had resulted in a national debt of around £900 million,[2] and Parliament was soon calling for the adverse affects of this to be countered by savings in public spending. As a consequence the Admiralty agreed to maintain a much-reduced peacetime fleet of 100 ships of the line with 160 smaller vessels being retained for use as cruisers and on other support duties. Such a force it was believed would be adequate in use, and in any case would still be superior to the combined forces of the next two largest naval powers,[3] which at this time were Imperial Russia and post-Napoleonic France, a country which on the ending of hostilities still retained many of the ships of its wartime battle fleet. The unwanted British ships were either scrapped or sold, with a proportion of those retained being mothballed and laid up in 'ordinary' rather than being commissioned on active service. The existence of this reserve meant that for the first thirty years of peace very few new ships were built within the British naval establishment. The effect of these savings on the navy's manpower strength was to drastically reduce it over a period of three years from 145,000 to 19,000,[4] a saving of close on 87 per cent.

Three-decked 100-gun ship of the line *Victory* photographed in her old age, long after her active career had ended, but with her lower masts, topmasts, topgallant masts, and associated yards all in position. Probably taken circa 1920 when she was moored near Gosport in Hampshire. (Author's collection)

The line-of-battle ship of the early nineteenth century and the frigates, brigs, schooners, and other smaller warships that together formed the fleet, had changed little in form, construction, and function from those that configured the British navy of a hundred or more years before, and this was true of the naval forces of every nation in the world irrespective of their size, importance, or economic position. Built of wood with masts and sails for motive power and with their muzzle-loading smooth-bore guns all arranged on the broadside, these ships were of near uniform design across all navies in the western hemisphere. There was, however, some variation in classes, with the larger ships having three gun decks and three square-rigged masts that additionally carried some fore and aft sails, whilst intermediate and smaller sizes were provided with one or two decks of guns and relatively fewer masts depending on the size and type of ship. The very smallest vessels were normally rigged with fore and aft sails only, although some square sails were still carried for use, for example when running before the wind.

Ships were rated according to the number of guns they carried, from the large 100-gun and above first rates like HMS *Victory*, Admiral Nelson's flagship at Trafalgar, through five more classes to the sixth rates of around 20 guns. The biggest size of guns carried were 42-pounders, that is each gun was capable of firing solid shot which individually weighed 42lb.[5] As a result of their great weight and bulk these massive pieces could only be carried on the lower gun decks of the largest ships, and as they were cumbersome and slow to operate, lighter but longer pieces that fired a 32lb shot at a higher muzzle velocity rapidly superseded them as the main armament of line-of-battle ships. In common with all other large guns in use at the time, 32-pounders were each served by up to twelve men who cleaned, loaded (by ramming powder charges and shot down the muzzle), aimed, fired, and controlled the bulky cast-iron pieces on their wood and iron gun carriages or trucks. Although solid round shot was by far the most common projectile used for penetrating a ship's hull, canvas bags of smaller shot known as grape were also used as anti-personnel weapons to clear decks. Double-headed shot consisting of two balls connected by bars or chains were utilised to smash rigging and break masts and spars.

Serving the guns in action was an extremely hazardous and difficult task, especially in the dark, restricted, and claustrophobic space of the lower gun decks of a heaving and rolling sailing warship under battle conditions, where enemy round shot might at any time burst through the near 2ft thick[6] combination of oak planking and frames of the ship's side, flattening all before it and sending a storm of lethal wooden and metal splinters and debris in all directions.

Sailing battle fleets were fought in line ahead, arranged in such a way that ships in the opposing lines sailed close-hauled on opposite tacks with their guns firing on the side nearest their opponents. In this way around half of all the broadside guns could be brought to bear on the opposing ships. Only the largest and most powerful ships were allowed to 'stand in the line', as smaller vessels were unlikely to survive

Quarterdeck of sailing warship (possibly *Victory*) showing three of her starboard side, muzzle-loading cannon on their carriages and with rear trucks in position. It was normal to carry the smallest size of guns on the quarterdeck but those shown in the photograph appear to be larger than that. (Author's collection)

being pounded by an incessant storm of round shot fired at close quarters. This dictum meant that ships with less than 74 guns were precluded from the line and could only act in a support capacity, or else in actions where single or small groups of evenly matched ships opposed each other. Fleet tactics developed over a long period, and although the British sailing battle fleet only fought six decisive battles including Trafalgar in the twenty years of war with France, by the time peace was declared, rigid line-of-battle arrangements had been laid down in Admiralty fighting instructions, and ships' officers were expected to slavishly follow these without showing much in the way of individual initiative,[7] although Nelson and a handful of other commanders appeared to flout such rules on occasion. Whilst tactical 'by the book' control of this type was invariably commonplace in multi-ship actions where the line of battle was used, the captains of frigates and other small ships that often had roving commissions were allowed more individuality, and this was especially the case when such ships were tasked with attacking enemy merchant shipping and engaging any escorts or enemy cruisers that might appear.

In terms of sizes of warships and their associated armaments, there was little to choose between the fleets of Britain and France, although for most of the French wars the British fleet was superior in numbers of ships. By contrast, however, the basic approaches of British and French navies when in action were very different. France often tended to follow a defensive strategy, which involved trying to disable enemy ships by firing at their masts, rigging, and sails, then breaking off action if they felt they could not board the immobilised ship, or were in danger of being overwhelmed themselves. In this fashion French captains sought to preserve their ships in a fighting condition for commerce raiding or for use in further fleet or individual ship actions. The British Navy, on the other hand, took an offensive approach that was highly aggressive and focused on sinking or totally disabling enemy ships by superior gunnery, including heavier broadsides at close quarters, and a more rapid rate of fire. A contemporary French naval historian defined the effect of this approach by noting that it was: 'to this superiority in gunnery that we must attribute most of our defeats since 1793, it is to this hail of cannonballs that England owes her absolute mastery of the seas … they strew our decks with corpses.'[8]

Although not occurring in every case, such winning actions were made possible by forthright, if sometimes brutal, leadership based on strict discipline, superior drilling and training of seamen, and the generally higher motivation and competitive spirit of the British gun crews, who would eventually share in the not insubstantial prize money that could accrue if an enemy ship was taken or sunk. In Britain legislation and associated administrative processes allowed enemy ships to be captured and sold as prizes as soon as hostilities commenced. The prize money received by the capturing ship as a result was divided in certain set proportions such that the captain received half, the officers and warrant officers received 25 per cent and the crew and marines received the remaining 25 per cent divided equally amongst them. An amount for any admiral on station, and the costs of prize courts and prize agents was met from the captain's share, sometimes significantly reducing it. This apart, an active frigate captain, for example, who often had great autonomy when cruising areas that enemy merchant ships frequented, could, over an extended period, amass a small fortune in prize money as a result of such actions. This did not of course apply in the case of individual sailors, as they all shared their proportion of the prize money with hundreds of others, but even in their case it was quite possible to increase annual wages by at least 50 per cent.

Merchant vessels with saleable cargoes when taken as prizes usually attracted more prize money than captured warships, especially if they were significantly damaged. However, the additional income that arose was still welcomed, and even if the enemy warship was sunk, a proportion of prize money was in many cases still paid, and this was based on the number of crew members originally carried by that class of ship. In the main though, warships taken as prizes were taken into the victor's fleet, and when crewed and provisioned were used against their former owners. In this way frigates in particular sometimes changed hands on more than one occasion, and British officers and crews often prized captured French ships for their speed and manoeuvrability. In most instances though this was not due to French ships being better designed and built, but purely to the fact that British warships tended to be heavier and more strongly constructed than their French counterparts, with a sturdier build and heavier scantlings in their hulls. This was because British ships were built for global service and had to be able to stand up to the worst weather and sea conditions and still survive, whereas the generally faster but more lightly built French ships tended to have more limited roles, being mainly used in coastal and Mediterranean waters.

With the ending of the long wars with France, the British people began to look forward to a period of peace and stability. As a consequence of her actions during the war years, Britain already held a pre-eminent position in Europe, and in addition to her superior naval forces had also been able to build up a strong mercantile marine. Using this position as a base, the British Government soon decided that national interests could best be served in the wider context by developing policies of free trade with each and every one of the world's main trading nations. In doing this it was reasoned that Britain's naval superiority was such that clashes of interest brought about by trying to achieve a trading monopoly at the expense of other countries, as had happened in the past, were not now necessary and would, in fact, be counterproductive. Great Britain would, for the foreseeable future, be at peace with all nations willing to trade with her.[9]

The achievement of this so-called period of *Pax Britannica* was not only due to superior naval power wielded with restraint by the self-appointed policeman of the world's sea lanes, but was also the result of Britain's increasing commercial and industrial development. This enabled her to take advantage of the ready markets that existed within a growing British Empire, both for her own goods and services as well as those of her erstwhile rivals. If due to Britain's superior position, naval and maritime power was not currently possible for other nations, the growth of free trade meant that they could at least share the economic benefits that the new arrangements made possible.[10] A further advantage, of course, was that costly and resource-consuming military conflicts could now be more readily avoided, although in practice a number of skirmishes and wars of limited objective did occur in the decades that followed the end of hostilities with France. Some of these involved Britain in both military and diplomatic capacities.

In addition to the occasional military adventure and to their trade related policing role, the ships and men of Britain's sailing navy at this juncture were involved in the suppression of piracy and slave trading on a worldwide basis, as well as occasionally being tasked with charting the oceans and coastlines of the world, and with carrying out expeditions and transporting scientific researchers to polar, and other previously unexplored, regions.

Even though such changes in the navy's role were taking place, the day-to-day life of seamen in the early nineteenth century British Navy was still exceptionally hard, having undergone little improvement over the years, and irrespective of the navy's so-called 'habit of victory'. Harsh discipline, brutal treatment, and poor working and living conditions were still all too common maladies that affected the service and the way it operated. Changing attitudes and expectations within both the officer class and the navy's rank and file, as well as within the Admiralty itself, were taking place, however, and these closely mirrored what was happening within a wider society that the long years of the French wars had significantly altered, and which was ready to take advantage of the opportunities and challenges that a new commercialism, and the fledgling Industrial Revolution, was creating.

Within this environment the need to extend the operational capabilities and range of British warships at sea was increasingly being seen as important by a naval administration that had slowly grown to believe that an ongoing dominance of naval sea power worldwide could best be achieved by ensuring that its seamen, as well as its ships, were better looked after. This policy, it was reasoned, could best be accomplished by making sure that ships' crews were well nourished and healthy, and the Admiralty organisation responsible for the often difficult job of feeding the fleet, initially known as the Victualling Board, was duly tasked with ensuring that this happened.[11] The Victualling Board was in fact generally looked on with derision within the service because of the frequent poor quality of naval provisions, and because of suspected corrupt practices by some of its commissioners and officials. In line with gradually enlightened Admiralty policy, however, the Victualling Board, which in 1832 was merged with the Admiralty Board, did introduce some important innovations and improvements, including the use of canned food.[12] As a consequence, and over an extended period, actions developed in line with such policies together with other improvements, such as better and more hygienic living conditions, curtailing the practice of flogging, and the ending of capital punishment for a whole range of relatively minor offences, improved working and other conditions within the naval service, and became the norm.

The Industrial Revolution had gathered force during the Great Wars with France, and as the nineteenth century progressed it was evident to all that Britain was the world leader where industry, commerce, financial matters, and shipping were concerned. It was also clear that no other power was able to sufficiently develop its industrial and other resources to offer Britain any serious competition. *Pax Britannica* thus represented a position where Britain's largely overwhelming naval forces could utilise worldwide harbour, dockyard, and other support facilities within its large Empire to protect an ever-increasing global trade. Naturally the various locations that constituted the British Empire rapidly became a focus for that trade, and provided essential raw materials and markets for a British economy bolstered by a growing Industrial Revolution, that poured its manufactured and other products into the rest of the world. It was an exceptionally strong framework for national and world power, and one that could remain effective, provided no unbalancing and undermining weaknesses occurred to cause or even threaten an eventual collapse.[13]

However it wasn't only the framework of *Pax Britannica* that enabled Britain to enjoy a period of apparently effortless naval supremacy after 1815, it was also because the governments of other nations made little effort, either individually or collectively, to mount any effective challenge. To a significant extent, therefore, Britain's monopoly position was made even stronger because her rivals were not prepared to spend the time and energy necessary to oppose and counter it.[14] Irrespective of this, worldwide winds of change were starting to blow, and around the middle of the century many European nations, in the light of their own progressive industrialisation and growing economic strength, began to follow Britain's lead and further develop and extend their own iron foundries, factory systems, and mechanical, civil, and marine engineering expertise. As a consequence competition became much stronger, and the period of *Pax Britannica* was gradually brought to an end.[15]

Apart from areas such as hygiene and other gradual shipboard changes, the British Navy, always highly traditional in its outlook and a firm believer in things needing to be tried and tested, especially where its ships were concerned, was at this time having to deal with, and absorb the effects of, fundamental changes in the way its wooden warships were being constructed. The existence of a reserve of ships that had been laid down during the French Wars had tended to curtail new construction work, with most dockyard resources being focused on repairs. Irrespective of this, new warship building was starting to be sanctioned, and a few hulls were being laid down in the dockyards, although there was little funding available to develop new ideas.

Suitable shipbuilding timber was, however, becoming more difficult to obtain, and it was also true that decades of bungling policies and mismanagement of the nation's home-grown timber resources, had more than once meant that a lack of this basic essential had left the dockyards in a condition where a defeat at sea might have led to disaster,[16] since repairs to damaged ships could not have been carried out due to the lack of suitable timber. To place timber supply issues in perspective, it should be noted that apart from the large volume of suitable and correctly seasoned timber that the dockyards required for repair work, over 3,800 fully matured oak trees might well be consumed in the construction of a single large ship of the line.[17] Timber, especially oak, in large quantities, was thus a basic requirement for Great Britain's wooden-hulled sailing navy, and in an attempt to alleviate some of the supply and other problems, Sir Robert Seppings, master shipwright at Chatham dockyard, who in 1813 became Surveyor of the Navy, had started critically reviewing the way ships were being built.[18] This task was far from simple or straightforward, especially in view of the long timeframes, high costs, and traditional, often near sacrosanct, building methods that over many years had evolved within the British dockyard system, and which had sometimes been given a legitimacy that was unwarranted in respect of economy and effectiveness.

But a general inertia and opposition to change, together with a lack of funds, and of course the critical timber supply problems, were not the only difficulties that Seppings faced and hoped to overcome with his reforms, and these revolved around matters associated with ship construction. It had been known for some years that wooden ships consistently involved in wartime blockade and similar duties were not always strong enough to bear the strains they were continually subjected to in heavy seas, and that the timbers in their wooden hulls 'worked', or moved, to such an extent that bows and stern could well droop. This condition was known as hogging, and excessive leaking and significant weakening of the ship's structure might well result unless remedial action was taken. This was a dangerous state for a sailing ship to be in, and leaking in particular had an added adverse effect in that it helped create an environment where both wet and dry rot could occur in and around the ends of frames and other structural timbers, with disastrous consequences if not discovered in time.

The method normally used to overcome such problems was to fit additional wooden or iron knees between beams and side timbers, iron standards on and between decks, and in some cases additional rider timbers in the ship's topsides, between decks, and in way of the hold. Any rotten timber found would be cut out if it could be reached, and new pieces fitted as replacements, using scarf joints. The value of these modifications was nonetheless temporary, as they only served to strengthen the ship's hull until the next time she was subjected to excessively heavy strains,[19] when further damage might well occur, and the whole process would need to be repeated all over again.

Wooden warship hulls were basically constructed by laying massive transverse frames across equally massive keel timbers to which they were fixed, before being topped with further large strengthening timbers, known as keelsons. The frames would then be covered with longitudinal planks inside and out, and strengthened and stiffened with beams, and other timbers. Seppings described the structure so formed as being like a five-bar gate without the diagonal members, as although the resulting hull was very strong there was very little in its structure to stop distortion such as hogging or 'breaking the sheer', as it was also called.[20] Over a period Seppings examined all these problems in detail, and was ultimately able to develop a new system of shipbuilding that included the use of shorter and more readily available timber for hull construction, diagonal bracing between all frames, filling between all the bottom timbers of the hull, and continuous shelf pieces instead of knees. He also redesigned the vulnerable bows and sterns of line-of-battle ships to strengthen them against gunfire.[21]

Further major changes in wooden ship design and construction were introduced some years later after Seppings had resigned, and Sir William Symonds had been appointed Surveyor of the Navy. The principle on which Symonds worked was to move away from the old established rules that dictated that a ship's beam, or width at the water line, should have a fixed relationship with its water-line length, such as for example three beams to the length where a ship with a 30ft beam would have a 90ft length. Instead he attempted to increase a ship's stability by increasing its beam, altering its hull form, and reducing the amount of ballast carried. In practice, however, ships designed in this way tended to roll very heavily, making gunnery difficult and creating rapid wear to the rigging.[22] Although significant, the changes that Symonds introduced were not universally supported, and his ability as a designer was limited by his lack of numeracy. This personal defect, which he was unable or unwilling to try and overcome, together with a total lack of interest in the technological changes that the Industrial Revolution was fast making possible, lost Symonds the confidence of the Admiralty, and in 1847 after much prompting, he tendered his resignation.

Warship design and construction had dramatically changed and improved under the influence of first Seppings and then Symonds, but was also due to the work carried out by the many talented dockyard naval architects and shipwrights who worked with these two men and designed, built, and modified Britain's wooden warships. The wooden warship of this era was much stronger than its predecessors and had been subjected to more change over a short period of tens of years, than had affected earlier ships over many hundreds. Additionally it was now possible to build bigger ships that were capable of carrying more guns of higher calibre, and of accommodating the larger crews that these changes necessitated.

A constant supply of good quality timber, especially oak, was still difficult to find, albeit that supplies were now procured from sources as far afield as Northern Europe and North America. But suitable oak was still difficult to source in the quantities required, so other timber such as pine was tried for building frigates and other smaller vessels. In practice, though, ships that were constructed of pine soon deteriorated in use, although vessels built in India from local teak were much more successful and longer lasting. Irrespective of all this, however, wooden ship construction remained a slow and laborious process, as ships had to be left in frame, sometimes for years, to allow their structural members to season properly.

It was also by this time widely accepted that the limit of wood as a building material had been reached, and that wooden ships that were larger than those that currently existed could not be constructed without creating major and perhaps unsolvable structural problems in the finished vessels. However, fundamental and far reaching change in the way ships would be built, the materials they would be built from, the way they would be powered, and the size and effectiveness of the armament they would carry, were just around the corner. Indeed the changes associated with this had in fact already started, having their roots in the work of Seppings and Symonds, although being far from fully recognised as such at the time, and in any case probably barely understood. This change process, that to those it affected might well have appeared to accelerate on nearly a monthly basis, forms the subject matter of the rest of this book. The reader should note, however, that the text mainly focuses on capital ship development during the nineteenth and early twentieth centuries. Consequently the associated history of cruisers and smaller vessels during the same period is not covered, and is only incidentally referred to as and when it impinges on the development of larger ships in the British battle fleet.

FROM SAIL TO STEAM ASSIST

With the ending of *Pax Britannica*, simmering national rivalries on the continent of Europe had gradually become more intensive as the nineteenth century progressed, and each great power both there and to a lesser extent in the Americas, faced the problem of confronting Britain over issues that had once been associated with prestige, but were now more about national existence. In so doing each national government encountered the problem of how to oppose this, the greatest of naval powers, with the inferior naval forces they commanded. Solutions to this problem could no longer be considered a luxury, for by now they had become a necessity where all Great Britain's potential rivals were concerned, and in the case of France in particular, the effort to find solutions dominated the history of its navy for the remainder of the century.[1]

During the first half of the nineteenth century the changes outlined in the previous chapter had altered the whole nature of the Royal Navy as a fighting force. Pressed to economise whilst at the same time being asked to take on fresh worldwide responsibilities, the Admiralty had no alternative but to repeatedly reduce the strength of a home fleet that had traditionally been seen as the main bastion of Britain's defences,[2] on the waters that surrounded the island nation. The somewhat weakened condition that this policy created for the navy, together with the emergence of other industrial powers and new rivalries in Europe, was seen as a real threat by both the British Government and the naval administration, as well as by numerous individuals within British society. These concerns became even more focused when in 1844 and again in 1852 the sabre-rattling and warship building activities of a resurgent France were viewed as possible precursors to invasion. Other invasion scares were to follow and the increasing nervousness in political and other circles generated a view that the navy was not now strong enough to defend Britain's shores.

France all the while had been providing the most advanced scientific training for both its naval officers and naval constructors, and was doubling its efforts to attain superior technical efficiency in all its naval resources. The French Navy counted modern science as one of its major weapons and under its new ruler, Louis Napoleon, followed what he perceived as being the three principles for successfully countering the Royal Navy, namely: near equity in numbers of warships, superior fighting efficiency, and the bold adoption of every new technical step forward,[3] and this included advancing the new technology of steam propulsion for French ships. On receiving news of these developments, Lord Palmerston, the then British Foreign Secretary, began to cry panic in the parliamentary debates that followed, and the Duke of Wellington, who by then was an MP, and never a great supporter of the navy, added to the scare in 1847, with the pronouncement that 'steam has bridged the English Channel to the detriment of Britain's security'.[4]

Steam engines had been in existence since the eighteenth century and were progressively used to provide power in factories, mills and mines, and for powering early locomotives. It was only in the last two decades of that century, however, that the practicality of using steam engines in river and canal boats was demonstrated, and this appeared to have happened simultaneously in France, Britain, and America.[5] Further development of those early marine engine and boiler arrangements took place in many countries over the next thirty years or so, with a number of private inventors and designers improving the construction and technical efficiency of 'those infernal machines'.

By 1830 Great Britain was starting to use steam power both commercially in its large merchant navy, where it was used in an auxiliary capacity to drive paddle wheels in what were essentially still sailing ships, and in the Royal Navy, where steam engines were installed in a few paddle tugs and other small craft. Mainly used for harbour and dispatch duties, these vessels could scarcely be classed as warships, at least not initially. In the next ten years a further seventy small steam vessels were added to the navy list, all of which had paddle wheels driven by slow-moving side-lever engines, that were based on those used ashore in mills, and as pumping engines in mines and quarries and on numerous canals.

The majority of these ships were provided with basic low-pressure flue boilers that delivered steam at a pressure of 4lb/per sq. in and which were individually built to fit the internal shape of each ship they were fitted in. Few of these vessels carried any significant armament, although two or three 6-pounder guns were sometimes installed. By around 1850 tubular boilers had been introduced, and these dispensed with the long winding flue, necessary to convey heated furnace gasses, that had been a feature of flue boilers. These new boilers were also more compact, so savings in weight and space were possible, and steam pressures could now be increased from 10 to 15lb/sq. in, with resulting increases in efficiency. Space for machinery, or the lack of it, was still an issue in these small wooden-hulled paddle ships, few of which exceeded 1,200 tons in weight, and the side-lever engines were eventually replaced by steam-powered oscillating engines that rotated the paddle wheels directly instead of via the cumbersome side-lever beams.[6]

Wooden-hulled paddle-wheel ships were not at first seen as independent fighting units, although they were often utilised to tow ships of the line in and out of harbour, or to help them move up into the wind, a position where normal sailing was impossible. In Britain funding for new construction was still scarce, although development work had been progressing for some years to produce a paddle warship that was large enough to carry a more effective armament, and take on more onerous duties. Initially this was achieved in 1843 by converting a 43-gun sailing frigate into a paddle steamer. This experiment was successful, although the frigate's broadside guns could not be retained, having been sacrificed to make way for the paddle wheels. In subsequent years other similar conversions followed, all of which involved cutting each ship in half and lengthening it by about 65ft to provide space in the middle for engines and boilers to be housed, and for paddle wheels in their boxes to be installed. The paddle frigates so formed were significantly larger than their predecessors, weighing around 1,600–1,700 tons.[7]

A number of new paddle-wheel frigates and corvettes were built in British dockyards during the following years, and were soon being employed in the normal reconnaissance, general cruising and other 'eyes of the fleet' work of a nineteenth-century ship of this type, that is everything but standing in the line of battle. By 1852, a total of seventy-two of these steam frigates had been built, as well as seventy-seven smaller paddle wheelers for dispatch and harbour work.[8] Those classed as frigates were normally rigged as three-masted barques, whilst the remainder were two-masted, and rigged as brigs, schooners, or sloops. Although rather ungainly, these, what were by now little warships, sailed reasonably well, irrespective of paddle wheels and surrounding structure, a distinct advantage in a vessel where powered propulsion was still considered secondary to that provided by sails.

At this juncture the majority of new-build paddle warships were constructed of wood but with double skins of planking up to 7in thick. Substantial frames were provided and under the Seppings System, wooden and iron diagonal straps were added to strengthen a hull structure that had to carry the weight of engines, boilers auxiliary machinery, and the great wooden-and-iron paddle wheels in their boxes, or sponsons.[9] Wrought iron for use as a constructional material had been around for some years, and its original poor quality was gradually improved as better methods of manufacture evolved, and importantly the technology necessary to roll iron sheets of dimensions suitable for ship construction, were developed. Records indicate though that by 1852 only seventeen iron-hulled paddle warships had been built,[10] possibly reflecting some reluctance on the part of the British Admiralty to heavily invest in metallurgical technologies and products that at that stage were yet to be fully proved.

Paddle warships had their armament arranged on the upper or spar deck, which in fact was the only through deck available. Once their military potential was established, these ships were fitted with four to six 18-pounder guns. Later on the frigate classes were fitted with up to four muzzle-loading smooth-bore 32-pounders on the beam, together with a long 32lb pivot gun that pointed forward, but which could also be used on either quarter.

Nelson class three-decked 120-gun ship of the line *St Vincent* probably during the period when her rig had been reduced and she was acting either as the flagship of the port admiral at Portsmouth, or in the capacity of a training ship at that port. Although at least one of her sister ships was converted to steam, *St Vincent* was not, and in the photograph she is shown being manoeuvred by two paddle tugs, one on either side. Even though she has been cut down, the complexity of her remaining rigging can still be clearly seen. (Author's collection)

Much of the ship's broadside was taken up by paddle wheels and sponsons and this severely limited the number of guns paddle warships could carry. In an attempt to counter this deficiency these vessels were sometimes fitted with large 8in or 10in shell guns[11] that fired spherical thin-walled shells. Each shell was filled with an explosive charge, detonated by way of a fuse that had to be lit before the gun was fired, so that detonation occurred as the shell closed on its target. The success of this action rested in the hands of the gun captain, who had to estimate target range and ensure that the fuse was cut to the right length to enable detonation to take place at the right distance. Due to the presence of large guns, all the standing rigging and sail handling gear, and on-deck coal storage facilities, the main deck of a paddle frigate was limited in terms of space. As all warships of necessity needed to carry launches, cutters, and other small boats, limited deck space could pose a significant problem where convenient storage of these for rapid use was concerned. This was overcome in paddle ships in a novel way by fitting specially constructed box boats that fitted upside down on the top of the paddle boxes that the boats were shaped to fit. These boats were launched as required using davits that had been specially adapted for that use.[12]

In response to the steam factory facilities that France had built in Cherbourg and at certain other of her dockyards, the British Admiralty established a steam factory at Woolwich, which became operational in 1843.[13] Similar establishments were subsequently provided at the other British dockyards. Whilst paddle warships were normally designed and built in the dockyards, the engines, boilers, and associated equipment were developed and built by private contractors that included Maudslay, Penn, Seaward, Rennie, and others. The dockyard steam factories, by comparison, were normally used for maintenance work only.

Having lengths of up to 220ft, paddle frigates, corvettes, and tugs were relatively small and rarely exceeded 1,500 tons in weight, as measured by what was known as builders' measurement or builders' old measurement, both of which were estimates of size based on volume. More accurate measures based on a ship's displacement were eventually introduced instead, and were soon universally utilised in all the world's navies. Although extensively used both in the merchant marine and in the navies of most seagoing nations, paddle-wheel propulsion possessed many practical disadvantages, and these limited its further development. For example, as the coal supply and stores were consumed during a voyage, the ship's draught was altered and the paddle wheels increasingly became less efficient as their working surfaces became higher in the water, creating a marked resistance to the ship's progress. For warships about to engage an enemy, paddle wheels were especially unsuitable, as they were in great danger of being rapidly damaged by shot and shell, as indeed was the paddle shaft and associated machinery. Furthermore the paddle boxes and associated structures interfered with the training and working of the guns to such an extent that the ship's fighting ability was adversely affected.[14]

These aspects, and especially the fact that sufficiently large paddle wheels would take up much of the space normally utilised by broadside guns, made paddle wheels most unsuitable for fitting to the navy's largest capital units, the mighty sailing line-of-battle ship. Consequently no ship of this type was ever built with paddles, the resulting reduction in broadside fire alone being enough to render the idea impossible.[15] In addition to the development and construction work associated with paddle frigates and corvettes, dockyard naval architects had for some years been making efforts to further improve the design and performance of the sailing fleet. However, although experimental vessels were sometimes built to incorporate and test new ideas, the only gains in practice were in the large amount of comparative data from trials that subsequently became available. It was true that the changes instigated by Seppings and Symonds, together with the latter's assistant John Eyde, had enabled

First-class paddle frigate *Terrible* of 1845. At 3,189 tons displacement she was the largest, and because of her massive wooden framing the most strongly built, paddle frigate in the British or indeed any other navy. *Terrible* was relatively heavily armed, with sixteen large calibre broadside guns. (National Museum of the Royal Navy)

cheaper, stronger, and slightly larger wooden broadside battleships to be built, but with the unsuitability of the paddle wheel, and in the absence of any suitable alternative power source, the vagaries of wind and tide still very much dictated the way that sailing battleships were moved and used.

Outside the confines of the British dockyard system, numerous engineers and inventors in Britain, America, France and elsewhere continued to work on alternative forms of water-based propulsion, and during the first part of the nineteenth century, some ninety-eight patents were taken out, or reports prepared in this respect.[16] Usually employing steam as an initial power source, by far the most popular focus of these patents was some form of screw propeller, although in practice very few of the patentees were determined and fortunate enough to turn their dreams into reality.

Where the Royal Navy was concerned it was John Ericsson who first demonstrated a screw propeller invention to the British Board of Admiralty. It was
Francis Pettit Smith, however, who, after showing his own propeller to the Board
during a number of demonstrations carried out over the space of two years, was
in 1840 appointed to consult on the fitting of his design to a prototype naval
screw steamer. Named *Rattler*, this prototype was of 888-tons displacement and
ran her first trials in 1843. Between that date and 1845 *Rattler* was used for an
extensive series of experiments in which screw propellers of various forms were
tested in different conditions of sea and wind. So satisfactory were these experiments that the Admiralty ordered twenty vessels to be fitted with one form of
Pettit Smith's screw, with the inventor himself being employed to superintend the
process. In all cases the screw propellers used were double threaded and set in the
deadwood of each host ship.[17]

Although there were still dissenters, including Symonds, who at that time still
held the post of Surveyor to the Navy, the acceptance that steam propulsion as
well as iron for hull construction was the way forward, was rapidly gaining pace.
It was gaining pace so much that eventually Symonds was forced to retire and in
1847 was replaced by a naval officer, Captain Baldwin Walker. However, Walker,
who would later be knighted and become an admiral, was not a ship designer
and focused his strong managerial talents on organising the work of his department and overseeing that of the dockyards, assuming the title of Controller rather
than Surveyor, whilst the department's Chief Constructor, Isaac Watts, was made
responsible for ship design, and the more recently established engineering function became the responsibility of the then Chief Engineer Thomas Lloyd.[18]

Whilst steam power in frigates, corvettes, and smaller vessels had been an
accepted part of the British Navy since 1830, its impact on the main battle fleet
was limited, and as paddle wheel propulsion was clearly not suitable, little thought
had generally been given to its inclusion in line-of-battle ships. It was true that
as a consequence of opportunities offered by screw propellers a few 74-gun ships
had been provided in their old age with steam engines to facilitate movement
in their capacity as floating batteries or block ships for harbour protection, and
a policy decision had been more latterly made to fit steam engines and screws
to all new-build ships that were smaller than fourth rates of 40 guns or less, but
in general the pace of steam-related development had been extremely hesitant
where ships of the line were concerned. Some associated development work had
however been carried out by John Eyde, the Assistant Surveyor under Symonds,
who, before he also retired in 1850, had begun the design of a line-of-battle ship
intended from the start to have a steam engine and screw fitted.[19]

This ship was never built, but in 1849 initial work started on the construction
of a screw line-of-battle ship to be named *Agamemnon*, that was based on Eyde's
design. Construction of this vessel was slow to start with, but when it was discov-

ered that the French fleet, that at the time consisted of some 105 paddle steamers in addition to 276 sailing vessels of all types,[20] was to have an addition by way of a newly constructed screw line-of-battle ship, things rapidly changed. Displacing 5,120 tons and carrying 80 guns, the new French vessel, *Le Napoleon*, had been designed by one of France's greatest naval architects, Dupuy de Lome,[21] and by 1850 construction was well advanced. Not wishing the French to move ahead in what was starting to become a serious arms race, the British Board of Admiralty put in place arrangements to speed up the construction of *Agamemnon*, which at 5,080-tons displacement was slightly smaller than *Le Napoleon*, but which carried more broadside guns.[22] In the event the British ship was completed only a matter of months behind that of the French one, but for some reason was not launched for another two years.[23]

Now that the die had been cast, the next few years witnessed a steady programme of screw steam ship building and the conversion of existing sailing ships to steam. This now included the great wooden ships of the line, which in addition to their three towering masts now also had tall narrow funnels to contend with. Although generally a quicker option, conversion work was not considered by Baldwin Walker to be the best way forward, and he advocated, and was mostly able to instigate, the building of an all-new steam battle fleet to counter the sudden progress in warship construction that had gripped the French Navy.

Although other manufacturers were sometimes used, the steam engines favoured by the British Admiralty for fitting to line-of-battle ships were trunk engines manufactured by John Penn, or by Maudslay, Sons and Field, at their Thames-based engineering works. These powerful engines were direct acting, with two cylinders arranged horizontally,[24] so that they could be placed safely below the water line, and thus be less liable to damage from shot and shell when ships were in action. In association with this it was soon realised that an added advantage of having large horizontal engines and boiler plant and auxiliaries situated low down in the hull, was that stability would also be increased, enabling such ships to carry heavier armament on the upper decks.[25]

Although most line-of-battle ships in the British fleet were eventually fitted with steam engines and screws, the widely held view still continued to pervade the service that steam was of secondary importance to sail, especially when passage making or travelling in fleet formation. This view, which would take many years to alter, was perhaps understandable at the time, not only because of the relatively high cost of coal and the difficulties often experienced in obtaining adequate supplies of that fuel in foreign ports, but also because of the somewhat unreliable nature of early marine boilers and engines, that could only be nurtured and coaxed to continue working by engineers whose role and skills were little understood by seamen officers. For the latter engineering was a singularly black art, while the vast intricacies of masts, spars, sails and rigging were second nature.

Three-decked 131-gun, steam line-of-battle ship *Duke of Wellington* of 1852. Originally intended as a 120-gun sailing ship of the line to be named *Windsor Castle*, she was converted to a steamer whilst still on the stocks at Pembroke dockyard, using the engine from an iron frigate. (National Museum of the Royal Navy)

Two-decked 86-gun steam line-of-battle ship *Royal George*, converted from a three-decked Caledonia class ship of 1827 without lengthening her. Her rather wide funnel can be clearly seen, and during conversion the foremast would have been moved towards the bows to make room for the funnel. (National Museum of the Royal Navy)

The apparently unreliable nature of early steam installation in ships was not necessarily due to poor manufacture of machinery, but rather the result of fitting engines, boilers, and pipe work that required a static environment to fully work efficiently, into wooden hulls that were prone to moving and flexing under the influence of the sea. It was nonetheless generally agreed that steam engines and screw propellers had an important part to play during manoeuvring, and when winds were fickle or blowing from the wrong direction for direct sailing.

To further facilitate voyaging under sail, screw propellers, which were thought to create drag and adversely affect sailing performance, were often located in a frame, which, when the propeller drive shaft was uncoupled and withdrawn, could be lifted vertically into a cavity positioned above the ship's water line.[26] Funnels that created windage, and by necessity were often inconveniently placed and got in the way when sails were being handled, could also be collapsed when not in use, and as these operations were possible when a ship was under way, a new order of 'down funnel up screw' became part of shipboard vocabulary.

British advances in metallurgy, and in casting and boring muzzle-loading cannon, meant that these guns were generally superior to those manufactured in other countries. By 1850 the artillery used in screw line-of-battle ships had been standardised, and a typical 91-gun three-decked vessel, for example, would carry 34 8in-shell guns on the lower deck, thirty-six 32-pounders on the main or middle deck, and twenty 32-pounders on the upper deck, all of which were loaded via the muzzle. In addition a large 68-pounder swivel gun might well be installed in what were by now much stronger ship's bows,[27] where it was used as a chase gun. Initially there was considerable opposition to the use of shells at sea due to a perceived risk of premature explosion, either accidentally or as the result of enemy fire. With experience and the introduction of improved magazine storage, as well as better training in handling and supply of charges, these fears were gradually allayed. Improvements in the way guns were sighted and ranges calculated were also introduced during this period, and percussion locks replaced flintlock-firing mechanisms. Finally gun carriages were modified to ease the task of aiming or training the guns.[28]

But on the continent of Europe war clouds were gathering, and in the winter of 1853 Turkey declared war on Russia, heralding the start of the Crimean War. For some years Russia had been trying to establish for herself a free access to the Mediterranean Sea, and the declining condition of the Turkish Ottoman Empire seemed to offer an opportunity. Using religious persecution of ethnic minorities under Turkish rule as an excuse, Russia sent Turkey an ultimatum and subsequently invaded Moldavia, forcing Turkey to in turn declare war on Russia. At the time, and mainly by virtue of their battle fleets, Britain and France were the strongest European military powers, and as neither wanted to see the Russian empire extend to the Mediterranean, they both offered support to Turkey. French naval expansion in pursuit of their aims to surpass Britain as the primary sea power had already created great anxiety, and the recent agreement by France's legislative assembly to make its then ruler Louis Napoleon an Emperor, set even more alarm bells ringing across the Channel. It was thus highly ironic that less than a year-and-a-half later the two lifelong enemies and totally mistrusting neighbours would, in allegiance with Turkey, be at war with Imperial Russia.[29]

At first much diplomatic wrangling between the Allies and Russia took place, but firm military action was finally initiated, and the battle fleets of both Britain and France, together with transports carrying their respective land-based forces, eventually sailed for the Crimea. Excluding troop transports, the combined British and French fleets consisted of 131 line-of-battle ships, most of which were screw driven, and 160 paddle and sailing frigates and corvettes. The Russian fleet, although the third largest at the time, was significantly smaller than that of the Allies, with forty-three line-of-battle ships and forty-eight frigates, few of which were powered by steam.[30] Turkey also had a small fleet, but this was totally destroyed during the second month of hostilities, when a Turkish force of some twelve frigates and smaller ships that were lying at Sinope, was surprised by a Russian squadron of six ships of the line and four frigates that entered the harbour and engaged them. The Turkish ships were completely outgunned and were soon destroyed, providing a very practical demonstration of the power of heavy shell guns against wooden ships that were not so armed,[31] and which, because of their wooden construction, were susceptible to the fires that exploding shells would invariably create.

The Crimean War was essentially a land-based conflict with most of the fighting carried out between the armies of the belligerents, and apart from Sinope no significant fleet actions took place. During hostilities smaller naval actions did though occur both in the Baltic and the Black Sea, and many of these involved blockade and attacks on coastal towns, villages, and shipping, as well as massed firing on forts and other such defensive strongpoints. In 1855 the focus of the naval war shifted to the Sea of Azov and numerous actions took place there including a blockade and an allied combined forces attack on the city and fortress of Sevastopol. In this action the Russian Black Sea fleet that was moored in Sevastopol harbour, together with the city's naval dockyard, was destroyed.

Most Russian coastal forts, of which there were many, had large shell guns installed as their main armament. After Sinope the French in particular hesitated to use their wooden ships of the line against shore fortifications that were thus defended, and started to consider what other means could be employed to more safely reduce fortifications that used shell-firing guns. Ordinary bomb vessels, which carried one or two large calibre mortars, were found in practice not to be suitable for such work, so plans were made to construct light-draft floating batteries carrying a number of heavy guns and armoured sufficiently to protect them against enemy shellfire. Iron armour was a new concept at the time but it was felt that batteries of around 36m in length and 13.4m beam could support armour made up of empty shell cases, a foot thick. Tests subsequently showed that 4in-thick solid iron sheets fixed to wooden backing was far superior to shell cases,[32] and could be more readily constructed.

Ten of these batteries that were to be fitted with boilers and steam engines driving a single screw were ordered, but as the existing French iron works were not capable of producing such a large order for iron armour plates in the short time available, Britain was asked to build five of the batteries. By the close of 1855 all ten had been completed and were eventually towed from France and Britain to the Crimean theatre of operations. The finished French floating batteries, which were larger than initially planned, displaced 1,575 tons and were around 51m long and 13m wide. Each carried sixteen, 50-pounder guns, and a crew of 280. Wrought-iron armour, 4in thick, covered their wooden framed topsides and extended below the water line. The British batteries were slightly larger and their armament consisted of fourteen massive 68-pounder guns, with wrought-iron armour, 4in thick, secured to thick wooden backing that in turn was fixed to the batteries' wooden topside frames.[33]

After the fall of Sevastopol an allied naval force that included some of the floating batteries sailed to Kinburn, a formidable fort to the west of Sevastopol. On arriving at Kinburn the batteries were anchored and began their bombardment, pouring some 3,000 rounds into the fort and reducing it to rubble in a matter of hours. Although also hit on a number of occasions by shellfire from the fort, the batteries suffered little damage, with the Russian shells being deflected or caused to harmlessly explode when striking the armour plating.

Both British and French floating batteries continued to be used in the Black Sea and also in the Baltic campaign of the following year, and indeed right up to Russia's surrender in 1856, repeatedly proving the defensive power of armour against heavy guns. The war produced no significant naval actions involving British or French ships, either between fleets or single combatants, but naval power had been exercised, and steam propulsion and the defensive advantages of armour plating had for the first time shown how industrial technology could prove decisive in a military conflict.[34]

The Crimean War had brought together the navies of France and Britain as allies, but after the war, rivalry between these two nations was soon resumed as the British became increasingly aware of the hostility towards them that existed in France,[35] and this was reflected in the numerous anti-British statements that appeared in the French press and in pamphlets and papers then in circulation. As a consequence invasion scares continued, although never materialising in practice, and the two rivals were soon again focusing on developing their naval material, with each nation planning to outsmart the other. Ongoing advances in marine steam engineering and in naval ordnance gave a new edge to the fast accelerating arms race that ensued, and importantly the increased potential of iron, both as a construction material and a means of protecting vessels from shellfire, was now clearly evident, and would play a significant role in the next stages of development, that of the seagoing ironclad warship.

THE BLACK BATTLE FLEET

In a somewhat nostalgic description written some years after the event, one contemporary author who would be very much involved in later developments in naval architecture, noted that: 'the introduction of the screw propeller in 1844 made a magnificent navy obsolete, and the realisation of the terrible effects of shellfire in 1854 again rendered the grand screw line-of-battle ships and sailing frigates things of the past.'[1] Whilst to some extent true, these statements were also backward looking, and the events to which they referred were in reality the basis for the next series of changes that were even more positive, fundamental, and far-reaching in their effects.

The success of the Crimean armoured batteries, and the necessity to protect warships against shellfire soon brought about an active interest in both France and Great Britain, and after the war was over, and extensive tests using different types of armour plates and backing material were carried out, French naval architect Dupuy de Lome was tasked with designing the first seagoing armoured battleship. This ship, *Le Gloire*, was launched in 1859, and as the French Government believed that by building sufficient steam-driven armour-clad warships their navy might achieve equality in sea power with that of Britain, three identical sister ships were also laid down.[2]

Constructed of wood *Le Gloire* was a three-masted vessel displacing 5,617 tons and her design was based on successful French two-decked line-of-battle ships, although in *Le Gloire's* case only one gun deck was provided. By reducing both the number of gun decks and the guns that would otherwise have been carried, Dupuy de Lome hoped to significantly reduce the weight of the ship's topsides, thus allowing armour plating to be fitted with no significant increase in displacement. *Le Gloire's* steam engine developed some 900 horsepower, and it was intended that her reduced barquentine rig would serve in a secondary capacity only, with her engine providing the main motive power.[3] The ship's armament was based on a single gun deck and consisted of 6.4in rifled muzzle-loading guns of which there were thirty-six, all arranged on the broadside. These muzzle-loading rifled guns proved very ineffectual in use, however, and they were all later changed for breech-loaders. In practice these replacement guns, the design of which was still very much at an early stage of development, proved to be equally ineffective, reflecting the inadequate heavy gun founding and machining facilities that existed in France at the time, and the lack of real knowledge of breech loading concepts.

Le Gloire's armour consisted of 4.3in-thick wrought-iron plates fixed with screws rather than bolts to 26in of wooden backing, and arranged in a belt that extended horizontally for the whole of the ship's length and vertically from 6.5ft below the water line to the upper deck, which was also lightly armoured. Given the limited power of naval ordnance that existed at the time Le Gloire was adequately protected above the water line, but although armour plated, the hulls of both Le Gloire and her later consorts were still constructed of timber, and were thus as vulnerable below the armour belt as those of any of the screw line-of-battle ships.[4]

During this period separate developments were taking place in America that would result in the Civil War clash of ironclad warships at the Battle of Hampton Roads. Ships of this type would continue to be used by both Union and Confederate navies up to the end of that conflict and beyond, however in all cases these vessels were low freeboard river monitors that, due to their shape and form, were incapable of being effectively used on coastal waters, let alone in ocean conditions. Le Gloire was thus the first seagoing ironclad to be completed by any nation. At first the British Admiralty, although curious about the French developments,[5] was inclined to consider the construction of Le Gloire as a costly and futile experiment, and a general view was held in Britain, and indeed by many French naval officers, that ships burdened with great weights of iron armour would prove both unstable and difficult to manoeuvre at sea. As a consequence Britain at that time tended to concentrate on steam line-of-battle ship conversions, and on building screw steamers of improved form and speed that had unarmoured wooden or steel hulls.

All the early French ironclads had hulls constructed of wood, although right from the start Dupuy de Lome had repeatedly argued for iron hull construction. However, higher construction costs, concerns about iron as a building material, and the current poor state of the French iron industry when compared with that of Great Britain for example, had meant that wooden hull construction was the option preferred by the French naval authorities. This position was to eventually change as more effective methods of iron working were introduced and the skills of iron workers improved, and in late 1860 a programme of building iron-hulled armour-clad ships was commenced in France, although in reality this took a long time to progress in any meaningful way.[6]

Long before Le Gloire and her sister ships were completed though, British opinion took a marked shift in favour of ironclads, and in the spring of 1859 the Admiralty ordered the construction of the first British warship of this type, which was to be named Warrior. This alteration in policy likely resulted from a change in government before the end of that year, with a correspondingly greater political will to counter the French lead in ironclad construction. As a consequence a further warship named *Black Prince*, together with two smaller ironclads, was also ordered, and thus after many delays, the ironclad reconstruction of the British Navy began.

Built with iron frames and plating rather than wooden frames and planking, as was the case with early French ironclads, both *Warrior* and *Black Prince* had three masts, all of which carried square sails, and each ship displaced just over 9,137, and 9,250 tons respectively. Designed on Baldwin Walker's instructions by Chief Constructor Isaac Watts in conjunction with John Scott Russell, builder of Brunel's *Great Eastern*, these two ironclads had single gun decks and their high length to beam ratio of 6.5:1, made possible by their iron hull construction, and meant that they were classed as frigates rather than battleships. Irrespective of this, at the time of their completion they were the most powerful warships ever built,[7] vastly surpassing any of the French ironclads then built or building.

Both the early French and British ironclads had what were known as broadside gun batteries, the guns being positioned along the broadside in a similar way to those of a wooden line-of-battle ship. In the case of *Warrior* and *Black Prince*, these batteries were protected by wrought-iron armour plates 4.5in thick that were arranged along the ship's sides, extended some way below the water line, and were mounted on 18in-thick teak backing. From tests carried out before and after construction, this combination of armour and backing was found to be sufficiently strong to resist not only all sizes of contemporary explosive shell, but also all types of round shot, even when these were fired at close range. In fact these ships were described at the time as being shot-proof frigates.[8]

Great Britain's very first ironclad frigate *Warrior* of 1860 with her 40 broadside guns, shown moored in front of a 74-gun ship of the line. *Warrior*, built at Blackwall, was constructed of iron as well as carrying iron armour, and marked a clean break with the traditions of wooden warship construction. (National Museum of the Royal Navy)

In the distribution of armour there was a marked difference between French and British vessels. *Warrior* and *Black Prince* had armoured belts that extended for the length of the battery only, leaving their ends unprotected, whilst *Le Gloire* and her consorts were fully protected from stem to stern.[9] This apparent discrepancy was due to the fact that at the time British designers considered it undesirable to load any warship's ends with heavy weights, although in France this was not considered to be too much of a problem. The safety of both *Warrior* and *Black Prince* were to some extent improved, however, by fitting a watertight flat below the water line, and watertight compartments below the machinery space. The lack of protection over and around the steering gear was nonetheless a major fault with the design of these ships.[10]

The designed armament for the Warrior class of ironclad was thirty-eight massive 8in 68lb smooth-bore muzzle-loading cannon on the main deck, some of the largest such guns ever made, and two pivot guns of the same calibre in the bows. Although some improvements to gun carriages and firing arrangements had been introduced over the years, and more recently large guns had metal hoops shrunk on to strengthen them, these weapons were still in effect merely huge blocks of roughly formed iron. Guns of this type though were considered quite adequate at the time, and a single calibre armament was always thought desirable as battery operations, including supply from magazines, could be simplified as a result.[11] But like France, Great Britain had been developing a new generation of guns that it was claimed could be more conveniently loaded using a breech arrangement. These weapons were also rifled, that is spiral grooves were machined into the inner surfaces of the barrels in such a way that protrusions, or soft metal coatings on the projectile, were forced into the rifling grooves as it was fired. This arrangement tended to impart a spin to the projectile as it left the gun's muzzle, which in turn improved accuracy.

During the period when *Warrior* and *Black Prince* were being built, the influential Select Committee on Rifled Cannon, set up by the government to consider submissions from inventors and manufacturers of prototype, rifled and breech-loading ordnance, carried out a series of trials. During the trials they compared the relative accuracy of rifled breech-loading and smooth-bore muzzle-loading guns in use, and found that the breech-loading rifled ordnance constructed from wrought-iron coils, and submitted by the Tyne based shipbuilding and ordnance company of Armstrong's of Elswick, at a range of around 1,000 yards was capable of placing every projectile fired into a rectangular target of about 23 yards long by 1 yard wide. Conversely with a smooth-bored muzzle-loading gun fired under the same conditions, the rectangle was about 145 yards long and 10 yards broad. As a consequence the committee unanimously recommended that the breech-loading rifled ordnance provided by Armstrong's should be adopted for use in the British Navy.[12]

Armstrong breech-loading rifled gun of the sort installed in *Warrior* and many other contemporary warships before the larger sizes were withdrawn from service due to problems with the breech mechanism. The gun shown is of the smaller 7in calibre size, a number of which were retained in use at the time. (National Museum of the Royal Navy)

Following this recommendation each of the two new ironclads were provided with rifled breech-loaders, but only to the extent that ten 110lb, 7in, and four 70lb guns of this type were substituted for muzzle-loaders, of which there still remained twenty-six 68lb cannon. In use, however, and to the great surprise of all concerned, it was soon realised that the new breech-loading guns were in fact far inferior to those they had replaced. The breech mechanism was found to be so badly designed that firing could occur before the breech was fully closed, a problem that in fact resulted in a number of serious accidents.[13] Additionally the lead-covered shells rapidly fouled the rifling, and, although accurate, proved to be incapable of piercing armoured targets during exercises. As a consequence an embarrassed Select Committee ordered that no more 110-pounders be placed aboard any other ships, although in practice some ironclads that had been laid down or built after those of the Warrior class did in fact have Armstrong breech loaders installed, albeit in the smaller and less problematic sizes.[14] Both *Warrior* and *Black Prince* were later re-armed and although these replacement guns were rifled, the breech-loading mechanisms, which to be fair were still very much in their infancy, were not utilised, the guns being loaded via their muzzles in the more traditional way.

At the point that these ironclads entered service, the British Navy included 599 steam-powered warships in its establishment. Some of these were screw line-of-battle ships, and some were paddle-wheeled frigates, corvettes, and smaller vessels.[15] All of these warships carried masts and sails, as engines were still considered to be secondary to sail power. At this stage in 1860 there were three main marine engine manufacturers that supplied the navy, Messrs Maudslay, Humphrys, and Penn, and both *Warrior* and *Black Prince* were fitted with Penn's single expansion, twin-cylinder trunk engines that at the time were the most powerful steam engines available. In line with general trends the boilers were of the box tubular type working at a steam pressure of 20lb/sq. in. This pressure was quite high for the time, as boiler development hadn't really kept pace with that of engines, and in the transitional period from paddle to screw propulsion, with its growing awareness of the need for greater efficiency in the generation of steam, there had been cases when new steam line-of-battle ships had had their original boilers and engines replaced soon after commissioning.[16]

In the two years from 1859 to 1861 the ironclad commenced to supplant the wooden and unarmoured capital ships in not only Great Britain and France, but also in the navies of other European naval powers such as Imperial Russia. After the Warrior class, four smaller ironclad frigates similar to *Warrior* and *Black Prince* were built in Britain, and, as in the larger vessels, the armour of these smaller ironclads did not extend along the whole water-line length. The main objective of the ironclad designers at the time was to protect the broadside gun battery, the gun crews, and the engines, boilers, and ancillary machinery. Whilst the idea of more adequately preserving buoyancy and stability and protecting the steering gear by armouring the ship's ends including bow and stern, was very much a secondary, and perhaps little understood, consideration.

Such reasoning reflected the need for cost savings, the requirement to keep displacement low, and a perception that, as was the case with wooden ships, temporary repairs could easily be made, and that bow and stern would still remain buoyant even when holed. It was soon realised, however, that ships constructed of iron behaved very differently to their wooden counterparts, in that shot holes in steel vessels were more difficult to repair in action, and might for example cause a significant change in a ship's trim from the ingress of water. Additionally, and probably more seriously, if the steering gear was damaged, the ship might well become unmanageable and easy prey for an attacker.[17]

As a consequence it was decided to give the *Achilles* of 1863 a complete belt of armour along the water line as well as around the battery. This increased both the draught and weight of this ironclad, which on completion displaced 9,829 tons, some 700 tons heavier than *Warrior* on a similar length between perpendiculars. Completed with four masts, the only British warship to be so rigged, *Achilles* had square sails on each mast, that in total presented the largest sail area ever to be provided in a British warship. *Achilles* was also the only such warship to carry four masts that were all rigged with square sails and as this proved unsatisfactory in use, alterations were made on a number of occasions. Eventually it was found that a four-masted barque rig suited her best.[18]

Although initially provided with breech-loaders, *Achilles* was, like *Warrior* and *Black Prince*, later fitted with muzzle-loading rifled guns. Unlike her predecessors, however, she was also built with a ram bow, an arrangement that after the Warrior class, was provided for all capital warships in the British and indeed many other navies, up to the middle of the twentieth century. It should be noted that the concept and effectiveness of the ram as a weapon is fully dealt with in the next chapter, so it is sufficient to say here that it was the combination of metal construction of ships and steam engine propulsion, that made the ram, which had been the main weapon in ancient oar-powered galley warfare, but which due to lower speeds and fickle winds could not be used under sail, an apparently feasible weapon once more.

The first iron-hulled ship to be built in a Royal Dockyard, *Achilles*, a belt-and-battery ship, carried 26 guns arranged on the broadside and originally had four masts, the first British warship to do so since the seventeenth century. Her masts were reduced to three in 1865, all of which were square rigged. (National Museum of the Royal Navy)

Achilles was the first of what was to be known as a 'belt and battery' ship, and all the ironclad frigates that followed had armour arranged in a similar fashion. By 1862 a good start had been made in constructing warships of iron, but the British fleet still contained a number of wooden ships either built or building, and for reasons of cost, and parity with France in particular, a decision was made to convert a number of these vessels, some of which had been laid down as 91-gun line-of-battle ships, into ironclads. This pleased the diehards in the service, as concerns still existed in some quarters about the suitability of iron for constructing ships' hulls. These concerns continued to revolve around problems of durability, higher costs set against possible obsolescence in a period of rapid change, an absence of consistently high quality iron, and the possibility of damage to bottom plates that in the absence of any anti-fouling arrangements soon became covered in marine growth, that in turn affected a ship's speed and manoeuvrability.[19] Wooden ships of course could have their bottoms covered in copper, which to some extent discouraged marine growth, but this was not feasible in an iron ship, as chemical reaction between iron, copper, and salt water tended to corrode the iron plates. When iron gave way to steel as a building material, however, this adverse chemical reaction did not occur and it again became possible for the protective properties of copper plates to be used.

Nine converted wooden ironclad ships of this type eventually entered service, and although most had 4.5in armour, two were further provided with armour that was nearly 6in thick. A number of additional iron-hulled, ironclad, frigates of the belt and battery type were also constructed during the period, the largest of these being the three ships of the Minotaur class, launched between 1863 and 1866. These three ironclads were each around 20ft longer than *Warrior* and *Black Prince*, and *Minotaur*, the named ship of the class, displaced 10,690 tons, *Agincourt* 10,600 tons, and *Northumberland*, the largest of the class, 10,784 tons. Thickness of armour on these three ships was increased to 5.5in amidships, tapering to 4.5in at the ends. Backing in all cases was 10in of solid teak fixed to their iron hulls. The armament of all three ships consisted of muzzle-loading rifled guns of various calibres, the largest of which were 9in, and with weights that ranged from 12.5 to 6.5 tons, these guns were truly massive. Although the ships were originally designed to carry fifty guns including breech-loaders, numbers were reduced during construction, and as a result *Minotaur* and *Northumberland* both carried twenty-six guns on commission, and *Agincourt*, twenty-eight. As was normal in the naval service, further changes were occasionally made to update this armament as time progressed.[20]

These three ironclads were the largest such ships to be built that were driven by a single screw, and in reality warships had now reached a size where twin screws would have been more appropriate. As in other ironclads of their type, two cylinder Penn trunk engines were installed, the absence of a conventional piston rod in this type of engine making a short horizontal engine well suited for the limited space available in the engine and shaft space of a single-screw ship. Ten rectangular boilers were utilised in each ironclad, and steam pressure increased to 25lb/sq. in. With this level of pressure trunk engines worked well, but difficulties with the trunks would become evident in future warships, when technical advances enabled higher steam pressures to be generated, ultimately leading to the navy's abandonment of the trunk engine type.[21]

The Minotaur class were the only British warships ever to be rigged with five masts, but with square sails on the first four masts and a spanker on the fifth, they were extremely poor sailors and were said to be virtually unmanageable under all plain sail. It was also said of them that no ship ever carried so much dress to so little purpose.[22] Over the years numerous adjustments to the rig were made, all to no avail, as these vessels remained poor sailors; they were though generally considered to be good sea boats and excellent gun platforms. Their appearance with five masts did though puzzle some seafarers, and one contemporary author noted that on one occasion a merchant ship, when approaching one of the Minotaur class at night, was fooled by the ironclad's great length and five masts into thinking that two ships were moored in line, one behind the other, and that their vessel could pass between. Apparently they realised their mistake in time, so that a collision was avoided.[23]

The name ship of the class, *Minotaur* was a broadside ironclad armed with thirty-six guns and carried five masts, the only British warship to be so rigged, and although some are partly obscured by funnel smoke, these can be clearly seen. (National Museum of the Royal Navy)

Agincourt was the smallest ship of the Minotaur class and is shown here with her rig reduced to three masts. Eventually ending up as a training ship, then as a coal hulk, before being scrapped, *Agincourt*'s pronounced ram bow can be clearly seen. (National Museum of the Royal Navy)

In 1868 when the last of the pure broadside ironclads entered service, the British Navy had an establishment of nineteen such ships and France had fifteen. The French ships had all steadily developed from *Le Gloire*, with many still having their armour fitted to wooden hulls. Few of these ships had any significant technical differences, except that two of them, *Solferino* and *Magenta*, had their broadside armament arranged on two decks.[24] Although approaching Great Britain's lead in numbers of ironclads, the French vessels were at this stage no match for those of the British fleet.

Although numerous tests and trials were carried out before and during construction of ironclads, the ability of armour to withstand shot, and of shot to penetrate armour, remained unproven in battle. In 1866, however, ironclad ships of the opposing Austrian and Italian navies were tested in action at the Battle of Lissa, where armour on the ships of both powers, many of which had been built in British shipyards, performed well against shellfire from heavy guns. Although damage to the ships of both forces was extensive, this only occurred in relation to unprotected parts of the damaged ships, where fires were a major problem, and where steering gear and other machinery suffered.

Some years before this action Baldwin Walker, who by then had been made Rear Admiral, had left the Constructors department to become Commander in Chief of the West Coast of Africa Squadron, and Isaac Watts had retired. The new Controller appointed in Walker's place was Admiral Spencer Robinson, an able and astute manager, once described as an iron-willed administrator for an ironclad age,[25] and Edward Reed was appointed as Chief Constructor in place of Isaac Watts. Reed was to enjoy a meteoric and turbulent rise to fame, but some years later in 1870, he was to resign his position over matters of policy, and as a result of conflict between himself and Hugh Childers, the then First Civil Lord of the Admiralty.[26] Reed later became a great critic of both the Admiralty and many aspects of the naval architecture of the day. During his period in office though, he appears to have been the first man to conceive of the ironclad as a separate and distinct entity. Previously to Reed having developed his ideas, the ironclad was viewed as merely being an ordinary steamer with some armour plating attached to her sides.[27]

The ironclad frigate type depended on their long thin hulls for speed, and under the power of sails this made sense, as a mathematical relationship has always existed between speed and water-line length where sailing vessels are concerned. Under engine power, however, this relationship tends to break down, and Reed appreciating this fact, believed that shorter, broader ironclads by a moderate addition to engine power, which technical advances were rapidly making feasible, could be driven just as fast as the longer vessels, and that in handiness and turning power under both steam and sail they would be superior.[28] In addition such ships were cheaper to build, and were capable of carrying the heaviest armour without undue increases in displacement, which at the time was always kept below 10,000 tons. Space constraints of course meant that smaller ships would have to carry fewer guns, but ordnance power was progressively growing in order to overcome the increased resistance of armour, and the combined power of even a small number of large rifled guns, especially if they were grouped together in a central battery or citadel, would still make short broad ironclads of this type impressive and efficient weapons of war.

Edward Reed was an inspired and creative designer and he developed and introduced both the central battery and then the breastwork monitor type of warship.[29] This latter form is fully described in the next chapter. Although responsible for the design of a number of ships prior to becoming Chief Constructor, Reed's first successful ironclad was the *Bellerophon*, a ship that heralded a new form of cellular construction on which the double bottoms in modern ships are still based. With a displacement of 7,500 tons *Bellerophon* was in fact a shortened version of the *Achilles* type and carried a similar rig.

Launched in 1865, *Bellerophon* was given a 6in-thick water line belt of wrought-iron armour that was carried up to form a central rectangular armoured box battery that included armoured bulkheads at its front and back. This so-called citadel, or casemate, was just large enough to hold ten 9in, 12-ton rifled muzzle-loading guns, and a few guns of this type were additionally placed in the ship's bow and stern, behind armoured screens. Although often debated, this latter arrangement constituted the first instance of protected guns for end-on fire being installed in a British warship. The *Bellerophon* was also the first Royal Navy ship to have a balanced rudder incorporated in its design. This was an important improvement because steering was at this juncture normally carried out by hand power alone, and a balanced rudder made this operation much simpler and less labour intensive. Previous ironclad warships had very unsatisfactory steering qualities and in the *Minotaur*, for example, as many as seventy-eight men were employed at the same time to work the steering wheels and auxiliary steering tackles when manoeuvring was taking place.[30]

Bellerophon was the first of the central battery type ships, but similar forms were subsequently adopted in France and other countries. The need for a warship to be able to train its guns in a forward, backward, and angular direction was increasingly seen to be important, and had always been a vexing problem that broadside arcs of fire could not solve. The arrangements in *Bellerophon* went some way to overcoming this problem of axial fire, and a number of other Reed designed ships were subsequently built with similar gun installations at bow and stern. However, due to operational restrictions that existed for guns placed in the narrow confines of bow and stern, and the adverse effect on a ship's motion that large additional weights at a ship's extremities could create, such arrangements were considered far from ideal.

A more advanced method of overcoming this problem was used in some of Reed's later ships, such as the *Hercules* of 1868. Each of the corner guns in the casemate of this ironclad had two gun ports, one for firing on the beam and the other for axial fire. With this arrangement it was necessary to shift the guns from gun port to gun port, an operation that was heavy and time-consuming, although made easier where turntables were fitted as gun mountings. In practice, however, the additional gun ports tended to weaken the armour protection, and mounting and serving the guns was made more complicated. In later ironclads of this type shifting of the guns was avoided by cutting large angle ports at each corner of the casemate; this arrangement slightly improved matters, although the problems associated with reduced protection still existed.

The manoeuvrability of steam ships independent of the wind, and the increasing power of so-called chase guns made the requirement for end-on fire increasingly important. Bow and stern mounted guns and angled casemate ports went some way towards fulfilling this need; however, it was becoming ever more evident that the issue of axial fire would never be successfully resolved whilst masts, sails, and rigging were retained and existed in such profusion over, upon, and around a warship's decks. Equally though, it was not readily apparent at the time as to how this problem could be overcome.

Considered to be one of Edward Reed's masterpieces, *Hercules*, a central battery ironclad, is shown moored alongside a quay. In the photograph the central battery can be clearly seen, as can the embrasures for giving some limited end-on fire towards both the bow and stern. (National Museum of the Royal Navy)

The Audacious class central battery ironclad *Iron Duke* is shown in this photograph with her forward torpedo net booms out on either side, although the nets are not rigged and the booms appear to be being used to moor a number of ships' boats, including a steam pinnace or launch. (National Museum of the Royal Navy)

In French casemate vessels a certain amount of axial fire was obtained by placing some of the guns on turntables in low circular breastworks on top of the casemates. Known as 'barbettes', these installations were often from necessity placed so far outboard that they projected beyond the ship's sides. Apart from the adverse effect on stability that resulted, such arrangements meant that the guns, which fired over the edge of the barbette, were unprotected, although the turning gear and turntable slides were at least sheltered. Barbette-mounted guns, being high up, could provide plunging fire, but they could not be fired directly forward or aft, or at angles of less than 45 degrees to the ship's centre line, without causing damage to the ship's own superstructure. Although barbette installations as they then existed were far from ideal, the concept on which they were based was sound and these early types were in essence the forerunners of more technically advanced barbettes that would eventually be used in most future capital ship classes[31] in all the world's navies, including that of Great Britain.

Although not called so at the time, in outward appearance the ironclad broadside frigates and casemate ships that constituted the mid-Victorian navy might well have collectively been called the Black Battle fleet, as indeed they much later came to be termed by historians. By this stage the chequered sides of the line-of-battle ship had gone and the white superstructure of later ships was still to appear. All ironclad hulls were now unrelieved black, apart, that is, for a narrow white stripe running around the ship's side outside the hammock storage nettings. Funnels and deck erections were black also, as were the larger boats, although masts and other spars were usually buff coloured.[32]

The weapons of the fleet at this time, like the ships that carried them, represented a midway stage in a complete transformation. It was the age of wrought-iron armour and rifled muzzle-loading ordnance that increased in calibre and weight some six fold over the period, and which stood somewhere between the cast-iron smooth-bore cannon of earlier times, and the later, re-engineered, breech-loading guns, that would, in a few short decades, develop into weapons of unimaginably immense power and range. This next phase of development and the technical and operational changes that accompanied it, not only where attack and defence aspects were concerned, but also for ship design and construction, and for numerous elements of marine engineering, form the subject matter of subsequent chapters.

4

OF RAMS AND TURRETS

As the development of ironclad warships advanced in the navies of the world it became clear that armour plating provided a defensive facility of great merit. Consequently as the quality of iron was improved over time, and foundry technology and processes were developed to more readily roll and shape ever thicker armour plate, the power of the gun as a weapon of attack appeared by mid-century to have been thwarted. For those in the British Admiralty and in the wider naval service who supported such a view, some alternative means of extending a warship's offensive capability seemed to be required. Iron hulls and the independent manoeuvring power of screw steamers appeared to provide the answer, in that ramming was once again considered to be feasible as a method of attack, and it was argued that irrespective of ordnance capabilities, it was now perfectly feasible for short, handy ironclads to themselves become the weapon, using their speed and weight to ram and cut down the most formidable of adversaries.[1]

Given the slow rate of fire and general inaccuracy of contemporary muzzle-loading guns, the ramming concept appeared to make sense, and in the true Nelsonian tradition, the ram was seen as a formidable weapon of close-quarters' fighting. Some even regarded the ram to be almost a weapon of both precision and first choice. Indeed one Chief Constructor would later boast that: 'one of my greatest personal efforts was to get the ram widely recognised as a proper weapon, and to secure its introduction in to every ship of war.'[2]

Whilst agreeing that all ironclads should be fitted with ram bows, some naval authorities additionally felt that even smaller handier types should be built, specifically as rams. Purpose built vessels of this sort would also, it was reasoned, be more effective if they were built without having any guns installed at all so that efficiency in ramming actions would not become compromised if a ramming ship became shrouded in gun smoke at a critical moment in the action.[3] In association with the singularity of purpose that rams were expected to provide, it was also commonly expected that personal dash on the behalf of commanders would be the principal quality needed for handling a ram, and that the occasional loss of such a comparatively inexpensive vessel would be of little consequence and a small matter, as compared with the loss or damage of a larger capital ship of the more normal type.[4] A few dedicated rams were in fact built, and for a short while were assigned a battle

The ironclad ram *Hotspur* of 1870 was not the most extreme form of ram in that she only carried three guns, a single, surprisingly large, 12in muzzle-loading rifle and two rifled 64-pounders in addition to her ram bow. (National Museum of the Royal Navy)

Built in a later decade in 1881, *Polyphemus*, a torpedo ram, has been included here so that she can be compared with *Hotspur*. Apart from six, twin-barrelled machine guns she carried no heavy guns, but in addition to her spur ram, was armed with four broadside 14in torpedo tubes, as well as one near her bow. (National Museum of the Royal Navy)

value that was completely fictitious, as in practice their size and specialist nature soon relegated them to the lowest category of armoured ship.[5]

Small dedicated rams aside, nineteenth-century tactical thought continued to hold ramming as a central concept in naval warfare and this was reinforced by a number of incidents over the years when ramming was successfully used. These included various naval actions during the American Civil War, and fighting at the Battle of Lissa in 1866, in which eight ramming incidents occurred, leading to the sinking of the Italian ironclad *Re d'Italia* by the Austrian *Ferdinand Max*. A series of accidental rammings had also taken place over the period, and these resulted in damage to, and in some cases the sinking of, a number of warships. One of these incidents led to a great loss of life when in 1893 the large battleship *Victoria* was accidentally rammed and sunk by the equally massive *Camperdown*.[6] Where that incident was concerned it has been estimated that for two large warships travelling towards each other at between 5 to 6 knots the ramming force involved was likely to be around 17,000 tons, much the same as that delivered by a shell from a heavy 12in 45-ton gun.[7]

Through all of the nineteenth century the bows of ironclads continued to be constructed in the form of a ram. This structure consisted of massive iron, and later cast steel, forgings, which were carried well down into the body of the ship, and secured and supported by keel members, bottom plates and decks. Due to difficulties in manufacturing such large and intricate castings, rams had to be made in two pieces that were joined using scarf joints and keyed together. This arrangement was a potential source of weakness that was not overcome until improved casting techniques eventually made it possible to cast rams in one piece.[8] The profile of the ram bow was a matter of considerable debate. Some naval officers preferred a ram projecting above the water so that the ramming ship could override and force its victim down, whilst a more substantial body of opinion favoured a more upright stem, with the more usual below-water spur.[9] Illustration of the structure of both types of ram bows are shown in Appendix 1 at the back of this book.

The underwater parts of a warship's hull were susceptible to ramming, as they could not be armoured to withstand attack without increasing displacement to an unacceptable level that would make them sluggish and slow to manoeuvre. Internal subdivisions were the accepted remedy for underwater protection against ramming, although it was also appreciated that such arrangements were not foolproof and that in an attack the opposing ram was certain to break a ship's outer skin and possibly also penetrate the inner skin. Where the ramming ship itself was concerned, however, whilst a glancing blow at low speed might well tear a large hole in the outer skin of the target vessel, only a direct blow of a ram moving at a high speed would be likely to fatally penetrate the subdivided inner skin of a well-constructed armoured ship.[10]

There was an ever present danger, however, that an attacking ship would itself be damaged when ramming was taking place. Given the speeds of nineteenth-century ironclads, it would take up to ten minutes to travel 2 miles, ample time for a stationary victim to fire six rounds or so at an attacker, and as the range decreased such fire would become more accurate. In the event it would likely be safer for the ramming ship's commander to attack his opponent with gunfire from a distance rather than exposing his ship to risk during a ramming attempt. Conversely, if the ship being attacked was free to manoeuvre it might flee, using its stern guns on its attacker when doing so, or it might attempt to move out of the way of the, what would be by then, fully committed enemy, and attempt to use its own ram if so fitted.[11]

Decisive results were thus difficult to achieve from ramming, and it was only in the unlikely event that the target ship was completely surprised, stopped or disabled, that ramming could succeed. It was also evident that the effective range of the ram was much less than that of the gun, and the possibility of failure in its use was high. Why then did the ram persist for so long when accidental and doubtful war experience apart, its weakness as a weapon could have been exposed by simple argument or trials?[12] Experience as a result of limited use in battle, and a few accidents that occurred over the years, appeared to show that in practice, ramming worked. Additionally, a ram bow was relatively easily provided, having little influence on the design of a particular ship, and in any case the concept easily slotted into the tradition of close-range fighting that was part of the mindset of many senior- and middle-rank naval officers at the time. Given this peripheral evidence it is perhaps hardly surprising that although a failed ramming attempt could bring immediate destruction of the ramming ship, the ram continued to be seen as an important primary weapon, and it would continue to be perceived as such until more appropriate short-range weapons such as torpedoes and quick-firing secondary ordnance became commonly available and fully effective in use.[13]

Edward Reed's central battery casemate ships continued to be built, but at the same time the perceived advantages from placing guns in revolving turrets was increasingly becoming an issue, albeit that it was realised in many quarters, including Spencer Robinson's department, that practical implementation would be fraught with difficulties. As far back as the Crimean War, John Eriksson, a Swedish engineer who had at a later stage tried to get the British Admiralty interested in his designs for a screw propeller, had discussed with the French Government a design for a low freeboard ship that carried one or two heavy guns in an armoured turret. The French, however, showed little interest at the time, but later in 1861, on the eve of the American Civil War, Eriksson was able to persuade the Government of the Northern States of America to build a turret ship according to his plans. This vessel was completed in 1862, and subsequently took part in a number of Civil War engagements. On Eriksson's suggestion this ship was called *Monitor*, which later became the generic name for all low freeboard armoured ships[14] that could be usefully employed for river and estuary operations, but were generally incapable of being used in offshore and ocean conditions. John Eriksson was thus the first person to practically develop a gun turret and see it utilised during hostilities.

Some time earlier in 1855 though, whilst the Crimean War was at its height, a British naval officer, Captain Cowper Coles, noticed that Russian shells were able to enter the gun ports of the new floating batteries, and was led to consider some way of overcoming this problem. After trials that he himself conducted, Coles, who was a very knowledgeable gunnery officer, independently formulated the idea of mounting guns in rotating cupolas or turrets, that not only more effectively protected the gun crews but also enabled a greater arc of fire, and facilitated the handling of the guns themselves. A committee of senior naval officers serving in the Black Sea area reported favourably on the scheme, and Coles was ordered back to Britain to lay his plans before the Admiralty.[15]

The sound arguments in support of his ideas that Coles put forward won support both in the Admiralty and in the wider service, and some months later a prototype turret was ordered and in 1861 installed on the armoured battery *Trusty*. Trials of Coles's turret proved successful, and as invasion scares and the perceived need for coast defence were at the time burning issues in Great Britain, the Admiralty ordered the construction of two ships incorporating Coles's turrets. In making this decision the Admiralty hoped not only to assuage public opinion, but also in part at least to limit the high cost of a programme of constructing coastal forts, the so-called Palmerston's follies, a scheme that had been put in train by Prime Minister Lord Palmerston, as a way of providing some defence against invasion.

The first of these ships, *Royal Sovereign*, was a cut-down wooden three-decker, armoured with iron plates and provided with four turrets, whilst the second ship, *Prince Albert*, was specially built of iron and also carried four turrets. In both cases the foremost turrets carried two 12.5-ton guns whilst the other turrets were all provided with a single gun apiece. The last of these two vessels was completed in 1864, and both underwent successful trials, and were considered adequate for their coast defence roles. Although having low freeboard and being without masts, neither were considered capable of extended voyages or service on foreign stations.[16]

But Cowper Coles believed that a seagoing turret ship was perfectly feasible, and being a tireless publicist and self promoter he persistently advocated this view, eventually enlisting the support of Prince Albert, who intervened on behalf of the inventor and pressed the Admiralty to concede to Coles's demands.[17] There was no denying that turrets facilitated the training of large guns smoothly and easily through large arcs of fire, as well as making the same guns available on both sides of the ship. But whilst in theory the same guns could be trained and fired near to the ship's axis to provide end-on fire, in practice masts, sails, and rigging made such unrestricted fire very difficult to achieve.[18]

The Admiralty were far less enthusiastic than the Prince Consort about the turret issue however, not only due to the above problems, but also because of doubts associated with the seaworthiness of turret ships, that to ensure stability was not compromised by great weights positioned relatively high up, had to have their turrets located low down near the ship's water line. These concerns were shared by both Edward Reed and Spencer Robinson who, during debates on the matter, informed the Admiralty board that: 'Captain Coles is completely ignorant of the very first principles of naval architecture as a science and from want of knowledge proposes designs which are utterly impracticable.'[19]

Masted turret ship *Monarch* of 1869 shown at anchor with her later 1872 barque rig on all three masts. The two turrets that housed her four 12in muzzle-loading rifled guns can be clearly seen in the illustration in front and behind the funnel casing, with a spar deck above them from which sail was worked. (National Museum of the Royal Navy)

This shows seamen and marines posing in front of a masted turret ship's turret. The ship is probably either the *Scorpion* or the *Wivern* of 1865, both of which were ordered in 1862 from British shipyards by the Confederate States Navy during the American Civil War but never delivered. (National Museum of the Royal Navy)

Notwithstanding the soundness of such an appraisal, the often forceful views expressed by both Robinson and Reed on this matter were generally construed by the British press as being counterproductive, and in an attempt to force the acceptance of Coles's designs, they conducted what was often a vicious journalistic campaign against the two Admiralty officers.[20] In addition, Coles himself used every avenue open to lobby Members of Parliament and other influential persons, and under all this political pressure, a reluctant Admiralty eventually decided to order the construction of a masted turret ship that could be used in other areas than coastal waters. This ship *Monarch* of 8,322-tons displacement, which was completed in 1869, was designed by Reed and when completed was the first British ironclad to carry 12in muzzle-loading rifled guns arranged in two turrets. In use *Monarch* steamed well and was considered the fastest ironclad in the fleet, although virtually uncontrollable under sail.[21] Her nine boilers provided a pressure of 30lb/sq. in to a return-connecting rod engine driving a single screw. This type of engine, manufactured by Humphrys and Tennant, had by this date started to supersede the trunk engine in British warships, as although it was still of a horizontal form, it was better able to cope with the higher steam pressures that then existed, without undue leakages taking place.

Reed himself, having been forced to design *Monarch* against his better judgement, was far from happy with his latest creation, or with the two monitor types that had previously been built, and later wrote that: 'most assuredly the building of such vessels was urged by many persons long before satisfactory methods of designing them had been devised and my clear and strong conviction at the moment of writing these lines is that no satisfactorily designed turret-ship with rigging has yet been built or even laid down.'[22] Long before *Monarch* was completed, though, Cowper Coles was once again lobbying, this time expressing a view that the new ship did not fulfil his requirements. These actions became highly personal, with further journalistic and public pressure being generated, so that eventually, overcome by the extent and vehemence of political, press, and public opinion, the Admiralty took the unprecedented step of allowing Coles's own turret ship design to be built. Although construction would be paid for using public funding in the normal way, it was considered that in view of the bad feeling that had been generated, the ship should be built by an external contractor rather than in a royal dockyard. Coles agreed with this view and Lairds of Birkenhead were eventually chosen to carry out the work.

Unfortunately, during the period when the new ship (which was to be named *Captain*) was being built, there were a number of changes in the appointment of First Lord, who was the political head of the Admiralty, and this may well have resulted at the time in a lack of overall direction where naval construction work was concerned. Additionally, as previously noted, *Captain* was not built in a naval dockyard and had been designed by amateur designer Cowper Coles, who, although an experienced naval officer, was not part of the naval constructors' department. Coles of course had also previously been a continuing source of aggravation for both Robinson and Reed, neither of whom was blessed with forgiving, tactful, or facilitating natures. As a likely consequence of all these factors, Admiralty supervision of the contract was not as rigorously carried out as would normally have been the case, and decisions and advice on subsequent design changes were not routinely provided by Reed and his team.[23] These aspects when taken together meant that certain critical design and constructional flaws were not identified during the building of the new ship, and as explained in the following paragraphs, were elements that unfortunately resulted in *Captain*'s early demise.

However irrespective of both this and the fact that Edward Reed still had doubts about many aspects of the design, the *Captain* was built and eventually completed in 1870. Guns by this juncture had increased so much in weight that it was necessary to limit the number of turrets in the new ship to two, both of which carried two 12in muzzle-loading rifled guns. Two smaller 7in guns were also mounted in unprotected positions at bow and stern. Displacing 7,767 tons and carrying wrought-iron armour up to 8in thick in a continuous belt, with armour of between 9in and 10in on the turrets, *Captain* had eight rectangular boilers and twin screws driven by two sets of trunk engines, that because of their small size were built by Lairds themselves rather than by a specialist engine-building company, as would have been necessary if the engines had been larger. *Captain* also carried three square-rigged tripod masts, the sails being worked from a flying deck located above the turrets so that masts and rigging would not cause an obstruction, and sail handling would not interfere when the guns were in use.[24]

Due mainly to the previously mentioned lack of supervision during building, *Captain* was completed nearly 1,000 tons overweight, and this meant that her freeboard was dangerously low, and inclining experiments carried out by Lairds indicated that she would become unstable at angles of heel of beyond about 20 degrees. This problem, although apparently not causing too much concern at the time, was found to be instrumental in *Captain*'s demise when in the winter of 1870, whilst under a press of sail during fleet manoeuvres off Cape Finisterre, she capsized and sank. Only seventeen of her crew of 472 survived. Cowper Coles, who was aboard at the time, perished with his creation.[25]

In accordance with prevailing custom, the inquiry that followed the loss of *Captain* took the form of a courts martial in which, as was normal practice at the time, the survivors were charged with losing their ship, although it was also recognised that in this case they were not to blame, and they were all acquitted.[26] The real cause of the disaster, however, rested elsewhere, and on summarising their findings the courts martial placed it on record that: 'the *Captain* was built in deference to public opinion and in opposition to the views and opinions of the Controller of the Navy and his department and that evidence shows that they generally disapproved of her construction.' The instability of the ship and the apparent incompetence of Coles to design such a vessel were also stressed.[27]

Captain Coles's masted turret ship *Captain* is shown here being loaded/unloaded from two lighters secured alongside. *Captain* was the result of Coles's ideas on low freeboard monitor type seagoing battleships, and as such was flawed right from the concept stage. (National Museum of the Royal Navy)

Captain is shown here in dry dock and her twin screws and high poop superstructure can clearly be seen. Although Coles criticised the high bow and stern superstructures at the ends of *Monarch*, he had them built into *Captain*'s design. (National Museum of the Royal Navy)

During this part of the nineteenth century there was generally a great interest in Britain in all things associated with the navy, and the tragic loss of *Captain* and her crew generated much concern and misgivings about the whole question of turret ships and their suitability as ships of war. This occurred within government circles as well as in the British press and public at large and as a consequence *Monarch*, in particular, was subjected to stringent stability and other tests. However, because Reed had designed her with more than twice the freeboard of the unfortunate *Captain*, these proved her to be satisfactory. The fact remained though that masts, sails, and turrets did not provide an easy partnership, especially for a ship that was to be used in ocean conditions. These factors together with open criticism in Parliament and in the press would later result in the Admiralty establishing a high profile committee to examine the whole question of warship design. The work of this body and the many recommendations it made will be outlined in the next chapter.

Some time before construction on *Captain* had commenced, however, Edward Reed and his team had been formulating ideas and developing designs for a new type of seagoing turret ship without sails, which they called breastwork monitors. This type of vessel was of general monitor form, but very different from the American riverine monitor, in that it was provided with a tall redoubt or breastwork amidships, at each end of which was mounted a turret. Although in true monitor style the freeboard at bow and stern was low, the high armoured sides of the breastwork ensured that when such a ship heeled no ingress of water would normally occur in the ship's hull, and this in turn secured stability at greater angles of heel than would otherwise have been possible. The turrets and the guns they contained were positioned considerably higher than in normal monitors, and the turret-turning gear was well protected.[28]

A number of these ships in smaller sizes were built in due course, although initially the design was received with little enthusiasm from the Admiralty and the first few completed were treated as prototypes and quickly relegated to duties associated with coastal defence in the Channel and elsewhere.[29] The first large seagoing ship of this type was *Devastation*, completed in 1871 and the result of a specific request by the Board of Admiralty for a monitor capable of easily steaming between Queenstown in Ireland and Halifax in Nova Scotia without the use of sails.[30] When completed *Devastation* became the first true capital ship built by any nation that carried no sails at all, and with her debut it was finally recognised that the advantages of the turret system could only be fully achieved in a ship that had no masts, sails, and rigging. Additionally, *Devastation* represented the first complete application to a seagoing ironclad battleship of the principle of mounting the main armament on top rather than inside the hull,[31] and although freeboard was still low, the absence of masts and sails allowed this factor to exist without creating undue safety problems.

With a displacement of 9,330 tons, *Devastation* carried a wrought-iron armoured belt that varied in thickness from 8.5in to around 12in with 16in to 18in of wood backing. The breastwork was covered with armour 10in to 12in thick and the two turrets with 10in to 14in. Her decks and bulkheads, especially those around the magazines, were also lightly armoured, and the lower hull had numerous water-tight divisions. Each turret carried two 12in muzzle-loading rifles,[32] and the guns in the after turret were so arranged that they could be fired at maximum depression over the stern if that proved necessary. At the time she was commissioned *Devastation* was considered to be the most powerful ship afloat.

Fitted with twin screws that not only improved her manoeuvrability but also provided insurance in the case of one engine breaking down, *Devastation* was initially provided with two sets of Penn trunk engines, and rectangular boilers that delivered 30lb/sq. in steam pressure. Much later she was re-engined with more efficient compound engines and cylindrical boilers, supplying steam at 60lb/sq. in, and this had the effect of enabling her to double the distance she could travel without refilling her bunkers with coal.[33] *Devastation* proved to be a steady gun platform in use, steamed well, and was not much affected by heavy weather. Her low monitor-like ends, however, meant that forecastle and decks at bow and stern became very wet in a seaway or when the ship was travelling at high speed.

But the whole saga of *Captain* had left a bitter taste, and this was evident in a surprisingly subdued and occasionally hostile reception from the British press and general public that accompanied *Devastation*'s launch. Reflecting on this some years later, one contemporary observer noted that: 'with such labour and travail was the modern British battleship born!' Irrespective of such a reception from a press and public, the bulk of whom were usually excited and even proud when a new iron-cased leviathan was born, two further ships of the Devastation class, *Thunderer* and *Dreadnought*, were both completed some years later in 1877 and 1879 respectively. In the interim though, public pressure and popular press outcry tended to decidedly modify decisions concerning matters of naval construction, until it was clear to most dissenters that all matters of concern had been addressed. This inevitably led to considerable delay in the building of *Devastation*'s two sisters.[34]

When turrets were first introduced, they were rotated and trained mechanically by means of a manually operated circular rack and pinion. Later on steam power was utilised, and some of the loading and other tasks associated with operating the guns themselves were also steam assisted. However, as the great muzzle-loading guns and their ammunition continued to grow both in size and weight, condensing steam in pipes, differences in steam pressures, and other associated problems, meant that this method of operation was becoming fraught with difficulties. Shipbuilders and ordnance manufacturers Armstrong's of Elswick, now back in favour after problems with their early breech-loading guns, were subsequently asked to examine these problems with a view to finding practical solutions. Based on work that Armstrong's had been carrying out on power transfer using hydraulics, the company's managing director, George Rendel, and his team of engineers were able to develop a hydraulic engine and ancillary machinery that to a large extent met the Admiralty's requirements, and these were used in *Thunderer*, the second ship of the Devastation class to be built.

Thunderer was completed to the same design as her earlier sister but mounted even bigger guns in the forward turret. These monster pieces were of 12.5in calibre, and weighed thirty-eight tons, a full two tons heavier than those of *Devastation*. It was this forward turret in which Rendel's hydraulic engine and ancillary equipment were installed, albeit in an experimental capacity, with the after turret having the usual manual and steam-assisted handling arrangements. The hydraulic installation proved so successful in use that every battleship of a future date would be provided with hydraulically operated gun mountings and loading gear worked on the same principle, but by then greatly improved.[35]

As was the case with *Devastation*, the boilers in *Thunderer* were eight in number and of the rectangular box type, producing steam at 30lb/sq. in. During trials in 1876, one of these boilers exploded, killing fifteen men. The steam pressure gauge on this boiler was known to have been faulty, but an enquiry found that due to the effects of corrosion the deadweight safety valves were additionally inoperable. This accident led to the introduction of spring-loaded safety valves into naval warships, together with a more stringent testing regime by boiler-

Devastation class turret ship *Thunderer* of 1872, shown during an important naval event, possibly a royal birthday or jubilee. This is evident from the large numbers of her crew on deck, and from the sailors manning the yards of all three masts of the steam line-of-battle ship shown in the background. (National Museum of the Royal Navy)

room staff. In fact at this stage it was becoming evident that box boilers were not really suitable for steam pressures much above 30lb/sq. in, and as ongoing advances in metallurgy and foundry practice had now made it possible to roll iron plates into shapes other than flat ones, oval and then cylindrical boilers could now be produced, allowing even greater steam pressures to be achieved as a result.[36] *Thunderer* thus became the last large British warship to be fitted with box boilers.

Apparently dogged with misfortune, *Thunderer* was the site of another major accident in 1879 when one of the 38-ton guns in her foremost turret burst, killing ten men and wounding many more. A subsequent investigation found that the explosion was not due to faults in the gun, but had in fact occurred as a consequence of a deplorable error in loading, when two complete rounds of powder and projectiles had been loaded and fired at the same time. This had resulted from a misfire in one gun of the pair when both guns were simultaneously fired. The concussion and smoke from the fired gun masked the fact that the other had not fired, and during the second loading a new charge was rammed down on top of the unfired one with disastrous results.[37]

Prior to the *Thunderer* accident muzzle-loading guns had been considered to be fairly reliable and could readily be fitted into all sizes of turret. With hydraulic assistance the loading and firing of such guns could also be performed comparatively quickly and conveniently, and they could be manufactured relatively cheaply at Woolwich Arsenal, where naval guns were by now normally built. This factor had not escaped the Ordnance Board or indeed the management of Woolwich Arsenal, where only limited facilities for building more complex guns such as breech loaders existed in any case, coupled with a far from progressive outlook by those in charge, meaning that little thought had been given to future service needs or advances in ordnance technology.[38]

It was generally agreed at the time, however, that an accident such as that which had taken place on *Thunderer* could not have occurred with a modern breech-loading gun, and as this belief gained strength it heralded the end of the muzzle-loading gun for British capital warships. France and some other European navies were already using breech-loading guns with greater or lesser success, and it is possible that this fact and a conviction, at least in the minds of their Lords of the Admiralty, that Britain should never be second to France in any aspect of the ongoing arms race, was also a contributory factor. In any event muzzle-loaders would now be phased out and breech-loading rifled ordnance would fast become the weapon of choice in the British navy.

The third ship in the Devastation class, named *Dreadnought*, was completed in 1879. Displacing 10,800 tons, this ship was very similar to *Devastation*, but her breastwork extended the whole breadth of the hull, further improving her stability as a result. Her side armour was increased to a thickness of 14in, and she carried two pairs of 38-ton, 12in guns in her two turrets. Utilising lessons learnt with *Thunderer, Dreadnought* became the first warship where guns and turrets were all entirely worked by hydraulic power, a system henceforth employed for all heavy guns in the British Navy.[39] *Dreadnought* was a successful ship, although subjected to many changes in subsequent years. A steady gun platform, she was well behaved in a seaway, although like all breastwork monitors she pitched a great deal and her forward and after decks became very wet when steaming at speed.

In his designs Edward Reed was able to provide many practical and often brilliant solutions to the warship requirements of the day, albeit that change would now advance at an even greater pace and complexity, and many new solutions would need to be provided as both technology and the requirements of the naval service continued to rapidly change over time. During the seven years that Reed was in office, he designed ninety-five vessels, twenty-five of which were ironclads. Where these latter vessels were concerned, displacement increased from about 7,000 to over 9,000 tons, the thickness of iron armour from 6 to 14in, and the size of guns from 12 to 38 tons.[40] In his later designs, turrets became practical propositions and masts and sails, now widely, but far from completely, accepted as being an encumbrance, were dispensed with. Although Reed may be criticised

The turret ship *Dreadnought* of 1879 shown here was a half sister of the Devastation class ships but was larger and had more powerful engines and heavier armour. *Dreadnought* had two turrets, each housing two 12.5in muzzle-loading rifles. (National Museum of the Royal Navy)

Originally designed for the Brazilian Navy the masted turret ship *Neptune*, shown in the photograph firing her starboard guns whilst in line-ahead formation with other British battleships, was later bought by the Admiralty prior to the Crimean War. (National Museum of the Royal Navy)

for retaining the box battery system for long after the advantages of the turret system were clear, his turreted and mast-less seagoing ironclads *Devastation* and her two sisters were of an advanced design, and can be seen as the forerunners of the twentieth-century battleship.[41]

In 1870, though, even before *Devastation* was launched, Reed had resigned from his post as Chief Constructor, prompting the Controller, Spencer Robinson, to describe the fact as: 'nearly a national calamity.' During his time in the department under Robinson's overall management, Reed had instigated, directed, and encouraged major improvements in all areas of design procedures. However, the bitter war of words with First Lord of the Admiralty Hugh Childers over the design of *Captain* had left him with little option but to vacate his post. It is also true of course that Reed's own wounded pride and often less-than-diplomatic attitude to such problems may well have contributed to his decision to go at that time. In any event, on leaving the Admiralty, Reed took on a number of senior positions in commercial shipyards where he designed ships for a number of foreign governments.[42] During the 1874 general election Reed was elected as a Liberal Member of Parliament, and he also continued to sit in the Commons after the next election in 1880. He frequently used his political position as a platform to criticise the Admiralty as well as to frequently attack the policies and warship designs of his successors in government service.

BEYOND THE FLEET OF SAMPLES

W hen Edward Reed resigned it was decided not to immediately fill the post of Chief Constructor. Instead, Nicholas Barnaby, who had been Reed's deputy, oversaw the work of a team of naval architects known as the Council of Construction, and this situation continued until 1875, when Barnaby was eventually appointed as Director of Naval Construction, with the somewhat outdated title of Chief Constructor being dropped.[1]

Other changes in the department were also imminent, and in 1871, a mere year after Reed had quit, the Controller, Spencer Robinson, was sacked from his post. This unfortunate situation occurred due to the constant friction and animosity between Robinson and First Lord of the Admiralty Hugh Childers, that the *Captain* affair had generated, and in order to stop the embittered but highly competent Childers from himself resigning, the then Prime Minister, William Gladstone, asked the increasingly volatile Robinson to resign.[2] In the circumstances, and faced with such a difficult decision, Gladstone was clearly hedging his bets, and perhaps taking a route of the lesser of two evils. Initially Captain Robert Hall became Robinson's successor, but a year later he was also succeeded when Rear Admiral William Houston Stewart took over. Houston Stewart remained in the post of Controller for the next ten years.[3]

During 1871, Hugh Childers, whose midshipman son had perished when the *Captain* sank, instituted an inquiry by Royal Commission into the whole question of ironclad design, and a special committee, known as the Committee on Designs of Ships of War, was appointed. By taking such action Childers aimed not only to vindicate the evolving principles governing warship design and to restore public confidence in the work of naval constructors, but also, as he had supported the work of Cowper Coles and the design of *Captain*, to attempt to move any blame associated with decisions to send that particular vessel to sea, to those who had been his subordinates at the time, namely Robinson and Reed.[4] These two had by now both left the service and were not in a position to adequately respond in their own defence.

The Admiralty instructed the Committee on Designs to examine particular named classes of warship and to advise their Lordships whether:

> with reference to the present state of the science of naval architecture and the
> requirements of naval warfare, the principles which should regulate the form

and type of warships to be built for the service of this country are fully satisfied by these designs, with the improvements recommended in them, or whether any further modifications are desirable.[5]

The committee itself consisted of senior naval officers, warship designers, and mathematicians. Robinson, Reed, Barnaby, and representatives of all the prominent naval and civilian authorities and private companies involved in designing and building warships at the time were summoned to testify.[6]

Considering the importance of the topic under review, and the vast amount of evidence gathered, it is surprising that once their analysis was complete, the committee submitted many of their conclusions in the form of 'a few suggestions', rather than in a series of firm recommendations. In their concluding report, however, they did call for the complete abolition of sails, and supported the design of *Devastation*, recognising that in her broad features she represented the capital fighting ship of the immediate future, and that as such her type should form the basis for subsequent first-class ironclad designs.

The necessity to continue building armoured ships was also recognised, although it was felt that due to the increasing thickness required to counter the growing power of the gun, the extent and effective distribution of armour was a major consideration if stability and speed were to be maintained. In addition to a ship's main armament of heavy guns, it was also considered that secondary batteries of smaller guns might well be required for use against high-speed unarmoured vessels. This secondary armament it was felt was unlikely to require significant amounts of armoured protection. In accordance with the general view in the service at the time, members of the committee also felt that the importance of ramming in future naval warfare was inevitably going to be so great, that in designing ironclad ships, particular attention should be paid to the best means of resisting ram attacks, including cellular compartments in the bow and stern of each new ship.[7]

Additionally the committee made a number of other design-related suggestions. These included the requirement for more accurate calculations of centres of gravity and metacentric heights, and the need to ensure that stringent tests were carried out so that during actual construction all these elements stayed within accepted parameters. In this way it was hoped that ships would not become unstable as a result of a mismatch between building and design, as had of course been the case with the ill-fated *Captain*.[8] Apart perhaps from the perceived importance of ramming as a central tactic, the committee's suggestions were generally sound, however the Admiralty did not choose to fully implement them for a number of years. One historian has suggested that this retrograde step was due both to conservative influences in the Admiralty, as well as economically minded political leaders in Westminster.[9]

Such influences might well have had an effect, but equally the committee's lukewarm suggestions rather than positive recommendations might also have played a part, as might the considerable disagreement that existed within the committee, as a result of which several members dissented from particular sections of the report, and two of the admirals declined ownership by refusing to sign the report at all. Equally those responsible for policy at the Admiralty likely believed that although ships like *Devastation* appeared to answer the dilemma that combining turrets with masts and sails had created, the strategic necessity for ships destined to serve overseas meant that an insurance against a breakdown of engines and boilers that could still prove unreliable, and a means of countering the continuing lack of good coaling facilities abroad, was still necessary. Until such times that greater reliability of engines, boilers, and ancillaries was achieved, and more numerous and effective coaling arrangements could be provided, masts and sails, in their view, provided the necessary insurance.[10]

Although the suggestions of the Committee on Designs were not immediately implemented in Britain, the navies of other European nations must have found the report, which was widely published and available, a most valuable guide to warship design, as well as to the general thinking on such matters of the naval administration in Britain, which, after all, was the main rival and potential antagonist as far as many of those countries were concerned. This aside, the committee's work did have a more immediate effect in that it began to create a new understanding, and a feeling of confidence in the ships of Britain's battle fleet, and this was the case not only for the navy itself, but also for the wider British public, as well as for many hitherto critical representatives of the national press.[11]

Before the Committee on Designs had presented its findings, Hugh Childers's attempts to find a scapegoat for the *Captain* fiasco had caused Edward Reed to resign from his post as Chief Constructor, and, as previously noted, Spencer Robinson was forced to leave the Admiralty soon after. Given the attitudes that prevailed at the time, both Reed and Robinson had been lateral thinkers, and between them they had ensured that British ironclads were more powerful than those of any other nation. Reed's successor Nathaniel Barnaby, though competent, was more conservative in outlook and exerted much less influence in the naval and administrative corridors of power.

After the exciting days of the introduction of the ironclad and the turret ship controversy, the decade from the early 1870s was less inspiring and has been called the dark ages of the Victorian navy.[12] For much of this time Britain was at peace and the navy attracted little public attention. When naval affairs were discussed they were done so with polite disinterest, as abstract matters of no great importance, with laymen and naval officers alike refraining from any questioning of the service's role and function.[13] This was very different from the attitude that existed in the previous decade, and also from that which would prevail a decade later, when naval reformers would be urging expansion with the fervour of men who vividly perceived the perils that threatened their country, albeit that most of these were in reality often imaginary.

The majority of naval officers at that time went about their duties without ever taking a strategic view of the navy's role or seriously considering how it would react if hostilities were resumed either with France or with any other power. There were some exceptions however, prominent amongst which were Admirals Alexander Milne and Geoffrey Phipps Hornby. Both of these officers represented a small but growing spirit of enquiry, and recognising the weaknesses in the Admiralty's organisation, worked to bring about reforms during the decade of the 1870s. The possibility of war and the need for planning to meet such an event was something Milne in particular had been focusing on for some time, and in 1872, soon after he became First Sea Lord, and professional Head of the Navy under the First Civil Lord of the Admiralty, he sent the then Controller Admiral Houston Stewart, together with the new Director of Naval Construction Nicholas Barnaby, to France to study the policies of Britain's most likely enemy. After some investigation these two officials concluded that in the event of hostilities between their two countries, the French would pursue a *guerre de course*, or war against trade,[14] and that due to the large number of smaller coast defence ironclads and cruisers they possessed, was in a position to pose a considerable threat to British merchant shipping. The provision of such information that was freely given by the French reflected the spirit of openness that then existed between rival governments and military services, even if a potential enemy benefited as a result. Unfortunately the bitter wars that the early twentieth century would bring would, in their turn, ensure that such arrangements could never openly happen again.

The intelligence gathered from France directed Admiralty thinking towards better protecting the nation's large worldwide merchant fleet. However, although the threat of a *guerre de course* did have some substance, it is also likely that it was not as serious or as immediate as was supposed at the time. This aside, both the Admiralty and a whole generation of 'navalists' would for many years believe that France and her allies, such as Imperial Russia, were poised to release vast fleets of small handy rams and gun boats that had the capacity to attack British trade and in so doing bring that nation to its knees. Concerns over French policy thus continued to significantly influence the design and development of British warships over this period, and led to the view that the more powerful ironclads should be retained in home waters and in the Mediterranean to counter any invasion threats, and that a large cruising fleet of unarmoured or lightly armoured warships should be used worldwide for trade protection.[15]

Barnaby, though, considered that cruiser work was not real warfare, and in conjunction with some other administrators and politicians of the period felt that because of their speed and endurance, lightly armed merchant ships were more suited to the trade protection role than naval vessels. Such thinking did not, however, take account of the vulnerability of these ships due to their unprotected machinery spaces and steering gear, and a bare minimum of watertight bulkheads.[16]

Where the larger capital ships were concerned Barnaby's views were also very different from his predecessor's. In Reed-designed ships offence was secondary to defence. Nicholas Barnaby, on the other hand, took the opposite view and placed attack before defence, seeing all naval actions as melees in which the ram was a prominent weapon.[17] In conjunction with other supporters of such tactics, the new Director of Naval Construction believed that warships built for ramming should forgo the use of guns, or at the most be only lightly armed. He also considered that the contest between larger guns and ever-thicker armour would lead to prohibitive costs and reduced speeds, which in turn would ensure that the ram could become even more dominant in naval warfare.[18]

Irrespective of the findings of the Committee on Designs, the naval administration of the 1870s appeared to have had little focus, although where warship design and construction were concerned, Barnaby was able to at least provide some direction, even if this was occasionally confused and often overly influenced by political whims and arguable logic. In a sense this was understandable, as he was given far less autonomy and authority than had been the case where Edward Reed was concerned. Barnaby had of course been previously involved as Reed's assistant in the design of *Devastation*, and later on had been responsible for making alterations and additions to the designs of *Thunderer* and *Dreadnought*, as well as overseeing their construction. Although the majority of Barnaby's designs were for turret ships, the first two ships designed by him in his new role were in fact enlarged versions of Reed's earlier central battery vessels, and as such were obsolete in concept even before they were laid down.[19] It seems strange that in view of the findings of the Committee on Designs, these ships should have been built at all, but in placing orders for them, the Admiralty Board appears to have listened to the small but clearly powerful minority view that still advocated sails and the retention of broadside ordnance. However, as no more ships of this type would subsequently be commissioned in the British Navy, the construction of these two vessels signified the final chapter in the history of the broadside ironclad.

Displacing 9,490 tons, *Alexandra*, the first of these vessels, was completed in 1876, and rigged as a three-masted barque. It was said that in practice her sails were rarely used, and in any case she performed particularly badly under sail. This mattered little, however, as *Alexandra* had twin screws driven by two vertical compound engines, the first British warship to be so fitted. Her twelve cylindrical boilers provided steam pressure at 60lb/sq. in, and when commissioned she was the fastest steaming ironclad afloat.[20] With her 6in to 12in thick armoured belt on 12in of teak backing, and 8in to 12in of armour protecting her gun batteries, this warship was considered by many to be the most successful central battery ship ever built.

Alexandra carried two batteries of guns, one above the other. The lower or main battery was divided into two sections, with the largest of these divisions containing three 10in muzzle-loading rifled guns on each side, whilst the smaller forward

Said to be the most successful central battery ironclad ever built, *Alexandra* of 1877 was in reality a step backwards and the arrangement of her ordnance was based on an obsolete design concept. Irrespective of this she served as a flagship for twenty-three years. (Author's collection)

section mounted 10in guns in the two front corners. The upper battery was smaller than the main one and had 11in muzzle-loaders in the forward corners and 10in guns of a similar type in the after corners. In this way some axial fire was provided, although blast damage from this arrangement was an ever-present danger when the guns were fired.[21] Irrespective of this problem, *Alexandra* was one of the only two ships ever to carry 11in muzzle-loading guns. She also carried a number of smaller 4in breech-loading guns as a secondary armament and at a later date was fitted with 4.7in quick-firing guns. Additionally four 16in torpedo tubes were later added,[22] and *Alexandra* became the first British ironclad to have these, what were then, state-of-the-art weapons installed. The development of quick-firing guns as well as torpedoes is more fully dealt with in later chapters.

The second of these Barnaby-designed central battery ships, *Temeraire*, which displaced 8,540 tons and entered service in 1877, was in fact a hybrid having two 11in muzzle-loading rifled guns carried in barbettes on the upper deck, as well as a battery that was similar in form and function to *Alexandra*'s with a mixture of 10in and 11in muzzle-loading rifles. The guns carried in barbettes were mounted on Moncrieff disappearing mountings, of the type normally installed in land-based forts. This arrangement allowed the guns to be loaded behind armour then raised to fire over the barbette lip, after which the recoil returned them to the loading position. The system worked well but took up too much space, and the great weight of the installation positioned high above the ship's water line was considered to adversely affect stability. As a consequence, disappearing mountings of this type were never again used in British ships, although barbettes later became very popular. *Temeraire* carried two masts and was rigged as a brig, possibly the largest brig ever built. Having similar engines and boilers to *Alexandra*, this ship was also slow under sail. Apart from her main engines she carried a further thirty steam engines that were used for auxiliary purposes when working ship.[23]

The decade following the laying down of *Alexandra* and *Temeraire* have been rightly termed the 'dark ages' of the Victorian navy, and for six years under Benjamin Disraeli's government the service was openly neglected and a policy of drastic naval economy was introduced.[24] Although costs of materials and labour were rapidly rising, the naval estimates were kept unnaturally low and one contemporary senior admiral commenting on this policy noted that:

> we have ships without speed, guns without range, and boilers with only a few months life in them. This is called economy, but it is really only not spending money, closing the purse strings, and keeping our Fleet in such a state of inefficiency and unpreparedness as to render it comparatively useless should we at any time become involved in a war with a maritime power.[25]

For at least part of this period new construction was drastically curtailed and the Admiralty Board, which at the time lacked any overall policy focus or leadership,

Rigged as a brig, but particularly useless under sail, the masted turret ship *Inflexible*, launched in 1876, has been photographed from the after starboard quarter. In the photograph one of her en-echelon positioned turrets, that housed two massive 16in calibre rifled muzzle-loaders, can be seen. (National Museum of the Royal Navy)

became very concerned about what they considered to be high-displacement ships, believing that major cost savings would accrue from building warships of a more diminutive size, irrespective of a lack of suitability for performing their 'command of the sea' role. In an attempt to meet this requirement, which he appeared to agree with, Nicholas Barnaby and his staff began designing short handy ships of relatively great beam, and although each of these vessels was different from one another, they all tended to be cumbersome looking and had confused and ugly profiles. Typically less than 8,000 tons displacement, most of these vessels were classed as second-class ironclads and in later terminology would have been considered as heavy cruisers rather than battleships. In fact, when discussing the approach taken at this time, one author has likened Barnaby's concepts and associated designs as being like a miscellaneous, bizarre, and ill-assorted fleet of samples that composed the navy's fleets and squadrons in the middle years of Victoria's reign.[26]

The restrictions on funding did, however, allow for one large ironclad to be laid down during the period, and this ship, *Inflexible*, although having turrets, was apparently built in complete disregard for the lessons so painfully highlighted with the *Captain* farrago, and was initially provided with masts and sails that were intended for economy when passage making, as well as for training purposes. In practice these encumbrances were found to be virtually useless and were later removed. Displacing 11,880 tons, *Inflexible* carried huge 16in 80-ton muzzle-loading rifled guns in two turrets arranged en-echelon. This arrangement was not successful in use and was not repeated in later British ships, although other navies, particularly that of Imperial China, did more extensively use such turret arrangements in their capital ship designs. *Inflexible*'s guns were so long that they could not be loaded from inside the turret, so during this operation the guns were depressed into fixed armoured glacis in the adjacent deck, where loading took place. *Inflexible* was also the first ship to carry submerged torpedo tubes, and the heaviest armour of any warship to that date. This consisted of compound armour that varied between 12in and a massive 24in, depending on whether it was fitted to the ship's sides or its turrets.[27] Compound armour made up of layers of iron and steel was a new concept at the time, and its development and use will be more fully covered in a later chapter.

The idea of combining barbettes with broadside batteries still appeared to have advantages, however, as large guns in the barbettes could be more readily combined with smaller calibre guns mounted in the broadside batteries, which it was thought could be more easily used against rams and other small assault ships. In accord with this thinking, the realisation dawned that it was high time that the long series of experimental and 'one off' types should give way to an improved homogeneity in design. As a consequence, and as more funding also became a reality, Barnaby was tasked with designing a single class of six warships that incorporated barbettes and broadside batteries. Collectively known as the Admiral class, individual ships ranged from 9,500 to 10,600 tons displacement, with the first of these, *Collingwood*, being completed in 1887, and the last to be laid down, *Benbow*, in 1888. Although there were some differences both in sizes and numbers of guns and thickness of armour between the six ships of this class, in general they all had a low short belt of 18in-thick compound armour bounded by transverse armoured bulkheads and covered by an armoured deck, above which were coal bunkers placed thus to assist in preserving stability in case of damage to the unprotected sides.[28] The extremities of these ships from bow and stern and up to the junctions with either end of the armoured belt, comprised of unarmoured cellular compartments.

These so-called central citadel ships carried two large barbette installations that were fashioned like pear-shaped polygons. These were situated at either end of the citadel and incorporated hydraulic gun mountings, with the gun loading gear at the back of the barbettes. The main armament consisted of two breech-loaders in each turret, breech mechanisms by now having been vastly improved, and these guns varied from 12in to around 16in calibre, depending on which Admiral class ship was being considered. In addition, numerous other secondary armament installations were provided with guns that varied between 6.5in and 3-pounder calibre, and these were largely situated on the upper deck or in the central citadels of each ship. In addition a number of 14in torpedo tubes were carried in all ships of the class, and the last to be built, *Benbow*, was fitted with quick-firing guns.

Although not the first ship to be thus fitted, *Benbow* carried nineteen of these handy weapons that would be installed in many other later classes of capital ship. The need for, and the development of, quick-firing armament, is more fully dealt with in a later chapter. Ships of the Admiral class were fitted with twin screws and compound engines, with higher-pressure steam being delivered from up to twelve cylindrical boilers. In addition the *Admirals* were the first British capital ships to be fitted with forced draft to the boiler installations. Although this had little effect in the earlier class members, once improved, this arrangement allowed greater speeds to be obtained in later units of the class such as *Benbow*.

Iron had been superseded as the construction material for warship hulls since around 1879, once improvements in the production of mild steel had ensured that uniformity in strength, ductility, and malleability had become a reality, and that high quality steel could be produced and sold at a price that was not prohibitive.[29] However, although a few individual warships had been constructed of steel, with mixed results in use, the *Admirals* were the first homogeneous, if not identical, class of warship to be so constructed, and with their compound armour could readily be defined as the first steel-clad rather than ironclad, class of battleship in any of the world's navies.

In considering the design of the Admiral class of battleships it must be said that they incorporated a good measure of the qualities demanded by the unsettled naval opinion of the day, although their minimalist systems of protection were somewhat flawed.[30] Changes in the make-up of the Admiralty Board, however, meant that the concept of guns mounted in barbettes was now frowned on, and the next two ships

Admiral class barbette ship *Benbow* of 1885, the picture taken off her starboard bow. The forward barbette, which housed a single huge 16.25in breech-loader, can be clearly seen, as can details of the port anchor and its lifting gear. (National Museum of the Royal Navy)

Photographed showing her two forward 13.5in breech-loading rifled guns positioned in their barbette, *Anson*, the fifth of the Admiral class barbette ships to be completed, can be seen about to launch or pick up one of her boats using her port derrick. A second boat can also be seen moored to a spar. (National Museum of the Royal Navy)

The 1887 turret ship *Victoria* is shown in Valletta harbour, Malta. Providing better protection than Admiral class ships, *Victoria* carried a main armament that consisted of two 16.25in calibre breech-loading guns in a single large turret that can be seen just in front of the superstructure. (National Museum of the Royal Navy)

to be laid down, *Victoria* and *Sans Pareil*, both of which displaced 10,470 tons and were completed in 1890 and 1891 respectively, were given turrets and complete belts of 18in compound armour, as well as thinner armour on the turret, redoubt, and decks, giving them the highest percentage of armour of any seagoing warship since the earlier Reed-designed *Dreadnought*. These ships, which carried two monster 16.25in, 110-ton breech-loading guns in a single turret, had ugly profiles and were in fact the last single turret battleships to be built for the British Navy. Both ships did though carry a secondary battery of one 10in and twelve 6in breech-loaders, as well as some thirty-two smaller guns and eight torpedo tubes.

Although having only eight boilers, both *Victoria* and *Sans Pareil* boasted triple-expansion engines, for the first time fitted in naval ships, and these drove twin screws making both ships powerful and relatively fast vessels. They were both, however, 'Board models', and it is unlikely that Barnaby had much influence on their designs, which were produced based on the instructions he received, albeit that he and his team prepared a number of different sketch plans for the Admiralty Board's consideration.[31]

In 1893, *Victoria*, the then flagship of the Mediterranean fleet carrying the flag of Admiral Tryon, became infamous when, under Tryon's orders, she was accidentally rammed by the battleship *Camperdown* when the fleet was manoeuvring prior to entering the port of Tripoli. It has been estimated that this collision created an impact force of some 17–18,000ft-tons, similar to the muzzle energy of a 12in, 45-ton gun, and the stem and ram of *Camperdown* created a huge tapering gash in the side of *Victoria*, measuring 12ft wide at the deck line and extending some 28ft down, with around 8ft of this gash below the water line, allowing water to flow through the hole at an estimated rate of some 3,000 tons per minute.[32] Whilst the bow sections of *Campberdown* were severely damaged in the collision, the ship did remain afloat. However the damage to *Victoria* was so extensive and the inflow of water so great, that she was quickly overwhelmed, capsized, and sank with a great loss of life that included her admiral. The subsequent courts martial found that some confusion existed in relation to Tryon's orders at the time, and that the fact that some bulkhead and watertight doors had been left open and could not be closed fast enough, was instrumental in the capsize and sinking of the battleship.

Whilst the supporters of the ram viewed the catastrophe as another example of its power as a weapon, there were still many questions that remained unanswered, and not unnaturally public opinion again became concerned as to the powers of resistance, and the criteria for design of what they had assumed to be state-of-the-art battleships. A full investigation based on the courts martial evidence was subsequently carried out at the Admiralty, and by the use of models and calculations it was shown that *Victoria* had few design flaws, and that the reasons for her demise were more to do with operational matters, as the courts martial had suggested, and that arrangements should be put into force to ensure that these shortcomings were overcome.

There were still, however, many critics of Barnaby's designs. Edward Reed, who was in fact Barnaby's brother-in-law, was one, and he totally refuted the findings of the *Victoria* investigation when it was considered by Parliament. Where other Barnaby designs were concerned Reed was even more critical, specifically stating that in his view ships of the Admiral class suffered from:

> a dangerous combination of long un-armoured ends comprising about forty-five
> per cent of the water line area with so shallow a belt of armour that when the
> un-armoured ends are injured and filled by the sea, as they would be in action,
> there would remain so little armour left above water that a very slight inclination
> of the ship would put it all below water. So great is the consequent danger of
> these ships capsizing, if ever called upon to engage in a serious battle at close
> quarters, that the writer cannot conscientiously regard them as armoured ships.[33]

Serving naval officers were also critical, with one eminent admiral summarising his views in a letter to *The Times* newspaper, and unhappily noting that: 'during the Barnaby era a number of false steps were taken where battleship design was concerned.'[34]

However in Barnaby's defence it must be remembered that this period was one of accelerating technical change, and in examining the attitudes that existed within the Admiralty and more generally in the naval service as a whole, it is evident that although the suggestions of the Committee on Designs had tentatively provided an initial focus, nothing approaching a basic idea as to what constituted the most efficient form of warship design had as yet been formulated. As a consequence it was almost impossible to produce a universally approved design, any

Better protected than previous battleships, *Trafalgar*, the named ship of the Trafalgar class of turret ships, is shown here with funnels that in 1891 were raised some 17ft in order to improve the natural draught to her boilers and so increase their efficiency. (National Museum of the Royal Navy)

consensus on design parameters, or even agreement on how warships should be tactically used in practice.[35]

Ordnance was increasing in size and power, yet there was great confusion on what the mix of large and small guns should be and how and where they should best be located on and in a warship's hull. In addition iron armour in all but the greatest thickness was seen to provide poor protection at the close-quarters fighting ranges that, owing to low standards of shooting and slow rate of fire, was all too common in the world's battle fleets, and the efficient production of sound composite armour was still in its infancy. The torpedo was also beginning to have an effect, though it was still feeble and inaccurate in practice, whilst the ram on the other hand was still perceived as a formidable weapon of attack.[36]

Combined with political and economic restrictions, reluctance on the part of the Admiralty to build ships that technical change might soon make obsolete, and the claims and counter-claims of various theorists, this position created an uncertainty amongst naval authorities that generated both inconsistent designs and construction policies during this period.[37] It is not surprising, therefore, that the 1870s and early 1880s saw a prolific variation in warship types, so that the so-called 'samples' within the fleet could each be used to test theoretical concepts enabling both their good and bad attributes to be observed in practice, before committing to whole classes of particular designs. In contrast, however, by the 1890s design had stabilised, theory and practice had become more closely matched, and as a consequence of increased funding and heightened political and public interest in naval matters, greatly stimulated by navalist propaganda, arbitrary displacement restrictions were lifted and the number of new ships being built was significantly increased.

THE PRE-DREADNOUGHT EMERGES

The decade of the 1880s began with the ironclad and ended with the steel-clad battleship, a change in terminology that through the 1890s corresponded with a significant crystallisation in warship design and function. Change and improvement would continue into the 1890s and beyond, but the 1880s saw the last violent swings between heavy guns and heavy armour, the last eccentric distribution of main armament and finally the end of sails for capital ships. It also saw the end of experimental designs for ships of different types, few of which were suited to working together in squadron or fleet formation.[1]

During the summer of 1885 William Gladstone resigned as British Prime Minister, being replaced by Lord Salisbury, and Lord George Hamilton became First Lord of the Admiralty. Pending a possible general election, the Conservative naval policy was only developed in a limited way, but in view of concerns about the effectiveness of the then naval administration, as well as management of the Royal Dockyards, where years of financial constringency had played havoc with both personnel and material, Hamilton pressed ahead with an initial series of changes prior to introducing a planned programme of administrative reforms and reorganisations. As a consequence all the naval lords on the Board of Admiralty were changed, and in arranging this, Hamilton ensured that from then on political considerations would have a much reduced part in Admiralty appointments.[2]

The new First Sea Lord was Admiral Sir Arthur Hood, and although the then Controller Vice-Admiral Brandreth initially retained his position, when his term of office came to an end, Vice-Admiral William Graham succeeded him. During this period Nicholas Barnaby, who would later be knighted, also handed in his resignation and retired from the naval service on the grounds that his poor health made it impossible for him to continue his duties. One historian has suggested that this was not the real reason for Barnaby's retirement and that the real cause was in fact the constant disagreements, quarrels, and open criticism with and from his brother-in-law and close neighbour Edward Reed, that was creating problems with family relationships.[3] Whatever the reason for Barnaby leaving, a new Director of Naval Construction was required, and William White, who had been a senior member of Barnaby's team, but who was now working at Armstrong's as that company's Chief Designer and Manager of Warship Building, was offered the post. Hamilton had to make some complex deals with Armstrong's and with White himself to facilitate this, but eventually later in that year White took up his new post.[4]

In his capacity as First Lord, Hamilton was a strong reformer and he did not fully subscribe to the generally accepted views that were originally put forward by Lord Randolph Churchill, when he defined the objective of administrative action within a government department as, 'the maximum of efficiency consistent with the amount of expenditure which the tax-payer or his representatives will tolerate'.[5] When White was appointed, however, and initially tasked with carrying out a review of Admiralty and Dockyard administration, Hamilton, who looked on Lord Randolph's synopsis as too restricting, promised his support to any arrangement that White's, 'varied experience in dockyard and private establishments would advocate as tending to economy and expedition and efficiency'.[6]

Work associated with the design of new warships did not appear to be pressing when White took on his new role as Director of Naval Construction, as a number of new ships were being built at the time. White's initial priority was thus the reorganisation of Admiralty Construction and Engineering Departments and the reform of dockyard administration. Soon after he had commenced this work White realised that whilst some parts of these functions could be readily improved, others, given the culture that then existed within the Admiralty, could probably only be gradually corrected with tentative steps towards reform. This was especially the case as the government was in a minority and would be faced with great upheaval in the event of a general election.[7]

The prevalent opinion at the time was that the closer the management and operations in the dockyards approximated to those of private shipyards, the more efficient they would become. White pointed out though that a royal dockyard differed from a private shipbuilding establishment in that it was also a royal arsenal, and its funding and operations were subject to the scrutiny and control of Parliament.[8] He also stressed that the dockyard organisation was by far the largest industrial firm in the country, employing over 6,000 staff in its five yards, and that as the greatest expenditure arose from the cost of labour and materials consumed in the work of the yards, these costs should not be hidden, as was often the case at the time, but should be clearly highlighted and reflected in separate management accounts. Other proposals included truly independent audit arrangements under the control of the Accountant General, a streamlined and more focused administration, more robust and clearer divisions of professional and other duties, better clarity of roles and communication arrangements, and more appropriate departmental organisation structures.[9]

In the early months of 1886 the Ritchie Committee, which had been set up to supervise the reorganisation, approved White's proposals, as did the Treasury. The proposals formed the basis of a general instruction that was then issued to all concerned, however before these instructions could be acted upon, the Prime Minister, Lord Salisbury, resigned, the government fell, a general election took place, and William Gladstone became the new Prime Minister, with Lord Rippon succeeding Hamilton as First Lord of the Admiralty.[10] As a consequence Edward Reed, very rarely a supporter of White, was promoted from the backbenches to become a Lord of the Treasury. Most of White's proposed changes survived, however, and were supported by the new administration, although his plans to bring dockyards under his own wing did become a casualty when an independent dockyards directorate, under Dr Francis Elgar, was set up instead. This latter arrangement, although criticised by White, might well have been a blessing in disguise for him as the normal duties associated with his naval construction role proved to be onerous and highly time-consuming in practice, and would have adversely affected White's ability to take on overall responsibility for the dockyards also. In the event, White was made Assistant Controller as well as Director of Naval Construction, and this meant that the Director of Dockyards post was inferior in rank to his in any case. It is evident, however, that White may well have considered himself the victim of a Treasury intrigue where this was concerned, especially as Reed was now in a position to make mischief, and was fully aware of the personal dislike White had for Elgar, who in the past had worked as Reed's assistant, and had been active in attacking both the Admiralty and White himself.[11]

Departmental politics aside the changes that were introduced at this time meant that for the foreseeable future the nineteenth-century British dockyards would develop to become the fastest and most effective warship builders in the country, if not in the whole world. A further positive change was additionally made when it was decided to alter the traditional arrangements whereby naval ordnance was ordered by the army-focused War Department, which also submitted the naval ordnance estimates each year. This arrangement frequently led to friction during periods when funds were scarce, and the Admiralty often felt that they invariably got the thin end of the wedge. Although some beneficial changes had been introduced in 1882 to alleviate some of these problems, the situation was far from ideal, so as part of the 1886 reorganisation, a separate Naval Ordnance department was created under Captain John Fisher. This meant that after a settling-in period, the navy was at long last able to achieve full control over the supply and disposal of its own ordnance and more appropriate management of all associated matters[12] then became possible.

The reforms instigated by William White ensured greater confidence that naval funding would in the future be used effectively. However, although a small building programme had been initiated for the construction of mainly cruisers to allay public fears that the strength of the British Navy was falling behind that of its rivals, many of the naval members of the Admiralty Board, who provided the civilian First Lord with professional advice, continued to believe that a large programme of warship building was still not required.[13] White soon came to disagree with this view, however, and a year after his appointment, when he had amassed sufficient supporting information, he took the initiative and submitted a detailed report showing the probable wastage in ships that because of age would become obsolete in the period 1888 to 1892. He also included a list of new ships that should be built to replace those removed, as well as to provide a more appropriate force of capital ships within the overall naval establishment. White's proposals listed some seventy-two ships of all types, including a number of battleships, all of which should be replaced with new construction at an estimated total cost of around £9 million.[14]

Initially the Board was unwilling to fully accept White's report, mainly because they baulked at removing so many well-known ships from the Navy List, but by the late 1880s a worsening international situation that included a war scare with France, a possible Franco-Russian alliance, which would have generated an opposing fleet that contained nearly as many battleships as Britain, and a resulting public clamour for naval expansion, forced them to alter their views.[15] On the strength of this, together with results of naval manoeuvres that indicated that the navy as it stood was altogether inadequate to take the offensive in a war with one, let alone two, great powers, and after much consideration, the Admiralty Board finally made a recommendation for an even bigger programme of construction than that submitted by White. This proposal, which was for the building of seventy-two ships between 1889 and 1894, including ten battleships, thirty-seven cruisers, and other smaller warships, at a cost of £21.5 million, was firstly submitted to the cabinet and then Parliament, and in the spring of that year was placed on the statute books to become the Naval Defence Act 1889.[16]

Prior to this new programme, the Navy Estimates always reflected immediate requirements rather than any comprehensive scheme or plan, and although not as bad as the days of the fleet of samples, this still meant that only a small number of capital ships were built at any one time, quite often as low as two or three from one design. As a consequence there was little homogeneity in the fleet and the armaments were often so different in character and disposition that there was little possibility of individual ships acting in unison during an action. In addition, there was no simultaneous provision of cruisers and other ships that could support the battle fleet when required. All this was changed with the Naval Defence Act and subsequent legislation, and from 1889 onwards huge programmes of construction embracing ships of all types meant that a truly modern fleet that was capable of combined action, could more readily be developed.[17]

Inconsistencies in warship design and development that marked the period up to 1889 were swept away by the designs of the next decade. Although much political infighting, differing views, and vested interests were still a reality within the Admiralty corridors of power, warship development progressed in a more effective, regular, and consistent fashion. Even though the challenge from the navies of other nations was growing, the Royal Navy was at the time still dominant in material and associated resources, as well as enjoying a level of support both publicly and politically as well as financially, that it had not experienced for many years. Together with changes that the ever developing technologies of the nineteenth century brought, this advantage allowed for the construction of large numbers of ships that where battleships in particular were concerned, were of significantly greater size and capacity than hitherto, enabling an improved balance in design to be achieved.[18] The new improved battleship types created as a consequence, and defined by future historians as pre-Dreadnoughts, would soon populate the world's navies, including the soon-to-be-powerful ones of Germany, America, and Japan, and for a relatively short period would be the favoured weapon at the forefront of naval strategy, that is of course until the even more advanced Dreadnought type made them, and all other capital ship designs, redundant.

The first battleships specified by the Admiralty Board, and designed as part of the new programme, were the eight ships of the Royal Sovereign class. Whilst generally agreeing on the form of these ships, there was still some dissention within the Board as to whether the main armament should be arranged in turrets or in barbettes. The biggest supporter of the turret option was in fact Lord Hood, the First Sea Lord at the time, and although he was in a minority, his position gave him a certain amount of influence. The matter was eventually settled when it was agreed that one of the new Royal Sovereign class would be built as a turret ship, whilst the remaining seven would be provided with barbette installations.

There was still, however, some related concerns within the naval service and to allay this and more importantly to counter undue criticism of the new designs, which Edward Reed, using his position as Member of Parliament and Treasury Lord, had raised in *The Times* newspaper, concerning cost, size, and fighting ability, White was tasked with preparing a comprehensive paper for presentation to the influential Institution of Naval Architects. This paper compared turret and barbette arrangements, described the main features of the approved designs, and in White's words: 'contrasted their protection, armament, speed, and coal endurance with the corresponding features in other battle ships designed during the previous twenty years, making it clear that there are good reasons why these ships surpass in size any previously constructed vessels of the Royal Navy.'[19]

The discussions that ensued after the presentation were lengthy and heated, but in his usual way White was well prepared, and was able to deal with and dismiss every point and argument raised by critics such as Edward Reed and his supporters. This was done in such a decisive and knowledgeable way that all opposition to the new ship designs and concepts was overturned, and Reed's views were seen as being based on resentment and bad feeling. As White's biographer later noted, Edward Reed had used his parliamentary seat as a convenient post from which to attack the work of one who was not only a professional rival, but as a civil servant debarred from the normal right of reply. Now that White had met his critic on a fair field, he had vindicated his methods completely. When he sat down his adversary had been silenced, and he had secured for himself an authority without rival.[20]

When, based on the Admiralty Board's requirements, William White designed the *Royal Sovereign* and her sisters he created the first true pre-Dreadnought battleships, and provided the British Navy with the finest group of fighting ships afloat at the time, which it was said sat on the water with majesty and distinction. For the first time since *Devastation* set a new standard for unsightliness, a group of British battleships provided a proud, pleasing, and symmetrical profile that was unmatched by any other warship in any of the world's navies.[21] That these ships were admirable examples of design was generally amply recognised within the naval service, and White received numerous letters of congratulation from serving officers after they had visited particular ships or became involved with them during periods of service.

Displacing around 14,000 tons, all the ships of the Royal Sovereign class apart from *Hood*, which unlike her sisters carried her main armament in turrets, were designed with high freeboard, allowing for greater speed, enhanced stability, and better performance in a sea way. These ships had 8.5ft wide water-line belts of compound steel armour with a maximum thickness of 18in, and covered in by a horizontal armoured deck 3in thick. The belt extended for two thirds of the length of each ship and armoured bulkheads of 16in and 14in thickness closed in the belt at forward- and after-ends respectively. Above the belt, from middle to main decks, 4in nickel steel armour was worked with the intention of providing protection against large shells bursting outside the ship, and to prevent the free perforation of the sides above the belt by quick-firing guns. The improved armour was such that only thin teak backing of around 2.5in was required, comparing starkly with the 15in of wooden backing required, for example in ships of the Admiral class. The barbettes were pear shaped and of very substantial construction, and carried a maximum thickness of compound armour of 17in that extended right down to the middle deck.[22] The turret armour of *Hood* was of similar type and size.

In numerous former ships, notably Barnaby's Admirals, the designed weight had been exceeded during construction with a deeper immersion on completion. This condition led to the top of the armoured belt being nearly on a level with the water line when all the coal bunkers were full, potentially affecting stability and laying bare and unprotected an important part of the hull to damage from shellfire. This problem was overcome in the Royal Sovereign and subsequent classes by allowing 500 tons for contingencies or other changes that might prove necessary during the construction process. The allowance was termed the 'board margin' and none of it could be appropriated for extra ordnance etc. without sanction of the Admiralty Board. If not utilised in a particular ship it was available for extra coal and additional bunker accommodation.[23] Owing to the existence of this margin as well as improved dockyard management arrangements, each one of the Royal Sovereign class achieved its designed displacement when completed.

The relatively high freeboard of these ships meant much of the pear-shaped barbette installation was hidden below decks with only their crowns showing. An

Royal Sovereign of 1891 was the named ship of what was to become the first class of true pre-Dreadnought battleships. Shown in the photograph under way in a calm sea her twin funnels and forward 13.5in breech-loaders retained in their barbette are evident, as is her relatively high freeboard. (National Museum of the Royal Navy)

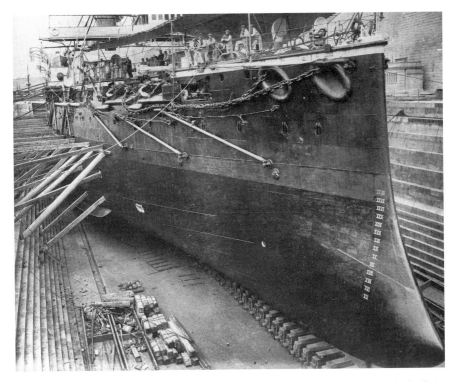

The photograph shows *Ramillies*, the second Royal Sovereign class battleship to be built, in dry dock undergoing some repair work. The shape and form of her ram bow can be seen, and the size of this protuberance judged with reference to the crew members on her foredeck. (National Museum of the Royal Navy)

upper storey contained the turntable for the guns, whilst the hydraulic turning and operating engines were situated at a lower level. Heavy armour protected the turntable and hydraulics and extended down to the armoured belt to alleviate any possibility of explosion damage by shells entering below them. Loading of the four 13.5in breech-loading guns was via fixed ammunition trunks when these massive weapons were brought to an end-on position. All the secondary armament consisted of quick-firing guns including ten 6in, sixteen 6-pounders, and twelve 3-pounders. The largest of these were placed in casements whilst the remainder were behind lightly armoured shields.[24]

In addition to their numerous heavy ordnance and quick-firing guns, all ships of the Royal Sovereign class were additionally fitted with seven 18in torpedo tubes, five above water and two below, although *Hood* carried two less than her consorts. In all cases one tube pointed astern whilst the others were fitted in the bows. Torpedo tubes of 14in diameter had been experimentally fitted to a few battleships previously but White's new ships were the first to carry torpedoes of the larger, more powerful kind. The original idea of end-on torpedo tubes was to provide an alternative to the ram, although all ships at this time were still built with ram bows. Although this arrangement continued for some time, bow tubes in battleships were never popular in the British Navy as the tubes were said to affect speed, and there were concerns that if a ship steaming at high speed fired her torpedoes, she might overrun her own torpedoes, which at the time were relatively slow, with very severe results. The stern tube appears to owe its origin to the idea that an overpowered ship running from a superior enemy might, at least in part, protect herself.[25]

The steam engines of the ships of the Royal Sovereign class were vertical three-cylinder triple-expansion units that drove twin shafts, and a mixture of natural and forced draught was used in conjunction with their eight return-tube cylindrical boilers. Electricity had first been used in the British Navy in the early 1870s, when electrical battery-driven gun-firing circuits and carbon arc searchlights were introduced. In the same decade incandescent and filament light bulbs became available, and later direct current distribution systems began to be installed in various ships. In 1895 *Royal Sovereign* herself became the first ship of the class to have her decks electrically illuminated at night to assist crew members when coaling was taking place.[26] Although the Royal Sovereigns had some critics, particularly Edward Reed, on completion they were found to be good sea boats, although they did tend to roll at speed. This defect was completely overcome by the subsequent fitting of bilge keels, whereupon these ships became very steady, and provided excellent gun platforms. The Royal Sovereign class ships were all well built, some in the royal dockyards and some in private yards, in fact they were all so well constructed that when they became obsolete and were scrapped in 1911–12, they were all practically as good from the point of view of construction, as when they were first built.[27]

Significantly smaller but similar in design to the Royal Sovereigns the Centurion class battleship *Barfleur* sedately steams past, driven by her triple-expansion engines, whilst a Maltese fisherman manoeuvres his highly ornamented and distinctly shaped boat with the aid of muscle power alone. (National Museum of the Royal Navy)

Apart from ships of the Royal Sovereign class a number of smaller second-class coastal defence battleships, as well as cruisers and smaller vessels, were designed by White and his team and built under provisions of the Naval Defence Act. This Act, however, did not have the restraining effect on warship building by rival nations, particularly France and Russia, that Hamilton and his Board had envisaged. During the period these two nations had become allies, and by 1893 had between them laid down twelve first-class battleships with a further five planned for the following year. Britain, by comparison, had ten first- and second-class battleships built under the Naval Defence Act, with a further three vessels laid down or projected under the estimates of 1892–93, and 1893–94, and whilst the Royal Sovereigns were generally considered at the time to be the finest capital ships in the world, this still left Britain two battleships short of the two power standard when measured in modern capital ships. Relationships between Britain and her two rivals had also seriously deteriorated over various territorial and other disputes, and although the new Liberal Government that had come to power in 1892, for a time resisted demands in Parliament and the British press for a further increase in capital ships, it finally agreed in 1894 to a further five years of planned warship construction to be named the Spencer Programme after the then First Lord. This programme and its associated legislation authorised the building of an additional nine battleships, as well as numerous cruisers and smaller craft, at an estimated total cost of around £21 million,[28] a figure which although considered large at the time, was in fact slightly less than that which had applied to the previous programme.

The nine first-class battleships built under the Spencer Programme were known as the Majestic class after the first of the nine to be laid down. These ships were enhanced versions of *Renown*, a second-class battleship designed on an experimental basis by White on the instructions of Admiral John Fisher, who was now the new Admiralty Controller, and White's immediate superior. In the Majestics the 13.5in guns, which had for so long been the standard guns for first-class battleships, were replaced by a new type of 12in gun that Fisher favoured, and which, although of a smaller calibre, was far superior to its predecessor.

The largest single class of battleships ever built, the nine ships of the Majestic class each displaced around 14,900 tons, and like the Royal Sovereigns were given high freeboard, although their disposition of armour was very different. White had come to believe that by reducing the thickness of the water-line armoured belt, and substituting a curved and stronger low-level deck, together with heavier uniformly thick side armour, that extended from the edges of the curved deck up to the main deck, overall protection would be improved.[29] This concept was built into the designs of M*ajestic* and her sisters, where the belt consisted of 9in-thick armour produced by the Harvey process, but equal in resistance to the 18in-thick compound armour of the Royal Sovereigns. The development of this type of armour is more fully dealt with in a later chapter.

The belt armour was carried up to the main deck for a height of 15ft and extended for about two thirds of each ship's total length. The protective deck between barbettes was run level across at the middle line, but sloped down to the bottom of the belt/side armour. This deck was 3in thick on the flat and 4in on the slope either side. Such an arrangement of armour it was expected would give protection against quick-firing guns in their larger calibres and would more effectively cater for the fact that due to additions and alterations, ships could well increase their draughts by up to an inch each year as time went on, and the value of the older form of armoured belt could progressively reduce as a result. Narrow belts were of course also prone to becoming ineffective if a ship was damaged in action or seriously overloaded,[30] and the belts of the Majestic class ships provided a marked improvement where these aspects were concerned.

The new and improved belts were closed forward and aft with 14in and 12in-thick armoured bulkheads, whilst the barbette armour was reduced to 7in, although the armour around the crown of each was 14in thick. In the case of the Majestics the barbettes were circular in form, thus allowing loading of ready-use ammuni-

Carrying a new type of barbette-mounted 12in calibre breech-loaders that were encased in thin shields that in effect formed light turrets, *Majestic*, the named ship of an exceptionally large class of nine similar battleships, is shown here tied up alongside a harbour wall. (National Museum of the Royal Navy)

Taken from a similar vessel steaming in front, an unidentified Majestic class battleship is shown in line ahead. Although some after-deck detail, including the end of the leading ship's main armament guns, is evident, the second ship is too far away to make out individual features. (National Museum of the Royal Navy)

The Majestic class pre-Dreadnought shown here is *Illustrious*, the third of the class to be built. She clearly has steam up, as can be seen from the funnel smoke, but does not appear to be moving. Perhaps she is about to get under way or has just arrived. (National Museum of the Royal Navy)

tion from a number of bins at positions that were not fixed, as was the case with the Royal Sovereign ships. This arrangement was achieved in practice by fitting hydraulic rammers attached to the turntable that revolved above the top of the barbette. All secondary armament was protected by 6in casements, and heavily armoured shields or hoods encased the normally open barbette tops, giving at long last at least some protection to the guns and their crews from the effects of plunging fire. Modified forms of these hoods continued to be used in later barbette installations and virtually turned the barbette into a turret, although it differed from the old type of closed turret in that the gun ports extended to the lower edge of the barbette front structure, so that the guns still fired over this heavily armoured wall.[31]

The operation of coaling the ship *Caesar* of 1896, the first Majestic class ship to be built. This was a messy and labour-intensive exercise. Coal was however extremely important, not only as fuel, but also as secondary protection when in the coal bunkers, and even occasionally as ballast to improve stability. (National Museum of the Royal Navy)

Instead of the usual 13.5in calibre ordnance, the main armament of the Majestic class ships consisted of four lighter and more powerful wire-wound guns of 12in calibre, arranged so that each barbette held two guns apiece. These weapons were mounted in trunnions at the centre of gravity of each gun and its slide, thus enabling the elevating gear to be worked by hand power. Secondary armament consisted of all quick-fire guns and included twelve 6in, sixteen 12-pounders, and twelve 2-pounders. Five 18in torpedo tubes were also fitted, four submerged and one above the water line. In later years electric ammunition hoists were fitted for use with the 6in quick-firing guns.[32]

Three-cylinder triple-expansion engines drove two shafts and steam was provided from eight cylindrical boilers using a mixture of forced and natural draught. All the Majestics proved to be good sea boats in use although coal consumption was always high, and later in their careers some of the furnaces were converted to oil firing, with a resulting increased efficiency and reduction in the maximum weight of fuel carried.[33] Ships of the Majestic class were considered to be the finest examples of naval architecture of their day, and with them William White introduced a general design that was often copied by other nations, and which, with certain modifications, served as the base design for all further battleships built during his term in office. The final costs of the Spencer Programme were around £31 million, much of which resulted from the building of the nine Majestic class battleships and although there was some, not too loud, criticism of their armour arrangements, this was soon overcome, for as White pointed out when describing *Majestic* the name ship:

> there would be no narrow belt, but instead a veritable wall of armour would rise nearly ten feet above water, and if in an extreme case an extra weight of some 400 tons were added, the extra immersion would only be about 8 inches, and consequently the special reasons that gave rise to the Board margin, the lowering of the top of the belt in narrow belted ships, would not apply to her.[34]

The same was of course true of all the other ships of the Majestic class.

THE GREAT ARMS RACE

In 1894 to 1895 a short but bitter war occurred in the Far East between China and Japan, over territorial and other related matters. The naval battles of this war took place between a well equipped, well led, and expanding Japanese Navy and the larger but poorly equipped navy of Imperial China. China's armed forces, whilst superior in number to those of Japan, were not so well organised or led and had existed in their present form for many years without taking advantage of new ideas or improved methods of waging war. The armed forces of Japan, however, had more recently been formed when that nation emerged from a state of feudal isolation earlier that century. During this transition the Japanese military had absorbed modern European ideas of both strategic and tactical warfare, with their naval and army officers being trained by European advisors, and their warships, many of which had been purchased from European shipyards, were of the latest form.

Japan was thus able to defeat her larger enemy in a series of overwhelming victories. Great Britain, who wished to extend her influence and operations in the Far East, had in the past provided technical support to, and constructed warships for, Japan. Whilst happy to continue with this arrangement after the war, Japan increasingly tended also to turn to an expanding Germany for advice, as that country's general philosophy of militarism appeared to appeal to the Japanese Government. Imperial Russia was expanding and gaining influence in the Far East also, much to the concern of both Britain and Japan, and although this appeared to indicate that Britain had a natural ally, and that Japan's ports and coaling facilities would be a great asset in the case of possible hostilities with Russia, there is no evidence that the British Government took any significant steps in courting Japan at the time, but instead decided to strengthen their own naval forces on the China station.[1]

In 1895 the British Conservative Government was returned to power with Lord Salisbury as Prime Minister, and George Goschen, who had been Chancellor of the Exchequer at the time of the Naval Defence Act, became First Lord of the Admiralty. This pleased the country's navalists, as Goschen was a supporter of naval expansion, and carried great weight both in the cabinet and in the wider political arena. In view of this, and because of what was seen as the pressing problems in the Far East, the government agreed to a further extension of the British fleet, and the estimates for 1896–97 provided for five new battleships to strengthen the squadron stationed in Far Eastern waters.[2]

These new ships were to be known as the Canopus class, and in their design William White proposed that they should have greater length to beam and that the copper sheathing with wooden backing, which was normally fitted to steel warships used in Far Eastern waters to discourage bottom fouling, should be left off. In this way, White argued, the ships would be lighter and have less draught, and would be more able to safely travel through the Suez Canal,[3] whilst good and convenient dockyard facilities in the area would allow ships' bottoms to be cleaned on a regular basis. At this time two battleships based on the design of the Royal Sovereigns were being built in Britain for the Japanese Navy, with further orders likely. White, who had recently been knighted, was of course fully aware of this and in designing the Canopus class he was clear that his new creations should at least be as powerful as those earlier, highly successful, Japanese warships.

As was by now common practice, White used tank testing during the design process of the Canopus class ships in order to establish the resistance of water to particular hull forms. Early work on resistance had been carried out by William Froude as far back as 1871 using completed ships, in which he was able to build up records of hull resistance at various speeds, and was able to clearly show that resistance increased very rapidly at higher speeds, with the result that much greater engine power was required to increase and maintain a ship's speed by even a small amount. It was clearly impracticable to extend this work using full-size ships, so scale models were built and tested in large tanks of water. Realising the benefits to design parameters that Froude's work signified, the British Admiralty soon sanctioned it, and a naval testing tank was established at Torquay. This was later moved to Haslar near Portsmouth, where it was known as the Admiralty Experimental Works.

By the time the Canopus class were built it was established practice to have models made and run in the Haslar experimental tank so that the resistance of various hull forms could be determined, and data provided to allow the most efficient hull forms, in terms of their resistance at least, to be incorporated into new warship designs.[4] Tank testing experiments were soon extended to include the design of propellers, rudders, the usefulness of bilge keels, and numerous other areas. William Froude's son Robert later continued his father's work, and in an attempt to compete with Great Britain, the naval authorities in a number of other countries also soon began to establish their own experimental tanks.

The first of the six Canopus class ships was laid down at the end of 1896 and the others followed early in the following year. Similar in design to the Majestics but of smaller dimensions, they displaced 13,150 tons and had a 6in-thick belt of the new Krupp armour, that was equivalent to about 8in of Harvey plate, and had a greater resisting power than the Harvey type. This belt was closed in with lightly armoured bulkheads and there were two protected decks. The two barbettes were circular in form and encased in armour some 12in thick, whilst gun houses and casemates for the smaller guns were covered with 6in armour plate,[5] and in *Vengeance*, the last of the class to be built, gun houses were protected with Krupp steel armour. As was normal practice at the time the belt did not extend for the whole ship's length so that the buoyancy of bow and stern would not be adversely affected. However, in the Canopus class the bows and stern were lightly armoured with 2in plate in an attempt to placate the somewhat un-informed public agitation against so-called soft-ended ships that was current at the time. This thin armour would in any case have provided very little protection against even light projectiles unless they were fired at very long range, and White never made a secret of his cynical disbelief in the arrangement.[6] The cast-steel ram on the other hand, which was much higher than in previous battleships, was additionally armoured with 2in nickel-steel plates over its normal skin.

Ordnance in these ships consisted of a main armament of four 12in, 35 calibre guns, two in each barbette, twelve 6in, 40 calibre quick-firing guns, and ten 12-pounders. Most of this secondary armament was located within the casemates or gun houses, and four submerged 18in torpedo tubes were also carried.[7] Although her sisters were not so fitted, *Vengeance* was provided with the newly developed Vickers chain rammer, for loading the larger guns at any elevation, and this successfully reduced the time taken to load the guns when in use. In addition, the Krupp plates, on the front of the barbette shields, were angled instead of curved, as this hardened steel, although superior in protective power, could not be bent as readily as Harvey steel plate. This arrangement set a fashion that was to become universal where battleship design was concerned.

Ships of the Canopus class were the first to have Belleville water-tube boilers installed and these were much more efficient than the other boilers fitted to previous battleships. Twenty such boilers were fitted, and provided steam to the three-cylinder triple-expansion engines that were coupled to twin screws enabling steaming to take place at full power speeds well in excess of those achieved by *Majestic* and her sisters for example. The development of engines, boilers, and auxiliaries in these and other capital ship classes is more fully dealt with in a later chapter.

In June of 1897 the British fleet assembled at Spithead to celebrate Queen Victoria's Diamond Jubilee. In this review some 165 warships including twenty-one first-class battleships, all of which had been gathered without withdrawing ships from foreign stations, were positioned in six lines that were each some five miles long, indicating the immense size and fighting strength of this, the mightiest of battle fleets, that in addition now enjoyed the strategic benefit of a number of worldwide naval bases and coaling stations. Reflecting on this great array of ships, a somewhat nationalistic *Times* newspaper correspondent noted at the time that:

Canopus class pre-Dreadnought *Goliath* shown in line abreast pounding through rough seas with some of her consorts in a battle squadron. Completed in 1900, *Goliath*, the third of the class to be commissioned was, like her sisters, a smaller and faster version of the Majestics. (National Museum of the Royal Navy)

A clear side view of *Ocean*, another ship of the Canopus class. The ship's high freeboard and large array of secondary armament, including some in sponsons to allow some end-on fire, is evident also, and she still has steam up and at least one of her port anchors is down. (National Museum of the Royal Navy)

Canopus, the named ship of the class, is shown here battling through rough seas. Although she was taking white water over her foredeck, her high freeboard, so unlike that of many previous capital ships, meant that her forward accommodation was likely to be relatively dry. (National Museum of the Royal Navy)

Such an assemblage of warships under the flag of any other power would have implied a direct menace. Our least friendly foreign critic can, however, find nothing to arouse his susceptibilities in the reassertion of a time-honoured national policy. A powerful British navy is the best guarantee of the peace of the world.[8]

A schematic of the Spithead gathering is included at Appendix 2, and this has been included in an attempt to indicate the vast array of British warships that were on show during that event.

Whilst such manifestations of Britain's naval power might have impressed the nation's public at large, longer-term prospects were far less favourable in view of the growing warship building programmes of almost every other industrialised nation in the world, and instead of reducing their naval aspirations, many of the representatives of other powers that viewed the vast Spithead display had their appetites whetted instead. Indeed the review seems to have been a major influence in accelerating the French, German, and Russian warship building activity for that and subsequent years, whilst industrial unrest and strike action during the second half of 1897 conversely retarded Britain's shipbuilding efforts.[9]

The British Navy was admittedly very strong, but it was evidently unlikely to be able to hold its position in all waters against so many potential rivals. Not only were the European powers extending their naval resources, but as Admiral Custance, the then Director of Naval Intelligence reported:

In consequence of the rise of the American, Argentine, and Chilean navies, the superiority which the British squadrons formerly enjoyed on the North America/ West Indies and Pacific stations had passed away, and they were now completely outclassed by the American fleet on the former station and were inferior to all three on the latter. On the southeast coast of America the British squadron was now inferior to Argentina as well as Brazil. The supremacy formerly enjoyed on the China station had passed to Japan, and the British squadron, considerably superior to the Franco-Russian combination in 1889, was hardly a match for them ten years later. Only on the East Indies, the Cape, and the Australian stations did the British squadrons remain superior to those of other nations.[10]

This report, whilst illustrating the extent of Britain's worldwide naval involvement, also indicated that all was not well, and that Britain's ability to contain both European and other powers in the way that she had been able to do in the eighteenth and most of the nineteenth centuries, was beginning to break down. Yet this was the result of only a few years of the new worldwide navalism of the mid-1880s, and this position was likely to become much worse when rapidly growing powers like the United States as well as Imperial Germany and Japan channelled even more of their national resources into developing their fleets. At the end of 1883 the number of British capital ships nearly equalled the total of all other naval powers combined. By 1897, some fourteen years later, however, this comfortable ratio had shrivelled away with Great Britain having sixty-two battleships and the six countries with the largest navies having ninety-six battleships between them.[11]

This position was worrying to all concerned both at the Admiralty and in Parliament, and irrespective of the great improvements in the fleet that had occurred since the 1880s, it appeared that much still needed to be done, and that further change was still required. The tremendous capital investment needed for replacement programmes made the Admiralty reluctant to scrap low value and obsolete ships, and some historians have claimed that naval tactics of the period lagged behind naval design. Admirals who had been raised in sail it was claimed were slow to adapt to the new conditions imposed by steam engines and other machinery and reforms were slow and often resented by the more conservative naval officers and strategists. In addition the dead weight of tradition which handicapped the British Navy was not felt to the same extent in the world's newer navies, which had no heroic past to obscure modern realities in a sentimental haze.[12]

Whilst there might have been some truth in this view, it was unlikely to have had a major effect on the excellence or otherwise of the British Battle Fleet. William White and those responsible for balancing design aspirations with political and other considerations were in general highly competent individuals with the interests of Britain and its navy at heart, and in any case most other European nations, apart perhaps from newer naval powers such as Germany and Italy, contained traditionalists within their naval hierarchies. In addition of course Britain spent much more on its navy than any other power. In 1898, for example, this was some £5 million more than the spending of France and Russia combined, and on average for ships of a higher displacement and motive power as well.[13] In accord with this position, and because Members of Parliament were aware of the issues raised in Admiral Custance's report, supplementary estimates were provided that year to enable the construction of a group of three battleships in addition to *Canopus* and her sisters. These new ships were to be known as the Formidable class.

For some time the British press, as well as many of the country's amateur strategists, had been calling for larger numbers of smaller battleships to be built, the argument being that most foreign nations were increasing their fleet numbers by doing just that, and to effectively counter this threat, British capital ships should follow the trend.[14] The British Admiralty, however, continued to believe that battleships of large dimensions made the most efficient gun platforms, and provided the best way of projecting superior naval power, even if they were somewhat fewer in number. The three ships of the Formidable class were, therefore, built to displace around 15,000 tons, and were thus even bigger than the earlier Majestics, and although similar to those ships in some other respects, were faster and more manoeuvrable in use, due to an improved hull form in which the deadwood at the stern was reduced.

Completed in 1901, *Formidable*, the named ship of the three-vessel Formidable class, is shown here under way. Similar to Canopus class ships, but more heavily armed with slightly longer guns in the main turrets and a larger secondary armament, *Formidable* and her sisters also carried more extensive Krupp steel armour than the previous class. (National Museum of the Royal Navy)

All the Formidable class ships were provided with Krupp steel armour through-out, that was said to have a resisting power some three times that of the similar size Harvey steel armoured plates fitted to *Majestic* and her sisters.[15] In these ships the belt was 9in thick for most of its length and extended to bow and stern, although beyond the citadel it was reduced to 3in towards the bow and 1.5in towards the stern. The decks were all armoured, as were the bulkheads fore and aft, but the armour on the circular barbettes was reduced from 14in to 12in thick in order to save weight higher up. Casemates were fitted with 6in armour, whilst gun shields carried armoured plates that varied from 10in to 8in in thickness.[16]

These ships carried improved forms of 12in guns that were 40-calibres long, and which were housed in the forward and after barbettes, two to each barbette. Loading arrangements were such that the guns could be loaded at any direction or elevation and their increased calibre enabled them to pierce a 12in plate at nearly 5,000 yards. The secondary armament of forty-three quick firing guns ranged from 6in to 3-pounders, and the two of the four 18in torpedo tubes were submerged and pointed forwards. Three of the four steam launches carried on deck were also fitted with torpedo tubes but at 14in these were much less powerful.[17] All members of the class were fitted with twin-screw triple-expansion engines, with steam being provided by twenty Belleville boilers. Although generally regarded as good, fast, steamers, the ships suffered from having experimental inward-turning screws that although increasing thrust and speed and reducing fuel consumption were trouble-some at low speeds, adversely affecting steering.

Whilst the three ships of the Formidable class were building it was decided to allocate funding from the 1898 to 1900 estimates to construct a further five bat-tleships to be known as the London class. These ships were of a similar size and

A further photograph of *Formidable*, this time in dry dock, where the crew members on deck, and those peering through the open scuttles, together with the dock workers and single sailor standing on the base of the dry dock, appear to be posing for what might be an official photograph. (National Museum of the Royal Navy)

Left: The after barbette turrets of *Formidable* are shown here with the ship's two large guns protruding from their light turret and extending over the rim of the barbette, whilst a large awning covers the installation and protects it from the sun. (National Museum of the Royal Navy)

Below: Battleship *Irresistible* of 1902, another pre-Dreadnought of the Formidable class, is pictured loading or unloading from two Thames sailing barges that would have been contracted by the Admiralty to carry out the work. (National Museum of the Royal Navy)

shape as those of the Formidable class and carried the same armament, engines, and boilers. Armour protection was also similar, however during their construction the opportunity was taken to improve bow protection by carrying its armour up to the main deck and gradually increasing its thickness to 7in where it met the citadel armour. In the region of the forward barbette, a thick sloping deck replaced the forward armoured bulkhead. In addition a greatly improved ram and stem was fitted in which the scarph at the water line was abolished and a heavy casting, which was shaped to carry back along the ship's sides for some distance, was made to form a very formidable snout with its strongest part where it would strike an enemy ship's armour when ramming operations were taking place. Many other minor improvements were incorporated in these ships, including improved subdivision and improvements in ventilation systems and with the extension of electrical power, the incorporation of refrigeration systems and cold storage rooms for perishable foodstuffs.[18] Later in its career *London*, the named ship of this class, was selected for the first experiments in naval aviation when in 1912 a sloping trestle runway was built from the front of the shelter deck to the bow, thus providing a launching ramp for early forms of seaplane.[19]

In 1896 the Admiralty Board received reports that Imperial Russia was building a number of cruisers. Later reports suggested that these were in fact much larger armoured cruisers, but when better intelligence was gathered it was revealed that these vessels were in fact a class of fast battleships of the Peresviet class. In practice only three of these ships were built and in use they proved to be an extremely unsatisfactory design with both armament and armour protection being poor and speed being rather mediocre. However the fact that these ships were under construction caused the British press, as well as scaremongers and doubters within the establishment, to again imagine conspiracies and invasion threats, and to bemoan a perceived inadequacy of naval resources to defend Great Britain against attack from its European rivals just across the North Sea.[20]

Bulwark, the first ship of the London class pre-Dreadnoughts to be built, and which was completed in 1902. *Bulwark* and her sisters were slightly modified repeats of the Formidable class ships. (National Museum of the Royal Navy)

The Duncan class pre-Dreadnought *Cornwallis*, completed in 1903, the second of a class of six, is shown here at anchor with a picket boat moored to a boom alongside. Built to counter a perceived threat from Russia, these ships sacrificed armour for high speed. (National Museum of the Royal Navy)

As a consequence of these manifestations and the resulting pressures of further public and service concerns, the Admiralty Board convinced the First Lord that six fast battleships should be laid down with their costs to be met under a supplementary estimate in 1898–99 and the normal estimates of 1900–01. Known collectively as the Duncan class, these ships were in fact repeats of the Formidable class with some modifications to their armour protection to enable displacement to be reduced to 14,000 tons with a marginal increase in speed as a result. In line with the requirement for extra speed the triple-expansion engines that drove the twin shafts of these ships were for the first time given four cylinders instead of three, and twenty-four Belleville boilers were provided. Although relatively fast in use these ships never in practice achieved their design speeds and should probably be considered as the least satisfactory battleships of the White era. Conceived as a response to faulty intelligence, their design suffered from an undue loss in protection in an attempt to achieve a marginal increase in speed that in reality was not attainable and probably not necessary in any case.

Where the ships and navies of other nations were concerned the reality was that although they were beginning to catch up with Britain, at least in terms of technology if not in numbers of ships, they still lagged behind, although some of them not by very much, and by this time of course pre-Dreadnought designs also made up the bulk of the capital ship fleets of these nations. French ships tended to be smaller than their British counterparts, and many had high sides that leant inwards, creating excessive 'tumblehome', reducing the effective beam, the size of deck working areas, and overall stability as a consequence. Twin barbette turrets carried 12in guns in a similar way to British ships but the secondary armament was normally quite weak. Many of the Russian ships at the time were based on French designs and although there were exceptions, a significant number were badly built. Italy, which tended to be on good terms with Britain and utilised British technology where it could, was constructing some fine ships but numbers were small due to funding issues. Germany was rapidly expanding its fleet under its 'navophile' Emperor Kaiser William, who at that time was very much opposed to Britain, and who had an expanding, well designed and constructed fleet of warships that had grown from small beginnings into a formidable force. Japan was developing its navy also, but was on generally good terms with Britain, with some of its larger ships being built in British shipyards. Across the Atlantic America was increasing its fleet, and although its ships tended not to be standardised into classes, it was constructing some large warships with very powerful armament.

By 1901 the heavy secondary batteries of 9in instead of 6in guns that were being fitted to both American and Italian battleships, was causing some concern in Britain and so it was decided that a further eight new battleships should be laid down to counter this. These ships were collectively named the King Edward VII class and the first three were to be funded under the 1901–02 estimates, a further three under the 1902–03 estimates and the remaining two under those of the following year.[21] These eight ships were in fact the last of the true pre-Dreadnought battleship types and, although William White was responsible for the initial designs, he was absent due to ill health for most of the design period, and his deputy, H.E. Deadman, took over his role. Later in the design process the head of the battleship section, J.H. Narbeth, also became involved. White later returned to work, however, and continued his duties, but long before all the King Edward VII class ships had been completed, his health problems had forced him to retire from his post as Director of Naval Construction, and from service at the Admiralty.

With a displacement of over 16,000 tons, the King Edwards were some 9 per cent larger than *Formidable* and her sisters, whilst their hull form was slightly finer to give the potential for greater speed. The disposition of armour was similar to the later vessels of that class although the side armour before the citadel was made thicker and the section of belt towards the ship's stern was increased to 3in in thickness. The casemate sides were completely plated from the main to the upper deck over the whole length of the citadel with 7in-thick armour, and the battery deck protection was improved by slightly increasing the thickness of plate used. However the main change in these eight battleships was in their secondary armament, where the four 6in casemate guns on the upper deck were replaced with four much larger 9.2in guns in well-protected turrets and on improved hydraulic mountings.[22]

The last of White's pre-Dreadnoughts the King Edward VII class of eight ships was seen as the culmination of his 'Majestic fleet' and is represented here by *Britannia*, completed in 1906, and shown with a boat about to be launched or picked up, together with a steam pinnace moored alongside. (National Museum of the Royal Navy)

New Zealand, completed in 1905, was the last of the King Edward VII pre-Dreadnoughts to be built. This ship's greater length, some 20ft more than those of previous classes, as well as the turrets housing some of the 9.2in secondary armament, can be clearly seen. (National Museum of the Royal Navy)

On board the class named ship *King Edward VII*, this shows a number of what are probably 12in calibre armour-piercing shells, shown here without the cases that held the propellant. The size of these large projectiles is evident when compared to the heights of the crew members. (National Museum of the Royal Navy)

In addition to these, the main armament consisted of four 12in, 40-calibre guns mounted in two barbette turrets fore and aft, and thirty-eight quick-firing guns ranging in size from 6in to 3-pounders were also carried. Four 18in submerged torpedo tubes rounded off the quite substantial ordnance facilities. In practice, however, it was found that the two sizes of big guns made fire control extremely difficult, even though improved fire control platforms were fitted on the two short masts in place of the fighting tops that were used in previous battleships.

Whilst four-cylinder triple-expansion engines similar to those used in earlier classes were used in all the eight ships of the King Edward VII class, the boiler installations varied considerably, with some ships being fitted with a mixture of Babcock and other cylindrical boilers, some with Babcock boilers only, and others with Nicklaus units. *Britannia*, the last of the class to be completed, was also provided with super-heaters on six of her sixteen boilers.[23] This all meant that a cumbersome mixture of boiler-room spares had to be carried, and likely advantages from standardisation could not be achieved as a result. In all ships of the King Edward VII class, hydraulic hoists were fitted for handling the ship's boats, thus facilitating their moving in and out of the water. To improve manoeuvring a very large balanced rudder was fitted and the deadwood redesigned and strengthened by installing a heavy casting to support it at the appropriate point.[24] Even with this modification though it was difficult to keep ships of this class on a steady course, and they soon collectively became known by those who sailed in them as 'the wobbly eight'.

Unhappily in his last years in office before he resigned in 1902, William White was plagued with increasing ill health and suffered a near nervous breakdown. This was likely brought on not only by the huge responsibilities he carried, but also as a result of controversy associated with problems in the design of the new royal yacht, *Victoria and Albert*, that had nearly capsized not long after launching. Following an investigation, the problem was shown to be serious errors in the calculations for weight and stability on which the design of the royal yacht had been based. Although he had not himself made these calculations, White's responsibility as principal technical advisor of the Admiralty was clear, and although he freely accepted this, he also to some extent became a scapegoat, as it is possible that others more senior to him could also have been blamed, especially if, as was likely, they had attempted to cater for the uninformed requirements of royal personages, and instructed more junior and less knowledgeable design staff without first clarifying what effect these requirements might have had.[25]

Sir William White's sixteen-year period as Director of Naval Construction was marked by an almost complete naval revolution. It began with the introduction of quick-firing guns, and the disappearance of low freeboard battleships. It ended with the pre-Dreadnought form of battleship, that was copied by all the major navies of the world, and which in Great Britain at least had achieved a pinnacle of design and technical excellence that had never before been seen. In between it included the coming of the torpedo, the rebirth of the armoured cruiser, unprecedented advances in ordnance as well as in armour, new forms of hull, the arrival of water-tube boilers, and the use of more efficient steam engine installations. Through this rapid period of change White guided the destiny of the British fleet and the many millions of pounds expended in the design and building of a range of capital ships, as well as cruisers and smaller craft. Although others were involved in the design and development work also, William White's name will always be synonymous with that of the pre-Dreadnought battleship type, which he more than anyone else was instrumental in creating, and which ensured that by the start of the twentieth century the British battle fleet was of a more balanced nature than it had been since the days of the sailing warship.

It would not be long, however, before the hinge of history began to swing again, and having perhaps achieved its pinnacle, the pre-Dreadnought battleship type would be subjected to fundamental and far-reaching changes that would in effect make the battle fleets of all the world's navies virtually obsolete at a stroke, although once more Great Britain would lead the way. The reasons for this new capital ship revolution, the way its associated aspects were implemented, and the short and longer-term effects it created will be briefly described in the final chapter of this book. However as a prerequisite to this, and in order to provide the reader with more specific detail than it has been possible to include to date, the next and subsequent chapters of this book will more fully describe the technical and associated advances that created the pre-Dreadnought battleship, how such ships performed in battle, and how for a short period before they too were eclipsed, these warships became the most powerful instruments of war the world had ever seen.

FORTRESSES OF STEEL

During the nineteenth and early twentieth centuries the three methods of attack that a warship was designed to withstand were gunfire, ramming, and much later in the period, the effects of torpedoes and stationary or floating mines. For protection against gunfire, armour was developed and additional metal plates were secured over as large a proportion of the ship's hull and superstructure as was considered practicable, and this was often backed up by large amounts of timber. Further protection was also provided by locating coal with its shock-absorbing qualities in bunkers behind the timber backing, although clearly as the coal supply was consumed during passage making, this additional protection was reduced also. Attack from ramming, torpedoes, or mines would cause damage principally at or below the water line, and as the armour only extended for about 6ft below water, additional protection at this point was eventually provided by the use of extensive and minute subdivisions and watertight bulkheads so that any ingress of water into damaged areas could be localised and pumped out before more significant adverse effects could occur.[1]

Each of these forms of attack could seriously affect stability and buoyancy if successful, and irrespective of the power of a warship's offensive capability, might well result in its disablement or complete loss. The development of armour, the way it was applied to a ship's hull to resist attack, and the constraints that affected its wider use, are thus of immense importance in tracing the development of the pre-Dreadnought type of battleship, and the subject is given significant coverage in the following paragraphs. To support this coverage and help illustrate some of the aspects concerned, Appendix 3 has been included, and this shows profiles and deck plans that indicate the main armament layout as well as the distribution of armour in many of the ships briefly described in the preceding, as well as later, chapters of this book.

As Britain's Industrial Revolution gathered momentum and manufacturing technology enabled their efficient production, wrought-iron plates were used to protect the hulls of warships, and although very early ironclads such as *Warrior* were only lightly armoured, the later and larger ironclads like *Minotaur* and her sisters were provided with heavier wrought-iron armour over most of the outer surfaces of their hulls. The increase in the power of naval guns and the use of improved projectiles steadily brought about an increase in the thickness of the wrought-iron armour used, and this meant bulkier more expensive ships of a greater displacement were now necessary to support the armour and its extensive backing. In fact a stage was reached in the early 1870s when the cost and weight restrictions these criteria imposed made it impossible to cover all the area of a warship's sides with iron armour thick enough to resist attack. The compromise adopted was to reduce the area protected and to use thick armour to protect a ship's vitals only. These included engine and boiler rooms, magazines and shell lifts, and gun operating machinery. An armoured deck was, however, often constructed just below the water line, as it was believed that such a provision would make the whole of the ship's bottom into a watertight raft.[2] This arrangement, the central citadel system, was originally proposed by the Committee on Designs in 1871 after the loss of *Captain*, and was based on the premise that it was better to adequately protect the mid-ship portion of a warship in way of magazines and propulsion and other machinery, than to cover a larger area with thinner armour that would be unlikely to keep out enemy fire. The turret ship *Inflexible*, of 11,800 tons, became the first of many capital ships in which this system was introduced.[3]

The main armour plates used in *Inflexible* consisted of two layers of 12in-thick wrought iron, pressure welded together when heated to the requisite temperature. The resulting 24in plates were fitted vertically to the citadel and extended from 9.5ft above water to 6.5ft below. On the turrets the armour was up to 17in thick and consisted of two layers of wrought iron faced with a thin layer of steel. The plates so formed were known as compound plates, and this improvement resulted from a growing understanding of the metallurgy of the relatively new material, steel, as well as better ways of manufacturing it. In the case of *Inflexible*, however, this improvement was only introduced after the ship was well advanced in construction. *Inflexible* was in fact the first British capital ship to be fitted with the new compound armour, and in addition to improved protection, use of this armour provided a saving in weight of some 600 tons displacement in the finished ship.

Cellular compartments at the sides and ends of *Inflexible* were provided to give a reserve of buoyancy and the side compartments were filled with cork packing so that even if holed, the compartments would not be deprived of their buoyancy effect. Over the years the cellular compartments of many of the ships that followed *Inflexible* were filled with a variety of different types of packing as alternatives to cork, and these included India-rubber bags and thin-walled metal boxes. Tests were even carried out using the French idea of compressed cellulose that expanded when subjected to moisture. This arrangement seemed promising initially but in practice the cellulose, being very buoyant, easily washed out if large holes were formed as a result of hull damage.[4]

The increase in resistance offered by compound armour was clearly evident, and in general its superiority over wrought-iron armour was calculated to be in the proportion of three to two. As a consequence it was soon universally adopted for use in the British Navy. On the Continent, however, compound plate was not seen as the answer, and experiments in the use of complete steel plates had been under way for a number of years. In 1876 trials carried out by the Italians indicated that the resisting power of steel was far greater than that of wrought iron, although the steel plates used in the trials were completely broken up during the process. This was because the manufacture of large masses of steel was still in its infancy everywhere, and the steel produced at the time contained impurities that created brittleness and a lack of ductility. This in turn meant that the resulting steel if incorporated in a warship's armour, was not tough enough to stand up to the racking effect of heavy projectiles.[5]

Considerable improvements were, however, being made in the east of France, where the Schneider company of Creusot, irrespective of the production and other problems inherent in many of France's iron- and steel-making industries at the time, were using more advanced production techniques to manufacture solid steel armour plates that were consistently of an apparently higher quality.[6] Consequently Creusot steel became the favoured type of material for manufacturing armour plate in both the French and Italian navies, with the Italians in particular using 22in-thick Creusot mild-steel armour in their 1876, 12,000-ton battleships *Duilio* and *Dandilo*.

The example set by France and Italy in adopting steel armour was not, however, followed at the time by Great Britain or indeed by any other great power. Creusot steel, although much superior to that produced by other manufacturers, was still far from perfect for producing armour plate, and in particular its tendency to cracking was seen as a significant difficulty. In view of this, and although experiments with steel armour continued to take place in Britain also, the British Admiralty was convinced that compound plate made up of iron faced with mild steel was more appropriate where armour for its own warships was concerned.[7]

The introduction of this type of compound armour was generally viewed as affecting a revolution in ship protection, and it was adopted in the British Navy over a long period of time. The two Sheffield firms of Charles Cammell and John Brown both independently conceived of and developed armour that consisted of a steel face intended to break up projectiles that was welded to a wrought-iron back to give toughness and stop the plate from cracking when subjected to a projectile hit. The method of manufacture employed by each company was, however, different, with the Cammell plates being made by casting a steel face onto a rolled-iron back, and the Brown plates by using a relatively thin mild steel plate at the face, with molten cast steel being poured between it and the iron back. In each case the compound plates were subjected to heavy rolling after the casting was complete. This type of armour was used for the first time in *Inflexible*, being incorporated into her turrets.[8]

Although French battleships tended to be built with mild steel armour irrespective of its propensity to crack, the French Admiralty also gradually started using compound armour, although during the period it was probably only incorporated in less than 50 per cent of their capital ships. Conversely, however, compound armour became the only type to be used in post *Inflexible* British capital ships up to and including the *Royal Sovereign* of 1889.[9] In continental Europe French armour manufacturers such as Schneider continued developing and improving their steel-making processes as well as their knowledge of metallurgy, and even in Britain exponents of compound plate such as Charles Cammell and the Vickers company were finding time to experiment with steel armour themselves. Numerous trials were held over the next eight years or so, both in Britain and on a more international basis in Europe, as well as more latterly in North America. These involved the use of both compound as well as mild-steel plate, and in an attempt to improve quality, sometimes included the alloying of other metals such as nickel during the manufacturing process.[10]

Various processes of face hardening were tried for compound, steel, and alloy steel plates, and air, steam, water, molten lead, and oil were all used with more or less encouraging results. But in Britain, compound plates, where the steel face was of cemented steel that had a significantly higher carbon content than normal mild steel, were starting to be utilised. During manufacture these plates were heated to the requisite temperature and subsequently hardened in cold water in such a way that steam could not form on the rapidly cooling face, and a glass-hard surface that readily broke up projectiles could thus be formed. Some leeway in the type of plate used by the British Navy was, however, accepted, as is evident from the First Lords' memorandum attached to the naval estimates for 1891. This expressly stated that: 'For the main defence of first-class battleships compound armour was to be preferred, but that steel armour had been adopted for the secondary defence of battleships, for the protection of auxiliary armaments, and for the protection of machinery in vessels of the cruiser classes.' In accordance with this decision the main defence of the Royal Sovereign class ships for example, consisted of compound armour, whilst the secondary armament was protected by 4in-thick alloy steel that contained a small percentage of nickel.[11]

It seems likely that the reason that alloy steel was not adopted for heavy armour at the time was the inability of British manufacturers to produce thick plate of this type that could compete with compound armour. The Admiralty was of course unwilling to purchase steel armour from its rival France, probably for reasons of national pride, but also because there was doubt about the quality of the French product. Certainly at the end of the 1880s, steel armour still had shortcomings and manufacturers both in Great Britain and elsewhere sought to produce superior armour plates that effectively combined great hardness with extreme toughness. The importance of this search soon became even more pronounced as recent

French tests had shown that chrome-steel tipped projectiles had the ability to peel the hardened steel layer off compound armour. Nickel plate, as used in the Royal Sovereign class, however, had not been so affected, and in any case was said to provide some 4 per cent improvement in hardness over current compound and steel armour, although still remaining ductile.[12]

It was clear that if nickel plate could be produced in greater thicknesses, it could effectively overcome armour manufacturers' problems, and further development work continued both in Great Britain and on the Continent, particularly in France and Russia, and to a lesser extent Imperial Germany. In Britain's case though, trials were also continuing to improve the chilling processes associated with compound plate. These developments apart, in 1890 an American Engineer, H.A. Harvey, developed a method of treating steel that enabled a plate to be produced that had a super hard face on a tough resilient back.[13] In the Harvey process a solid steel plate was pressed and rolled and its face was highly 'cemented' by increasing its carbon content. Once cemented the plate was bent and cut to the required shape and all bolt holes pierced. It was then heated and quenched in water to harden it, and this produced a glass-hard surface in the normal way. However the next stage involved heating the plate again and allowing it to cool naturally, and this annealing process had the effect of toughening the back whilst allowing the face to remain glass hard. This new type of armour was subjected to numerous trials over the next year or so, and as these proved its superiority, the Harvey process was subsequently adopted in all the major navies of the world.

Many of the British pre-Dreadnoughts of this period were armoured with the new Harvey steel that allowed much thinner plates to be used, with corresponding savings in weight. In the Majestic class of 1895–97 for example, William White was able to use side armour made of this material that was reduced to 9in in thickness, allowing two tiers of plate to be fitted over a much greater length than would have been possible with compound plate. A Harvey steel plate had a hardened face about 1in deep, and tests carried out in Britain by both Cammell and Vickers in 1892 showed that with repeated firing at a velocity of nearly 2,000-feet-per-second, a 6in diameter projectile was unable to perforate a 6in-thick Harvey plate. By comparison it was estimated that the same 6in shell travelling at the same velocity would have readily perforated 11in of wrought iron.[14] The new steel was generally considered to have a resisting power that was 50 per cent greater than compound armour, but William White put its superiority even higher, referring to experiments which showed that so far as resistance was concerned, 6in of Harveyed steel was equal to 10in of compound armour.[15]

The best results by the Harvey company themselves had been obtained by including nickel in the manufacturing process, as although an ordinary Harveyed plate was 15–20 per cent harder than a straight nickel-steel plate, tests at the time on nickel plates submitted to the Harveying process indicated that they could be provided with a further 20 per cent improvement over straight Harvey plate.[16] In Britain though there was a view that the later American results were not wholly proven, and in any case the high cost of nickel was prohibitive where British manufacturers were concerned. Further development work by British armour plate makers, aided by Admiralty funding,[17] showed that although there was some tendency for plates with no nickel in them to crack, pure Harvey steel plates did in point of fact have a greater resistance to penetration than nickel plates.[18]

The new Harvey plate with all its merits did, however, have one major flaw and it was later found during further testing that the higher calibre, more power-ful, guns and more effective projectiles that were being developed as part of the ongoing competition between attack and defence, could cause the toughened back of unalloyed Harvey plate to fracture under the racking effect of a heavy bombardment. In an attempt to counter this defect, the German steel founders and armour manufacturing company of Friedrich Krupp of Essen developed an improved method of armour manufacturing in which the crystalline nature of the back of a Harvey plate could be made tough and fibrous in nature so that cracking was prevented, and the stresses due to the impact of projectiles could be distributed over a wider area, thus reducing penetration.[19] In the Krupp process, mild steel was alloyed with small percentages of nickel, chromium, manganese, and possibly molybdenum, and the principle of differential treatment during the final stages of the process was adopted for the first time. This process resulted in armour plates that had tough non-carburised backs with deep hard, cemented faces. As the process was complex and time-consuming, the cost of Krupp plates was significantly greater than those produced by the Harvey process.[20]

Krupp plate offered great resistance to penetration, 6in of Krupp steel being considered to be equivalent to 8in of Harvey, and the backs of each plate remained virtually free from cracking when being racked by projectiles. The Krupp process of manufacture was soon universally adopted by all major navies,[21] includ-ing Great Britain, and by 1896 the three main British armour manufacturers, Cammell, Brown, and Vickers, had all acquired the rights to use the Krupp pro-cess and had installed the necessary equipment and operational arrangements.[22] By the end of the 1890s, therefore, armour was decidedly superior to ordnance, which for a temporary period at least had slipped behind in the ongoing compe-tition between attack and defence.

The Krupp process required enormously more care and accuracy in the fab-rication of armour plates, as well as more expensive materials. As a consequence the price of armour, which had been declining as the result of more efficient production, again increased. Irrespective of this the benefits in terms of greater protection and coverage of a warship's vitals, with the added advantage of reduced weight and associated displacement, was considered to be well worth the extra cost. In Britain, Krupp steel armour was first used in the belt of the Canopus class battleships of 1896 and from then on in the Formidable, Duncan, London, and King Edward VII classes, right up to the end of the pre-Dreadnought era and beyond, although the disposition and thickness of armour sometimes changed from class to class in response to design and current cost criteria.

From about the year 1900, however, technical and other advances meant that the penetration power of the largest naval guns rapidly increased, and irrespective of the considerable progress made by armour manufacturers up to around 1906, the gun and its associated ordnance gained ascendancy over armour once more.[23] During the nineteenth century, the naval constructor was forced by new developments in gunnery to continually increase the thickness of a warship's armour, and this in turn frequently meant that fundamental alterations in design might have to take place. Conversely, after first iron and then steel became the materials of choice for gun construction, ordnance engineers were not impeded by any other consideration apart from the progress of their own science and its associated technical changes, in designing and building ever more powerful guns.[24] The way this occurred and the process by which naval guns developed from smoothbore, muzzle-loading weapons that fired solid shot over relatively short distances, to massive breech-loading rifled guns that could fire an armour-piercing shell over distances measured in miles, is the subject matter of the next chapter.

THUNDER OF THE GUNS

In the competition between armour and ordnance, the naval gun, except for a few brief interludes, led the race. Armour had to be distributed over a large area, and any increases in thickness meant that there was a corresponding increase in weight, and to meet this additional burden, larger warships would need to be built, or weight savings made in other areas such as machinery, numbers of guns, etc. Attempts to anticipate future developments in ordnance by increasing armour protection were naturally very costly, whilst a warship's armament on the other hand formed a much smaller proportion of the burden each ship carried. Guns could for example be doubled in weight with an associated huge increase in power, without greatly increasing a vessel's loading, but to make an equivalent increase in the armour of a particular ship would have likely been beyond the realms of practical shipbuilding as it existed at the time.[1]

In the later pre-Dreadnought battleships ordnance increasingly comprised of three classes of gun. First there was the main armament of strongly protected heavy guns that alone had the power to attack the vital parts of an enemy ship by what was known as 'belt attack'. Then there was the secondary armament usually mounted in casemates, and these guns could deliver many more, smaller, projectiles in a given time, maybe thirty-two shells as compared with three from guns of the main armament. Lastly there was the third division, consisting of light quick-firing guns placed behind shields. Designed to defeat ram or torpedo boat attack, and as anti-personnel weapons, these guns were intended to deliver a hail of fire at close quarters. The development and use of this third category of naval artillery, though having appeared at a later date than their larger counterparts, soon accelerated to a marked degree, and they were considered an essential asset in late-nineteenth-century warships.[2]

For a period of some hundreds of years prior to the 1850s and indeed right up to the Crimean War, very little development had occurred in naval ordnance. In fact *Duke of Wellington*, a large steam line-of-battle ship commissioned just before the outbreak of that war, carried smooth-bore guns that although much larger, were in essence similar to those used in Nelson's flagship *Victory* at the Battle of Trafalgar. These guns were merely heavy blocks of iron roughly cast to the required dimensions and form, and the only machining to which they were subjected consisted of rough finishing of the bore and drilling of the vent hole. The wooden carriages on which many of these guns were mounted were equally crude, initially built of oak, but more latterly of teak and mahogany. These carriages were moved on four wooden trucks or wheels, the rear pair of which was frequently replaced by wooden chocks to ease movement when laying or aiming the gun. The recoil once a gun of this type was fired was initially controlled by the friction of large wooden axles and big wedges under the trucks, whilst final control was exercised by the rope breechings that secured each gun to the ship's side. Elevation and training on a target was made possible by the use of wooden wedges known as quoins and by the use of iron handspikes. For running each gun out prior to firing, block and tackles were generally employed, and to work with any degree of success, these technically simple weapons had to be served by a large gun crew, of which each member had a particular job to do, and who virtually surrounded each gun when it was in use.[3]

Smooth-bore guns of this type fired solid shot, and those used in the larger sizes of gun were very heavy indeed. Increasingly though it was found that hollow spherical shells, filled with explosive and fitted with fuses, could also be fired from the larger smooth-bore guns. In addition, developments had been taking place to create shorter and lighter forms of gun that had large diameter bores or calibres, and were known as carronades after their originators the Carron Company. Many of these weapons were also being installed in British sailing warships, although the carronade was never considered to be an official part of a ship's armament, and in many cases they were provided at a naval captain's own expense. The likely reason for this was that to add to the listed armament of a warship at that time meant that the ship in question would probably need to have its 'rate' re-classified, and this could lead to all sorts of complicated adjustments to equipment and ship's complement. Administratively it was far easier to stick with the established number of long-guns that a ship carried when fixing its rate, and to look on the additional carronades as a sort of armaments bonus.[4]

After the introduction in 1856 of William Armstrong's method of fabricating guns, wrought iron, in conjunction with steel that formed an inner tube, superseded cast iron, and by the 1880s steel alone had become the only material used for the construction of guns.[5] In 1859 the 8in, 4.75-ton, cast-iron, smooth-bore guns of Great Britain's first ironclad *Warrior*, were the most powerful weapons afloat, but it soon became evident that the heaviest spherical projectile from a smooth-bore gun of their type was quite inadequate to pierce the newly adopted armour plates if they were fitted to an enemy ship. As a consequence ordnance manufacturers began to focus their attention on producing weapons that would once again be powerful enough to turn the scale in favour of the gun.[6]

The only type of large projectile that could be fired from a smooth-bore gun was spherical in shape and due to the problems of 'windage', was quite inadequate to pierce even the thin armour plate used at the time. Windage was associated with the necessary difference that existed between the diameters of barrel and round shot, which caused an escape of gas and thus a loss of power, as well as an irregular and erratic flight after the shot left the gun's muzzle. Experiments soon showed that an elongated form of projectile, if given a spin or rotation about its longer axis, could travel through the air with its point always ahead, without much loss in power, as well as following a more accurate path and trajectory over a longer distance. In order for this to consistently happen though, the gun from which the projectile was fired had to be fitted with groves or rifling within its barrel to impart the required spin to the projectile as it travelled up the bore of the gun.

The British Admiralty were very interested in these developments, and conscious that a number of ordnance manufacturers were involved in developing their own solutions to the problem, decided in 1858 to set up the Committee on Rifled Cannon, to receive submissions on the various forms of projectile and rifling that were being developed at the time. During these submissions it became clear that the superiority and accuracy of the gun type submitted by the Armstrong Company of Elswick, was so conspicuous, that the Committee unanimously recommended the adoption of that company's guns. In fact with regard to range, accuracy, and penetrating power the Armstrong rifled gun was so great when compared with similar sized smooth-bores, that members of the Committee, many of whom were serving naval or artillery officers, became convinced that the days of the smooth-bore gun were numbered.[7]

Additionally though, in the mid-1800s, William Armstrong was experimenting with different methods of loading, and developed the first rifled guns that could be loaded via a breech rather than via the muzzle, making the whole loading exercise very much simpler. In view of these new developments the Committee on Rifled Cannon in 1858 recommended the introduction of breech-loaders into the British naval service. These guns, apart from being easier to load, were more accurate in use, although disappointingly, velocities of projectiles were not much improved. This problem was overcome eventually by fitting obturators that enabled post-firing pressures to be increased. The breech mechanism of these early breech-loaders proved unsatisfactory in use, however, owing to a tendency for the breech block to occasionally jump out of its place when the gun was fired, and this fault subsequently resulted in a number of serious accidents.[8] Such difficulties increased with the size of gun, and although William Armstrong believed that all the associated problems could be overcome, he eventually yielded to the opinion of naval authorities in Great Britain and agreed to concentrate his resources on manufacturing improved rifled muzzle-loaders instead of focusing his company's expertise on developing better breech mechanisms.

Over a period of some years breech-loaders were consequently withdrawn and removed from British ships, with the Admiralty replacing them with the newer types of Armstrong rifled muzzle-loaders, which were soon extensively introduced into the service. The new gun was of the built-up type, depending for its strength on wrought-iron coils shrunk onto an inner steel tube, and was so constructed that when complete the inner parts were left in a state of compression whilst the outer parts were in tension, thereby balancing stresses in the metal that firing the gun created. This principle of 'initial tensions' was universally adopted and used in the manufacture of all subsequent guns. The rifled muzzle-loader became the standard gun in the British Navy up to the end of the 1870s, and as manufactured on licence by the Royal Gun Factory in Woolwich, became known as the Woolwich gun. This version was constructed with a few thick coils instead of a number of thin ones and was thus cheaper to manufacture than those produced directly by the Armstrong company.[9]

Britain continued to use rifled muzzle-loaders for many years, irrespective of the difficulties that loading the longer guns entailed, and which meant that this operation had to take place outside the turret using a raised glacis in the adjacent armoured deck. Many other countries meanwhile developed their own breech-loading systems and, unlike Britain, completely built their guns of steel. Foremost amongst these was France, who irrespective of initial problems caused by the black powder used at the time, which tended to kick rather than push shells out of muzzles, sometimes bursting the early inferior steel guns in the process, persevered with steel production and improved breech design, eventually producing good quality homogeneous steel as well as serviceable breech-loading guns well before Britain was able to do so.[10] In support of Britain's position, the advocates of muzzle-loaders claimed that such guns were relatively simple to use, could be more readily housed in smaller turrets, were less vulnerable, and once hydraulic power became available, could be loaded as quickly as breech-loaders.[11] Although all this may have been true, the reversion to an earlier form of weapon for quite a long period caused Britain to fall behind both France and an expanding Germany, in the art of naval gun construction.[12]

Prior to the introduction of rifled guns all the world's navies used smooth-bore cannon, and for the sake of economy many countries attempted to convert them into rifled pieces. Cutting rifling grooves in existing guns, however, tended to weaken them, and various ways of strengthening the guns were experimented with. Different methods such as shrinking on steel rings, encasing each gun in a steel jacket, or inserting metal liners, were all tried with varying degrees of success. In Britain guns were lined using the Pallister principle and this worked reasonably well. Under this system, cast-iron guns in particular, were lined with coiled iron barrels that had rifling cut into their inner surfaces, and these were fitted comparatively loosely into each gun until expanded by heavy proof rounds being fired from them. In 1865, however, the first British heavy rifled guns specifically built as such were constructed, and these marked a new departure in gun making. These weapons were just over 10ft long, weighed 6.5 tons, and had a calibre of 7in. Even larger calibre weapons were subsequently produced over the next few years, until by 1874, 12.5in guns weighing 38 tons that could throw a projectile of 820lb in weight, were being manufactured.[13]

In 1873 it was proposed to construct an even more powerful rifled muzzle-loading piece, and in 1875 the first 80-ton gun having a calibre of 14.5in, was completed. After a series of experiments this huge weapon had to be re-bored twice, being finally completed with a calibre of 16in. This mighty gun that had an extreme range of some seven miles was the largest muzzle-loading weapon ever used in the British Navy, and was first mounted in the turrets of the battleship *Inflexible*. However, in 1878 William Armstrong's company constructed some even bigger guns that weighed 100 tons, and had a calibre of 17.5in. Four of these were bought by the British Government, but never installed in British ships. Instead they were used in shore emplacements at Malta and Gibraltar. The Italian Navy did, however, purchase some of these gigantic weapons and installed them in the turrets of *Duilio* and *Dandilio*, two of that country's earlier large battleships.[14]

Progress where ballistics was concerned would, however, eventually create a position where even in Britain muzzle-loaders would no longer be tenable. Experiments had been progressing over a number of years in an attempt to overcome the damage to gun barrels that the rapid expansion of gunpowder often caused when a large gun was being fired. These experiments and subsequent tests resulted in the development of large grain prismatic powder, and then in the early 1880s German scientists made further improvements to produce prismatic brown powder. Prismatic brown was introduced into the Royal Navy in the mid-1880s, but was superseded in 1887 by a type known as slow-burning cocoa powder.[15] With this new propellant the initial velocity of the projectile could be significantly raised and its perforating power greatly increased. But for this to take place, larger powder charges, that required correspondingly larger chambers than those that existed in existing muzzle-loaded rifled guns, were required. In short the new conditions called for a new type of gun that was much longer, with powder chambers of a larger diameter than that of the bore, and these requirements could only be provided if the gun was loaded at the breech.

Thus for Great Britain a return to breech-loading ordnance became necessary, although the old type of Armstrong movable vent piece and breech mechanism was avoided, and conscious of the accident that had occurred on *Thunderer*, the Admiralty set up trials of the two main breech-closing systems that were in use at the time, viz. the German wedge type and the interrupted screw system of the French. As a consequence the French breech-closing system, together with the De Bange's obturator to stop any gas escaping, both of which had proved superior in the trials, were adopted.[16] At the same time the Woolwich system of gun construction was abandoned, and a decision made to use steel for constructing all parts of the new guns. These decisions were to have far-reaching consequences for the British Navy, and for the foreseeable future they would not again fall behind their continental rivals where the power of heavy ordnance was concerned.

The Admiralty again chose Armstrong to design and build the new guns using their version of the French breech. These guns consisted of a thin inner steel tube with a long steel jacket shrunk on to provide longitudinal strength, and with a further layer of superimposed steel hoops shrunk on the outside of this. Considerable difficulties were at first experienced with building these guns, especially those designed for *Collingwood* and other ships of the Admiral class, but after a few years' experience, satisfactory results were achieved and there followed a growth in size of this type of ordnance that culminated in the 16.25in, 110-ton breech-loaders of *Benbow*, *Victoria*, and *Sans Pareil*. At the end of the 1880s though, and into the 1890s, a reaction set in against such massive guns both in Britain and where the navies of all the great powers were concerned. This was due to a number of reasons such as the drooping of the barrels in super large 110-ton guns, a slow rate of fire due to the heavy nature of the ammunition, a short operational life for the guns due to erosion of the bore, and the extended length of time it took to manufacture these large pieces. Moreover the advent of smokeless gunpowder made it possible to achieve adequate perforation with guns of smaller calibre, and as a consequence sizes were gradually reduced until the 12in calibre was reached, and this remained the standard in most navies until around 1910.[17]

The smokeless powder introduced at the end of the 1880s was in fact cordite, and this soon completely superseded the old-time gunpowder, and when combined with increased gun length and more advanced gun construction permitting higher pressures, soon allowed projectile velocities in excess of 2,000ft per second to be achieved. Cordite being smokeless, slow burning, and efficient, allowed longer gun barrels that, in turn, enabled a more effective build-up of pressure to take place when the gun was fired, maximising the increasing energy of the gun and the velocity of the projectile as it sped up the barrel. While the early breech-loaders had a length equivalent to 30 calibres or 30ft, the 12in guns of the Formidable class ships built as part of the 1897 programme, were 40 calibres long and the muzzle velocity was around 2,500ft per second. From that stage guns progressed even further, and in the *Collingwood* of 1908 for example, the 12in guns were 50 calibres long and fired 850lb projectiles at a muzzle velocity of close on 3,000ft per second. The muzzle energy of these powerful guns was estimated as being more than seven times greater than the 12in muzzle-loading guns of the 1860s.[18]

In the last decade of the nineteenth century further advances were made when wire-wound construction of heavy guns was introduced into the British Navy. The idea of strengthening guns with steel wire was not new, and experiments on wire winding had taken place in Britain as far back as 1855 and in France some years later in the 1870s. In most cases these experiments had involved smaller guns of the sort included in secondary armament, but as these weapons were more expensive to build than conventional guns, they were not at the time adopted for use in the Royal Navy. In 1893, however, the Admiralty, conscious of the superiority of such weapons, approved a design for the first wire-wound guns that were to be used for battleship main armament. These were the 46-ton, 12in Mark VIII, which had a length of just over 35 calibres, and which were mounted in the fifteen ships of the Majestic and Canopus classes. Most of these guns were built at Armstrong's and Woolwich Arsenal, but the later 12in, Mark IX of 40 calibres in length, and weighing 50 tons that was approved by the Ordnance Committee in 1898, was a Vickers company design. This type was mounted in ships of the Formidable, London, Duncan, and King Edward, classes.[19] In all cases wire-wound guns were utilised for both main and secondary armament.

Although some modifications were introduced during the period when wire-wound guns were in use, the basic construction was to build up two forged nickel-steel tubes, one inside the other, and on the outer tube wire of a tensile strength of around 100 tons/sq. in was wound from the muzzle to the breech end using specially adapted lathes. The wire winding was then covered by a chase hoop and a metal jacket, shrunk on in such a way that stress was made uniform throughout the whole of the structure, a condition impossible to achieve when guns were built up from steel hoops alone. Wire-wound guns were the best form that could be manufactured at the time, and were in fact much stronger than guns of a solid steel construction,[20] although due to a lack of longitudinal strength, drooping of the barrel was greater than in other types. This did not, however, cause too much of a problem, as the heat and other energy created in the barrel caused barrels to be temporarily straightened when each gun was being fired. On the later wire-wound guns of first-class battleships there were some fourteen layers of wire, and no less than 113 miles of wire were used for each gun. Around thirty-six, eight-hour days were required for each gun winding, and one gun could take up to nine months to complete. In practice though it was estimated that the total cost of building these later and improved wire-wound guns was not much more than the cost of building a more conventional type of breech-loader.[21]

As previously noted, up to around 1860 naval guns were mounted on a simple gun carriage constructed of wood, which ran in and out on small, low wheels known as trucks. The recoil was controlled more or less by the friction produced by making the axles oversize or by the use of wooden chocks under, or even instead of, the rear trucks, and was finally checked by the use of rope breechings secured to the ship's side. In use each gun was trained or aimed by the use of handspikes and levers that were used to move the carriage from side to side, whilst elevation was achieved by the use of wedges, or in later pieces by the use of simple elevating screws under each gun's rear end. The substitution of iron for wooden carriages in about 1864 and the use of inclined slides fitted with rollers that ran on concentric iron tracks sunk into the deck, signified a major advance, especially as various compressor brakes were developed to control the often violent recoil that occurred when the larger forms of these muzzle-loading guns were fired.[22]

When the weight of guns reached about 25 tons, and even heavier pieces were under consideration, it became clear that hand power was no longer sufficient to manipulate guns, and that some form of mechanical assistance was required. In addition the increased speed and manoeuvrability of steam-driven ships of war, due to improvements in propulsion and other associated machinery, meant that a corresponding rapidity in both the rate of fire and the training of the guns was required if an adversary was not to retreat out of range before a second shot or shots could be fired. For the same reason it was also stipulated that new guns should have a training arc of 120 degrees instead of 90 degrees, which had been the case previously.[23] It was generally agreed that the best way to achieve these criteria was to mount the guns on turntables, to utilise steam to provide power, and to use the emerging science of hydraulics to transmit that power as required.

Turntables were initially mounted in closed turrets that offered perfect protection to the short guns of that period, as well as to the crew who could serve the guns under cover of the turret armour. Protection for the turntable and its associated operating mechanism was provided by sinking this below the armoured deck, or more latterly by the use of raised redoubts. For reasons explained in previous chapters, turrets eventually gave way to barbette installations, where although the turntable etc. was protected, the guns as well as the loading operations, were not. Later, though, lightly armoured cupola-shaped screens were fitted over the guns. Attached to the turntable in its barbette, these provided some additional protection and became known as barbette turrets.[24]

With the advent of rifling the longer muzzle-loaders required complicated hand and steam operated mechanical methods using rack and pinion and winches for running guns in and out and for reloading and training. However, with the advent of breech loading, there was no longer any need for such arrangements, although it was now necessary to provide hoists and methods by which ammunition could be delivered to guns in their barbettes and turrets.[25] Where breech-loaders were concerned the trunnion pins of earlier installations were replaced by straps that allowed the guns in twin turrets to be set more closely together, with a consequential saving of space and better positioning, that allowed turret guns to be fired through smaller ports. Irrespective of whether turrets, barbettes, or barbette turrets were used, the recoil from breech-loaders was in all cases absorbed by hydraulic pistons encased in cylinders that were positioned below the gun slides. Hydraulic pressure was also utilised to depress the tail-heavy guns, whilst the controlled release of hydraulic fluid was used to elevate them.[26] Additionally the friction plate compressors and breeching ropes that had controlled the movement of the earlier muzzle-loading guns as well as the now defunct early Armstrong breech-loaders, were not now necessary, and in their place hydraulic buffers began to be used that incorporated relief valves that operated in the same fashion as the spring-loaded safety valves fitted to steam boilers.[27]

Later improvements enabled even more efficient use of gun-mounting hydraulics, and as associated arrangements became more sophisticated, hydraulic power was used for other operations such as washing out the guns, opening and closing the breech, and for handling ammunition, including lifts from magazine and shell room, as well as all loading and ramming operations. The result of all these incremental improvements was that the speed of serving, aiming, and firing a 12in breech-loader, for example, came down from about two minutes per round in the 1880s to three rounds every four minutes in the mid-1890s, and by the beginning of the twentieth century, with the aid of flexible chain rammers that were carried around with the revolving barbette turret, a speed of one round every thirty-five seconds was achieved.[28]

The underlying concept in the armament arrangements of pre-Dreadnought battleships was that their mixed calibre battery of guns would provide a balance between hitting power and rate of fire. In use the heavy guns of the main armament pounded away relatively slowly, in an attempt to penetrate an opponent's armour, whilst the medium power guns of the secondary armament, and more latterly the quick-firing ordnance, would on the other hand deliver a hail of projectiles, wrecking unprotected superstructure and undermining morale by inflicting heavy casualties on crew members.[29] In application though this general concept was subjected to a number of changes during the nineteenth century, and where disposition of armament in particular was concerned the principle of concentrating guns frequently oscillated with the opposite principle of distributing them. Similarly, reducing the number and increasing the power of large guns was for a long while considered to be the best approach, although towards the end of the century this tendency was reversed and with the increased sophistication of secondary armament, the number of guns was increased whilst their sizes were generally reduced.[30]

The issues associated with the design and manufacture of large guns already outlined, applied to the secondary armament also, although because of their smaller size and associated costs, they were the first type to benefit from changes such as the return to breech loading. Typically the size of these guns was up to about 8in in calibre, although larger calibres were sometimes used in a secondary capacity. Eventually 6in became the favoured size and towards the end of the nineteenth century the secondary armament of most battleships was based on these. Mountings were arranged in batteries and casemates, or less frequently in the open with steel shields being used to give at least some protection. During the

muzzle-loading period, guns of the secondary armament were mounted on carriages and slides to which compressor brakes were fitted. After the introduction
of rifled breech-loaders, though, the energy of a gun's recoil after firing became
so great that increased braking power could only be obtained by the addition of
more friction plates. The number of plates that could be used in practice was limited by the slide width, so that the friction type of compressor became inadequate
and new forms of mounting had to be developed.[31]

Various arrangements were tried in an attempt to overcome this problem, but
it wasn't until the 1880s that Joseph Vavasseur, who worked for the Armstrong
Company, was able to develop an effective hydraulic mounting for secondary ordnance. These mountings, which were further improved as a result of experience
in use, were made for a whole range of different sized guns, but all incorporated
a central pivot arrangement that was anchored to the deck, and this carried a
pedestal on which the slide unit operated and was rotated by the use of a hand
wheel. A compressor brake consisting of a pair of hydraulic cylinders formed part
of the carriage, with their piston rods attached to the mounting. The slide unit
was inclined upwards at a considerable angle so that gravity assisted in running
the guns out when in use. Gearing was used for elevation and training, ensuring
the guns could be rapidly used in action, although the training gear was dispensed
with altogether in smaller gun mountings, where training was carried out using
a shoulder piece only. Vavasseur mountings were eventually used by most navies
and in Britain were mainly utilised for 4in to 6in calibre guns. They were also
used for some 9.2in ordnance and even for the single 10in guns in *Victoria* and
Sans Pareil.[32]

Apart from their mountings, guns of the secondary armament were in essence
scaled-down versions of their larger main armament counterparts, albeit often
based on less complex construction. The newer form of quick-firing weapons
that were introduced towards the end of the nineteenth century was though very
different and more innovative in nature, soon becoming an essential part of the
pre-Dreadnought battleship's armament.

In the 1870s machine guns of various sorts made their appearance, as it was
thought they could provide a defence against the perceived new threat of fast
torpedo boats. Although the torpedo was not yet a significant weapon, developments in torpedo technology were taking place and larger, more powerful boats
were increasingly being utilised as fast-attack craft that were capable of being
used at close range, thus avoiding the usual methods of defending itself that a
warship might use. In practice though the multi-barrel machine gun that existed
at that time was not really powerful enough to deter such an attack if it was
determinedly carried out, and so during the 1880s frantic development work
resulted in Armstrong's building the first medium-calibre quick-firing gun at
their Elswick factory.

A number of improvements and developments were subsequently made, both by Armstrong and other manufacturers, but in all cases the essential aspects of a quick-firing gun were that it should have a calibre of around 5in, and use a brass cartridge that incorporated its own primer instead of utilising the multi-part loading arrangements that were more common with larger guns. A mounting suitable for allowing rapidly aimed fire, and fast-loading breech mechanisms were also required, and the latter facility was achieved by the use of a coned screw in the single barrel Elswick guns, and a cylindrical block or Krupp wedge, as it was called in other patterns.[33] The increase in power these innovative guns provided was different to that for which larger guns of primary and secondary armaments were developed, for where the quick firer was concerned it was frequency and speed of hitting that was important rather than large scale destructive power, and where this former attribute was concerned, some Elswick guns were reported as being capable of keeping three shots in the air at the same time, a considerable performance for a weapon that was of a comparatively light weight but that still had adequate penetrating power.[34]

In the mountings of quick-firing guns every effort was made to ensure rapidity of fire, and the weapons were so robustly constructed that in the absence of any other arrangements, the gun itself could absorb the recoil. The use of cartridge cases was an important aspect, as not only did these facilitate handling and load- ing of the ammunition, as well as rapidity of fire, but the cartridge also formed a perfect gas check and rendered it unnecessary to clean the gun between rounds. In 1889 Armstrong's made several important improvements in the central pivot system of mounting that contributed greatly to the success and power of quick- firing guns. These included arrangements that allowed the gun to recoil along its own axis, enabling mountings of a more compact nature to be used, taking up less space, and allowing smaller gun ports to be utilised. The guns recoiled in a slide or cradle supported by trunnions resting on a saddle and pivot stand, and at first this was simply a plate attached to the deck or fitted on a low structure. In 1890, however, after some further development work, a pedestal stand was introduced and this was much more robust and less liable to damage than its predecessors, enabling a greater arc of fire for a given size of gun port to be provided.[35]

With some further minor modifications the gun mounting and operating sys- tems as well as those associated with ammunition delivery and handling outlined in the preceding paragraphs, continued in use for all British battleships up to and including the early years of the twentieth century, and ensured that these warships were not only provided with a powerful primary and secondary arma- ment, but also with an array of quick-firing guns for use in the event of torpedo boat attack, even if this in reality, and with the benefit of hindsight, was a vastly exaggerated danger. This apart, the quick-firing guns of the later Armstrong type were formidable weapons that were capable of penetrating armour of light and medium thicknesses and of demolishing unprotected structures by a great volume of rapidly fired shells.[36] For reasons of comparison, the most significant gun types and their associated installations as mentioned in this chapter, are illustrated in Appendix 4.

It should be noted though that irrespective of the improvements and major engineering achievements attained, warship designers and builders experienced a number of frustrating difficulties associated with the supply of guns and mountings that often extended the construction of warships by time periods that sometimes equated to more than nine months per gun installed. This is evident from William White's address to the Institute of Civil Engineers in 1904, when conscious of the hostile world and ever accelerating arms race that existed at the time, together with the need to keep ahead of potential adversaries, he stated that:

> These changes in guns and mountings have greatly influenced the rate of construction of warships, and seriously affected costs as well as progress. The complaint is not a new one, but it is no less true. So long a time is frequently occupied by Committees and sub-Committees in working out details of new guns and ammunition before actual patterns are finally settled and manufacturing begins, that in many instances in my experience, ships have had to wait for guns, and in others to have considerable modifications made in consequence of changes in gun designs.[37]

White also made a plea that in the interests of speed and cost, the design, construction, and supply arrangements for guns' ammunition and mountings should all be finally settled and put in train before the work of building an associated warship was commenced.[38] Irrespective of this, design and supply problems appeared to have continued well into the early years of the new century, and were only eventually overcome by the reforms initiated by the then First Sea Lord, Admiral John Fisher, as part of the next major stage in battleship development: the Dreadnought revolution.

TO PIERCE THE ARMOURED WALLS

The advances in size and destructive power of naval guns between 1840 and 1905 were very much greater than that which had occurred in any previous century. In association with this, developments in the chemistry of propellants and explosives led from black powder that had been around since at least the thirteenth century to the slower burning powders, and then to the smokeless types of the nineteenth and early twentieth centuries.[1]

Small-grain gunpowder that was produced by combining saltpetre, charcoal, and sulphur in specific proportions, had been used as an explosive and propellant in the world's navies for most of their histories, and in its basic form was bagged into made-up charges or cartridges that were rammed down the barrels of the broadside cannons used in sailing warships, after which a fibre wad, and then the actual round shot was, in turn, rammed down on top of it. Each gun was now prepared for firing by pricking the cartridge through the weapon's touchhole, before a quill filled with fine gunpowder was inserted. Firing could then take place, and this was carried out by igniting the powder in the quill using a slow match, or later by the use of a flint or percussion gunlock. The basic black powder available at the time was quite adequate for such use. However, as ordnance developed and guns became larger and more powerful, it became more and more apparent that black powder was no longer the most effective propellant, and the turning point eventually occurred with the introduction of rifled muzzle-loading in naval guns.

To be fully effective in use propellant needed to produce an even, low, continuous pressure on gun bore and projectile, giving the latter a high velocity as it left the gun barrel. Small-grain powder gave a large igniting surface and was consumed before the projectile had travelled very far up the gun barrel, creating wave pressures that could potentially damage the gun. Whilst this was not a major problem where the older smooth-bore broadside cannon were concerned, larger pieces, especially those that fired shells, required a slower ignition so that greater pressure could be created. In an attempt to overcome these problems the size of black powder grains was increased during manufacture so that less burning surface was exposed in total, and larger chambers were built into guns so that extra air space for the charge could be provided. Although these measures helped, the position was still not completely satisfactory, as large quantities of unconsumed powder tended to exit gun muzzles with the projectiles, or was deposited on the inside of barrels after firing had taken place.[7]

Built-up charges of powder formed into a prism with a hole bored in the centre of the prism were then introduced, the idea being that as the prism burned from the outer and inner edges, a constant area of burning surface would be exposed for the generation of gasses that would result in all the prism being consumed as the projectile exited the gun muzzle, and that a constant and low pressure would be exerted on the projectile while it travelled up the barrel. Black prism powder was used initially but as the size of guns and charges continued to increase, it was found that this type of prismatic powder created too great an initial pressure. As a result prismatic brown, a much slower burning powder, was developed by the German manufacturers Krupp of Essen, and later still a derivative of this, known as slow burning cocoa powder, became the favoured type in all navies.[3] Although more effective in use than previous types, this latest slow burning powder was still problematic, as less than half of each charge was burnt when a gun fired, the remainder creating dense clouds of black smoke as well as heavy deposits inside the barrel.[4] In addition there were concerns about the powder's general stability and safety when stored, and confusion over this led to a number of accidental explosions during the period.

Slow-burning gunpowder of this new form did, however, have the effect in use of increasing the velocity of the projectiles fired from the rifled muzzle-loading guns of the day, increasing their energy by nearly 75 per cent. Such higher energies could not, however, be fully generated in a relatively short gun barrel, as they had to build up gradually, and to allow this to happen it was necessary to significantly increase barrel length. It was difficult, however, to load such guns at the muzzle, and although various loading methods were developed, the only really effective way that these weapons could be practically used was to incorporate the new and improved breech-loading arrangements that were by now being developed.[5]

The fact that clouds of dense black smoke was invariably generated when guns, including breech-loading ones, were fired, was though still a major problem, and made aiming and assessing the range, as well as manoeuvring the ship under battle conditions, quite difficult. In view of this further research was carried out in order to develop a smokeless powder that could be more safely stored, yet still retain the benefits of current types. In 1885, France became the first country to manufacture an improved form of smokeless powder that was based on nitrated cellulose mixed with guncotton, but to the British industrialist and armaments manufacturer Andrew Noble is due the accolade for combining nitroglycerine with guncotton for the production of a highly effective form of smokeless explosive that was known as ballistite. It was later discovered, however, that camphor, which was used by Noble as an agent for enabling the two base elements to chemically join together, tended to evaporate over time, adversely altering the explosive and other properties of the ballistite. Irrespective of this though the British Government continued to hold Noble's work in high esteem, and in view of this the War Department Chemist Sir Frederick Abel was asked to work with Noble to overcome the problem.[6]

This partnership soon resulted in the creation of a more stable explosive called cordite, that was subsequently proved to be capable of withstanding severe climatic changes without serious deterioration, either chemical or ballistic, and was capable of developing much greater velocities for the projectiles used with it. The energy of this new explosive was in fact five times greater than normal black powder and it was completely smokeless. In addition, due to its efficient combustion properties, no residue was created, so there was now no need to sponge out guns each time a firing took place. Operationally this meant that the firing sequence could be speeded up, and soon all the navies of the world had adopted either cordite or the French variation based on nitrocellulose.[7]

Where projectiles were concerned the solid iron balls used in the smooth-bore broadside-mounted guns of wooden ships were increasingly found to be of little use when used against ironclads, although canister and other smaller types of shot could of course still be utilised to clear decks or bring down the vulnerable rigging and spars. Hollow balls filled with bursting charges that were ignited by a fuse were also used at the time and these included shrapnel shells, where the fuses were cut to explode the shell just before it struck its target, releasing numerous smaller balls that had a devastating effect on crowded decks. With the onset of rifled ordnance, however, major improvements were made possible by the introduction of elongated projectiles that had pointed heads of ogival form and carried studs, or bands of copper on their bodies, that located in the gun's rifling grooves so that the necessary spin could be created, and the shell would follow a normal trajectory instead of tumbling in flight once it had been fired. In later shell patterns studs were omitted and the gun's automatic gas check imparted the necessary rotation.

Projectiles for rifled ordnance occurred in three different varieties. Firstly there were the armour-piercing shells that by the 1890s had further developed from the chilled cast-iron Pallister type into shells made of forged and hardened chrome steel. In practice, however, when used against hard-faced armour, the points of armour-piercing shells were often found to break off on hitting the target, greatly reducing penetration and diminishing the shell's effect. Although this problem had been recognised some years previously it wasn't until the late 1890s that a solution was perfected. This involved the use of a steel cap that was fitted over the nose of the shell and which had the effect of providing lateral support to the point,[8] increasing penetration power by around 15 per cent. The second variety of projectile was an improved form of shrapnel shell that was longer than an armour-piercing shell, and contained many more, small diameter balls than its earlier smooth-bore counterparts. Lastly there was what was termed common shell for use against unarmoured ships. These were made of cast steel and were much longer than either armour piercing or shrapnel shells, so that a maximum bursting charge could be incorporated.[9]

The high explosive bursting charges in the shells varied in strength depending on the type of shell in use. In Britain this charge was normally based on picric acid or lyddite as it was more commonly known, and in armour-piercing shells the charge was ignited when the projectile's hardened nose struck, or alternatively pierced, its target. Shrapnel and common shell on the other hand had fuses fitted in their noses, and these could either be time-or-percussion, or alternatively time-and-percussion types. Time-or-percussion fuses used arrangements whereby the shock of discharge as the shell left the gun allowed a hammer to cut a thin wire and fire the detonator mechanism. The more complicated time-and-percussion fuses on the other hand utilised a needle held by a spring that was forced by impact with the target into the detonator, thus exploding the shell. Later forms of armour-piercing shell had delayed action fuses that were used for bursting the shell beyond the armour plate through which it had passed.[10]

This latter arrangement was designed to create a maximum of localised damage on the target ship, but it is interesting to note that where time-or-percussion types of fuse were concerned, the use of slow-burning powder as a propellant created problems in that the forward momentum of the shell now became so gradual that the inertia of the hammer in the fuse was not sufficient to cut the wire that fired the detonator. This problem was finally overcome by fitting replacement wire in each fuse that was thinner and at least one-tenth the strength of that originally used.[11]

Cast-iron common shells that had such a devastating effect on wooden and unprotected iron ships were practically powerless against ironclads that carried large areas of armour. In view of this, and as a result of advances in metallurgy, more costly steel shells were constructed and these allowed greater bursting charges to be used. However as the thickness and cost of armour increased it became necessary to concentrate armour so that although it covered a warship's vitals, large areas were left unprotected. As a consequence it became possible once more to use cast-iron shells, especially when fired from secondary armament, but by this time quick-firing guns were also in vogue, and these could be used to even greater effect against unprotected structures.[12]

Whilst the projectile with its bursting charge, and the linen or canvas cartridge holding propellant that were utilised in the main and secondary armaments of warships up to and including pre-Dreadnoughts, were separately loaded into the muzzle or breech, the ammunition used in quick-firing guns used a brass cartridge case into which the projectile was fixed. This arrangement was very effective in use, allowing for much faster loading and firing of the guns, as well as safer and less labour intensive storage of the ammunition. In fact this combination of projectile and cartridge into one entity that was first used with quick-firing guns, paved the way for similar arrangements to be eventually introduced for the primary and secondary ordnance of warships in all the world's navies.

It is surprising to note, however, that during a period that saw such vast improvements and change in both armour protection and the power and effi-ciency of guns and their mountings, very few commensurate advances in the technology of projectiles occurred. It was true that improvements in the chem-istry of propellant, and the process of capping projectiles to improve penetration had taken place, but the armour-piercing and common shells used for example in the Admiral class of the late 1880s were very little different from those used in ships of the Majestic class of more than a decade later. Indeed the problem of designing a shell and appropriate fuse that would penetrate thick armour and effectively burst inside the target ship was not completely solved until long after the pre-Dreadnoughts had been superseded as first-class capital ships. The same was not, however, true of another high explosive weapon that, although at this time in its infancy, would develop to become one of the most deadly and feared weapons of nineteenth and early twentieth century naval warfare, that so-called 'devilish and damned ungentlemanly weapon', the torpedo.

The term torpedo is now only used for mobile torpedoes, but in its earli-est form it was the name given to a submerged explosive device similar to the twentieth-century mine that exploded when a ship travelled over it, and was used thus by the Confederates during the American Civil War, and by the Russians during actions in the Baltic. This type of torpedo was, however, too passive, and its successful operation too uncertain, and something better suited for offensive warfare was required, so as a result the spar torpedo was devised. This device was simply an explosive charge fixed to the end of a long pole carried in the bows of a launch or similar small craft. Under cover of darkness the target ship was approached, the pole and charge immersed in the sea, and the explosive ignited by an electrical wire when in contact with an underwater section of the victim's hull. In the confusion that would follow the assailant might well escape, but the risks for the attacker, both from enemy counter action, and the explosion itself, were enormous, and it was soon evident that effort needed to be focused on some means of discharging a torpedo at a distance from its target.[13]

During this phase of development, a British naval officer, Captain Harvey, pro-posed a new form of torpedo. This weapon consisted of an explosive charge fitted into an elongated, somewhat streamlined casing, that was towed behind a fast attack vessel, and when the attacker was about to pass the target ship the towed torpedo was partly released so as to cause water resistance to force it sideways towards the target as it slowed down. In this way it was possible for the device to make contact, usually at the target ship's bow or stern, whereupon a contact fuse would ignite the explosive it carried and the attacking boat could make its escape. The Harvey torpedo was, however, little more than an experiment, and was quickly succeeded by a much more superior weapon, known as the Whitehead torpedo.[14]

Created by English engineer Robert Whitehead, who managed an engineering factory at Fiume in Austria, a prototype of this weapon had been developed by 1868, and Whitehead was keen to sell his torpedo to the British Admiralty. Irrespective of this though it took some considerable time to convince certain members of the Admiralty Board who assessed all new weapons, of the new torpedo's worth, and exhaustive trials had to be carried out before the Admiralty finally agreed to fully adopt Whitehead's invention. The body of the device consisted of a steel, cigar-shaped cylinder, driven by a small compressed-air operated engine that was attached to a small screw propeller, and which was located in the after section of the torpedo itself. Horizontal rudders adapted to the pressure of water at different depths, and regulated the distance below the surface the torpedo was to operate. At first the explosive used was gunpowder but this was later changed to guncotton, and this was packed in the fore part of the torpedo's body. Firing of this charge occurred on impact with a target by the use of a striker mechanism and a detonator cap. The original Whitehead torpedo could travel at a speed of 8 knots per hour within an extreme range of a quarter of a mile, but on further development the weapon was provided with a range of about half a mile and a maximum speed of 30 knots.[15]

Initially this form of torpedo was far from perfect, but after its adoption by the Admiralty it was continually improved, and after testing in Froude's experimental tank at Portsmouth, was redesigned and given a bluff-shaped head. As a result of this and other improvements the Whitehead torpedo eventually became a most efficient weapon of considerable range and great speed. Although the diameters of these torpedoes varied, by the end of the nineteenth century two sizes were in use in ships of the British Navy, the 14in and the so-called 18in, which in reality was actually 17.71in in diameter.

Whitehead torpedoes were built not only at Fiume, but also at the naval gun factory at Woolwich, as well as at a number of other locations in Britain, and amongst the improvements of the last few years of the century was the fitting of a gyroscope to assist steering and automatically correct any tendency of the weapon to deflect from its original line of fire. Whitehead torpedoes were usually discharged in one of two ways, either from ejector tubes using the initial impulse of compressed air that started the torpedo's engine, or from the use of dropping gear by means of which the torpedo was lowered overboard into the water and then started and released. In capital ships torpedo ejector tubes were normally used, and these could be mounted on deck and trained through above-water ports, or by the use of submerged tubes that were fixed in position, and could only be aimed by movements of the vessel's helm. Towards the end of the nineteenth century and into the twentieth, the tendency was to fit submerged tubes in preference to deck-mounted types, as it was recognised that a projectile striking the detonator or compressed air chamber of a torpedo sitting in an above-water tube would likely detonate it, with what could well be disastrous results where the ship on which the torpedo was being carried was concerned.[16]

Once Whitehead torpedoes began to be installed in capital ships, it became clear that they could also be readily fitted into small fast-attack craft, which in the hands of a determined opposing force would provide a major threat to larger ships, especially if those ships were at anchor. In fact where the earlier threat from flotillas of small ram-bowed craft had eventually been seen as erroneous, the threat from torpedo boats designed to dash in within effective range of an enemy's large warships, discharge their torpedoes, and then quickly sheer off out of range of hostile fire, appeared to be a much more realistic proposition. The anxiety this realisation generated in all levels of the naval service, including the members of the Admiralty Board, was palpable, and many wondered at the apparent mixed blessing the torpedo had bestowed. Recalling this some time later, the then First Naval Lord Sir Frederick Richards noted with reference to Robert Whitehead, that: 'No man ever did his country a worse service … the millions which his invention has taxed his country up to the present would have built a large fleet.'[17]

Ideas surrounding the use of torpedo boats would continue to develop both in Britain's navy and in those of the other great powers, and in an attempt to counter the sometimes exaggerated threat that these vessels posed, torpedo catchers and then the more significant torpedo boat destroyers would later become important additions to all nations' battle fleets. Whilst the history and development of these smaller ships is interesting in its own right, it falls outside the remit of this current work, however the various methods and arrangements that the British Admiralty and its naval service used in an attempt to protect its capital ships from the possibility of torpedo boat attack do not, and these are outlined below.

The Torpedo Committee, set up on behalf of the Admiralty Board, and which consisted of senior naval officers and other interested parties, had been established to consider evidence on torpedoes and their use, before agreeing that the rights to manufacture Whitehead's torpedoes for use by the British Navy should be acquired. This group was also tasked with considering the question of defence in the event that British capital ships were attacked by foreign torpedo boats that either carried Whitehead torpedoes or something similar. Where this was concerned the Committee found that: 'the protection from offensive torpedoes of our ships at sea is by far the most important branch of enquiry submitted to the committee and one requiring immediate attention; it is moreover the only one on which they are unable to make a confident recommendation.' They further concluded that, 'the most powerful ship is liable to be destroyed by a torpedo projected from a vessel of the utmost comparative insignificance', and that this would result in a 'tendency to reduce to one common level the naval power of the greatest and most insignificant nations'.[18]

The underwater parts of a warship were not covered with armour plates as this, all agreed, would increase displacement and therefore construction costs, affect the efficiency of the armoured water line belt as the ship would sit lower in the water, have a detrimental effect on speed, and make a ship very sluggish and difficult to manoeuvre. In view of this it was evident that the thin metal plates of the underwater body were very prone to damage from the explosive effects of torpedoes or mines, and in view of the Torpedo Committee's findings, many in the British naval service considered this form of below-the-surface attack incomparably more dangerous than the more usual above-water attack from naval guns.

At first when the maximum range of torpedoes was relatively small it was thought that attacks could be fully countered by the use of quick-firing guns, with the addition at night of powerful searchlights fitted with dioptric projectors, the use of which advances in electricity had now made possible, and which could be utilised not only to pinpoint the attacking torpedo boats, but also to make it difficult for torpedo boat crews to manoeuvre and aim their weapons. However as the power and versatility of the torpedo developed, and ranges significantly increased, other methods of protection had to be considered. Numerous experiments were carried out during the period to try and develop a method of stopping torpedoes, but the only one that appeared promising was the use of booms that projected some 40ft from a ship's side and carried steel mesh nets that hung vertically in the water alongside, and extended to a depth that was adjusted to correspond with the bottom of the ship's keel. The booms were hinged at their heels and when not in use, as would be the case when the ship was under way, were stowed along the ship's side after being lifted and swung in by use of the ship's derricks or other lifting devices.

Whilst the use of such arrangements in trials appeared capable of stopping torpedoes, this could in practice only occur when a ship was at anchor, as dangling nets would have been too much of a liability when a ship was under way, as they might foul the screw during course changes or get in the way of a ship's secondary armament. In addition, the cumbersome steel crinoline that formed the nets and which was stowed when not in use around the upper deck edges, took a lot of effort and time to secure for use, longer still to re-stow, and was prone to being damaged or even completely swept away during periods of rough weather. Finally, with the onset of automatic wire-cutting devices that were installed in a torpedo's nose, and later developments in the power of the torpedo that allowed it to smash through the net defensive screen, the function and utility of nets was brought into question. As a consequence torpedo nets were generally discarded as a practical means of providing protection against torpedo attack.

As nets became obsolete together with the realisation that the latest generation of torpedoes could not be stopped, attention was focused on minimising
the damage that might accrue from a torpedo strike. Protection against possible damage from rams had previously been thought possible by subdividing the
underwater hulls of warships into sealed compartments, so that the ingress of
water could be localised and pumped out, and many in the service felt that similar
arrangements could be used for protection against torpedoes.

The explosive nature of the latter weapon, however, meant that such methods
were not wholly practical, that is until the idea of building longitudinal torpedo
bulkheads was developed. Usually extending from the aftermost machinery spaces
to the ship's bow and encompassing boiler, as well as engine and other machinery rooms, these bulkheads were set far enough inboard to prevent them being
breached in the event of a torpedo exploding against the outer or shell plating.
Although sometimes filled with coal, the outboard space formed by the bulkhead
and the ship's side was better left empty, as the void so-formed would allow the
explosion to vent itself. Whilst this arrangement did meet with some success it
was still not ideal, and it wasn't until the First World War in 1914 that further
developments resulted in the construction of warships that carried underwater
steel protrusions along their sides known as torpedo bulges, and the thin, unarmoured outer skin of these together with the void that existed behind, fulfilled
their expected function in that they tended to absorb the shock of an external
explosion without in most cases damaging the hull proper.

OF BOILERS, ENGINES, AND STEAM

Steam is a gas formed when water is heated to, and maintained at, boiling point, and the steam engine is basically a device that converts heat energy in the steam into work. The operating principle of the non-turbine or ordinary steam engine is that an expanding force or pressure of steam acts on one side of a piston contained in a cylinder, forcing it to move. In doing this it does work, and as a consequence other mechanical parts that are linked to the piston via its connecting rod are forced to move also, and this latter motion can be linear or rotary, depending on the mechanisms in question. In vertical engines the piston motion is up and down, and in horizontal engines backwards and forwards. In all cases the pistons' reciprocating motion is achieved by alternatively opening passages to steam and exhaust in either ends of the cylinder. To produce this effect a system of side valves is used.[1] As steam engines became more sophisticated during the nineteenth century, multiple pistons that were each encased in their own cylinders were used, so that the expanding and cooling steam could continue generating work over a longer period.

As noted in earlier chapters, the first steam engines were simple reciprocating devices that were used at the time for many applications on land. However until some means of turning reciprocating into rotary motion had been discovered, no progress was possible in adopting the steam engine to the propulsion of either inshore or sea-going vessels. Early in the nineteenth century, though, experiments in Great Britain and Europe as well as North America, showed that steam engines driving paddle wheels could be used to power small, then increasingly larger, boats and ships, and from that date the success of steam navigation can be said to have been secured.[2]

As far as the British Navy was concerned there were four main periods of development with respect to the steam power of capital ships. These were marked by: the evolution of the paddle-wheel frigate, the introduction of the screw propeller, the conversion or construction of sailing line-of-battle ships into auxiliary screw steamers, and the development of various types of screw-powered warship. In accord with these divisions it should be noted that marine engines were generally divided into two classes: those adapted to drive paddle wheels, and those best suited to driving a screw propeller, the chief difference being that the early engines used for driving paddle wheels acted via side-levers, although later on early forms of direct-acting engines were employed. Engines used with screws on the other hand were always direct-acting, in that their piston rods were directly connected to a crankshaft that provided the requisite rotary motion.[3]

Steam vessels were first introduced into Britain's naval service in 1820 and between that date and 1840 some seventy small paddle-wheel ships were built. These early steamers were mainly used for towing, dispatches work, and general-purpose duties, and as they carried little if any sort of armament, these small vessels could hardly be classed as warships. In the main these little ships were fitted with primitive flue boilers and slow moving side-lever engines worked by steam at a pressure of around 4lb/sq. in.[4]

Side-lever engines were basically modifications of the beam engines that were used for pumping water out of mines, and for adjusting the water levels of canals and other inland navigations, but in the case of side-lever installations, the normally overhead beams were placed alongside the cylinders, condensers etc. so that the engines would fit into the much-restricted space available in the hull of a small ship. In addition, the usual movement of the ordinary beam-type pumping engine was modified by the use of side rods, crossheads in guides, and overhead crankshafts, to provide the requisite rotary motion[5] needed to turn the ship's paddle wheels.

The flue boiler used at the time was similar to those used on land, but because of the fear of fire in wooden and even iron ships, the lower part of the flue was wholly contained within the boiler itself rather than being positioned above it, as was the case with shore installations. In this position it was surrounded by water and this enabled the flame and hot gasses generated in the furnace, and which were confined in the narrow flues, to heat the boiler water until nearly dissipated, and to create steam as a consequence. At this point any gasses left were led up through the uptake at the bottom of the ship's funnel, and vented to the atmosphere. Although relatively easy to operate, flue boilers were heavy and took up a great deal of space in a small ship, even when formed to fit the hull, and although used for a number of years they were eventually superseded.[6] As a general point it should be noted that illustrations of some of the engines and boilers mentioned in this chapter are shown in Appendix 5 at the back of this book.

No great advance was made in the flue boiler until about 1840, when multi-tubular boilers started to be introduced. This type was of a rectangular, box shape and contained a large number of tubes through which furnace gases and flames passed on the way to the uptake and funnel. These tubes were generally horizontal, and as they passed through the boiler they heated the water that surrounded them, creating steam that, when collected in a steam drum, was fed off to the engines. This form of fire-tube box boiler was in use in the Royal Navy up to about the middle of the 1870s, and with certain improvements allowed steam pressures of around 35 to 40lb/sq. in to be achieved.[7] The *Thunderer* of 1876 was the last capital ship to be fitted with box boilers, and was the subject of the worst boiler explosion in the annals of the British Navy, in which forty persons were killed. A subsequent inquiry, however, found that faulty boiler construction was not the reason for the explosion and that errors in operating, combined with faulty safety valves, had alone been the cause.

In paddle ships space was always at a premium, and engine side levers and their associated linkages in particular, took up a great deal of room. This problem was finally overcome by the introduction of direct-acting engines for rotating the paddle wheels. A number of engine builders had been involved in these develop-ments but the British Admiralty chose the Thames-based firms of Maudslay, Sons and Field, and John Penn to supply engines for their ships, with the Penn type, due mainly to its simplicity, being the one in most demand. The Penn engine was of the oscillating form in which the normal connecting rod was dispensed with and the upper end of the piston rod fitted with brass bearings and allowed to act directly on the crankpin. The cylinder itself was carried on trunnions to enable its oscillation to suit the motion of the crank, and as the trunnions were hollow, steam could be admitted to, and exhausted from, the cylinder through them. Although it was normal for two cylinders to be provided, the use of direct-acting engines allowed significant savings in both space and weight, that in turn affected displacement, and these engines were soon installed in the majority of paddle-wheel ships in place of the now defunct side-lever types.[8]

As noted in a previous chapter, paddle wheels had many disadvantages, the great-est of which was the unequal 'dip' or immersion of the paddle boards brought about by the varying draught of water as coal and stores became used up, and this could have the effect of slowing a ship down quite significantly.[9] Additionally of course paddle boxes, and indeed the paddles themselves, created resistance to a ship's pro-gress and for the relatively larger paddle warships, which by now were being built, the paddles in their boxes with their exposed shafts were highly vulnerable to attack, and made it difficult to train and work any guns that were being carried.

Early increases in steam pressure were closely associated to the type of condenser in use. At first engine and boiler installations utilised what were known as jet-con-densers, where steam having passed through the cylinders was condensed back into water by having a jet of cold water injected into it, and the condensate produced as a result was recirculated and mixed with the salt water used to feed the boilers. Salt deposits in this feed water caused corrosion in boilers and pipes but whilst boiler pressures were low, this could be allowed for and arrangements put in place to minimise its effect. However, as steam pressures and temperatures increased, it was found to be impossible to prevent heavy corrosion and other damage from the increased build-up of salt deposits, and the jet-condenser had to be abandoned. In its place the surface-condenser was developed, and first introduced into the British Navy in the latter half of the nineteenth century. In this system the exhaust steam was directed through a series of tubes surrounded by cold water, condensing back into fresh water as a result. This condensate was then used as feed water, and as no mixing with salt water occurred, the corrosion problem was, in the main, overcome. Later on, the development of evaporators in which sea water could be made into fresh water meant that large quantities of fresh boiler-feed water were made available. This facility was further refined and augmented at a later date by the introduction of distilling units, supplemented by reserves of fresh water for boiler feed purposes carried in a ship's double bottoms or other tanks.

The adoption of the screw propeller in place of the paddle wheel was arguably the most important step taken in the progress of marine engineering, as this allowed many subsequent developments in both marine engines and boilers to take place. The principal advantages of the screw over the paddle wheel were that it was little affected by a ship rolling or the draught decreasing as coal and stores were used up, and it was capable of being used, irrespective of the power of the engine driving it. In addition, it was not normally affected by damage from projectiles, and warships in which it was installed could readily use their armaments without obstruction. It also permitted engines to be fitted in such a way that being low in the hull, they were more readily protected by deck and belt armour. As a consequence of these advantages screws were increasingly being used and from 1840 the British Admiralty acquired the rights to use Pettit-Smith's form of screw propeller and began introducing them into the service.[10]

New forms of engine were required to drive the screw propeller, especially as by its use it had now become possible to install an appropriately designed engine below the water line, although due cognizance had to be given to restrictions that existed in a ship's hull, and which made it difficult to get a connecting rod of suitable length to work between the piston and the crank.[11] This problem was overcome by engine builder John Penn, who developed the trunk engine, in which a hollow cylindrical casing or trunk was bolted to the upper face of the piston, and working through a steam-tight stuffing box on the end of the cylinder cover, took the place of the piston rod, whilst the lower end of the connecting rod worked through the hollow trunk and was connected to a gudgeon in the centre of the piston itself.[12]

These engines were installed horizontally in a ship's hull and were quite efficient in use, although like all steam engines and boiler installations, they suffered from being installed in wooden hulls where flexing and movement of timbers due to the action of wind and waves caused breakdowns, and damage to steam pipes, joints, and couplings. Later, with the introduction of higher-pressure steam, trunk engines became obsolete as it was found to be impossible to keep the trunks steam-tight. Trunk engines were, however, extensively used over a long period, being utilised in steam line-of-battle ships, and in large ironclad frigates like *Warrior* and her consorts. Return connecting-rod engines, that enabled horizontal cylinders to be brought close to the crankshaft, and direct-acting types that, whilst still horizontal, had their connecting rods between the cylinder and the crank, were both later utilised in many British capital ships.

The simple expansion engine of the 1870s, with steam at around 30lb/sq. in, using surface condensers, and fitted with steam jackets to retain heat, were fairly economical and were a considerable advance on those that had gone before. After the success of the surface condenser, renewed attention was given to achieving higher steam pressures and the efficiencies that could then accrue due to greater expansion of the steam. In line with this though, boiler design had to be considered, and when steam pressures rose from 30lb to 60lb/sq. in, boilers were changed from the box type to the cylindrical, so that the increased steam pressure could be safely carried. At the same time compound or double-expansion engines were introduced, and in the period up to about 1885 were fitted to nearly all warships in the British Navy.[13]

In this type of engine the expansion of the steam happened in stages. Initially steam was admitted to a small diameter cylinder and, once expanded, was allowed into a second cylinder of a larger diameter, where it was allowed to expand even further before being exhausted out to the condenser. By comparison, in earlier simple expansion engines, even if they had two cylinders as was latterly the case, the steam passed into each identically sized cylinder directly from the boiler, before being exhausted to condenser or the atmosphere without allowing the full work potential of the steam to be achieved. In compound engines, however, the different sized cylinders allowed much more of the steam's energy to be utilised, and were thus more efficient in use.

Once compounding was introduced and found to work in practice, it became possible to increase the power of steam engines by adding more cylinders, each one of a larger diameter than the previous one, so that every ounce of work could be wrung from the expanding steam that passed through them. If the steam passed through and was expanded in three cylinders in succession, the engine was called a three-stage or triple-expansion engine; if it had four cylinders it became a four-stage or quadruple expansion type.[14] Three-cylinder triple-expansion engines were fitted to many of the pre-Dreadnoughts up to the London class of 1902, but from then on quadruple-expansion units became the norm for battleships and were fitted to all later pre-Dreadnoughts up to and including ships of the King Edward VII class.

With the introduction of compounding it became necessary to build vertical engines that had their crankshafts directly below the cylinders. This arrangement had been introduced for merchant ships long before the Admiralty agreed to follow suit and use them in warships, because for reasons of security during an attack it was thought necessary to locate machinery below the water line in ships of war, and only horizontal engines appeared to meet that requirement. Vertical engines, however, possessed many practical advantages both in relation to their more efficient operation and to their better accessibility, and less space requirements. When, therefore, twin screws were introduced in battleships, vertical compound engines began to be fitted, but with a central vertical watertight bulkhead between the two sets of engines. Apart from its increased operating efficiency, this type of installation had the added benefit that by dividing the overall engine power into two, each engine, even in the largest of warships, would be of moderate size and, although it was unlikely that all the machinery would fit below the water line, the parts above would be protected by the better armour arrangements that then existed, as well as from coal bunkers and similar hull spaces located either side of engine and boiler rooms.

The generation of higher pressure steam that these improved engines were capable of working with could not, however, be readily achieved with the cylindrical fire-tube, or water-tank boilers that were in use at the time. Once steel began to be used for both engine and boiler construction though, it became possible to develop a very different type of boiler that, although cylindrical in form, was the converse of the preceding forms, in that the water was carried in tubes, whilst the flames and hot gasses from the furnace surrounded them. The hot gasses outside the tubes were, however, confined within the boiler casing, and from there were led to the funnel by an additional casing provided for that purpose. This arrangement was in effect the reverse of that which occurred in fire-tube boilers, and as water-tube boilers were further developed, steam pressures of up to 300lb/sq. in became possible.[15]

Advantages claimed for water-tube boilers included greater strength, lightness, greater safety in use, enhanced power, durability and ease of repair, as well as greater economy in the use of fuel.[16] Where this latter was concerned, however, other developments also had a significant effect. To produce more steam from a given size of boiler was achievable if more coal could be burned, but this required a greater supply of oxygen to the furnace than could be provided in an open stokehold utilising natural draught, and some form of forced draught arrangement was clearly required. Various methods of achieving this were tried but in 1882 the system of making each stokehold into a closed compartment, and keeping them under pressure by the use of large steam-operated blowing fans was adopted, and this innovation allowed the steam-generating powers of all subsequent boilers to be significantly increased.[17]

Water-tube boilers had been fitted in merchant ships long before they were introduced into the British Navy, but in practice many of these early types were problematic in use and often failed due to rapid corrosion of the tubes that carried water and steam. Eventually though, with the advent of cylindrical multi-tubular boilers, and by the use of fresh, rather than salt, water for boiler feed purposes, these difficulties were overcome. Although the advantages of water-tube boilers was soon apparent, naval opinion as to their suitability for use in HM ships was mixed, and doubts as to their continuing effectiveness remained within the service for some time.

A water-tube boiler consisted of a steel container through which steel tubes carrying the feed water passed and which were exposed to fire, gasses, and intense heat that boiled the water and turned it into steam that was then fed into a receiver from which steam was drawn by the operation of engines and auxiliaries. In practice the water tubes could be combined in a surprising variety of forms.

These included round- or flattened-tube coils arranged vertically or horizontally, straight lengths of tube or tubes in lengths that were slightly curved, or conversely elaborately bent, all of which could be placed at any number of angles,[18] and large- or small-bore tubes of various dimensions.

Numerous firms of boiler manufacturers in Great Britain, as well as on the Continent, and in North America, vied with each other to develop the most advanced form of water-tube boiler, all claiming that they were able to best combine the various elements to achieve near perfection. At the time British firms that were competing included Yarrow and Thornycroft, and later Perkins; in France, Normand, Du Temple and Belleville;[19] and in America, Herreshoff, a company more usually associated with development and construction of early and highly successful America's-Cup racing yachts. Irrespective of this often-competitive activity, though, the first water-tube boiler suitable for service in large warships was constructed by Belleville in France. This was of the large tube type and was introduced into French warships at the beginning of the 1880s, after having been used and tested in French naval launches for a number of years. In Great Britain, by this juncture large-tube boilers were being built by Niclausse, Babcock and Wilcox, and Yarrow, and all these were tried in British ships, but in practice each type was found to be problematic. By the middle of the 1890s, therefore, the British Admiralty had decided to take the unheard of step of acquiring the rights to build the French Belleville boiler for use in its capital ships,[20] and this arrangement continued for some years, although water-tube boilers manufactured by some of the other makers were also occasionally used.

The Belleville had appealed due to its apparent sturdiness and because it had already been successfully used in the French Navy, and in addition required no access space at sides and back, apart from that taken up by casings and firing space. More room was consequently available for the fire-grate area than any other boiler then in production, and the elements that made up the installation could be readily removed during maintenance etc. through ordinary hatches, making large openings in the armoured deck that other designs required, completely unnecessary.[21]

Numerous tests had been carried out by the Admiralty before making the decision to fit these boilers in British capital ships, and these took into account the increased piston speeds that reciprocating engines were then capable of, as well as the difficulties that leaking steam joints sometimes generated, due to increased speeds and boiler pressures. Unfortunately when the Bellevilles began to be fitted in some smaller warships it was found that so much space was taken up by the boiler installation that access to auxiliary machinery was cramped, making maintenance difficult and causing operating problems for engine room staff. Problems experienced in the dockyards when constructing these boilers soon indicated that insufficient briefing by the French had taken place, and this lack of information led to deviations from normal French good practice, and errors both in construction and fitting of the boilers into British capital ships,[22] became commonplace.

By the early 1900s though, many warships, including the twenty pre-Dreadnought battleships that made up the Canopus to the Duncan classes, were fitted
with Belleville boilers. As the new ships with these boilers came into commission,
several experienced problems over and above those which would normally be
called teething problems, and in some cases these involved serious breakdowns.
Although in a few instances the breakdowns were in fact associated with the
Belleville boilers, in many others they were due to other causes. Irrespective of
this, however, the general view was still that the French boilers were at fault. This
led to the Admiralty being openly and heavily criticised for its policies associated
with Belleville boilers, both within the House of Commons and in the wider
naval service, as well as by the British popular press. In addition, publishers of
influential professional journals like *The Engineer*, were highly scathing in their
criticism, and as a consequence a Committee of Enquiry under the chairmanship
of an eminent admiral was appointed, with committee members being drawn
from both the Royal and Merchant navies as well as from mercantile insurers
such as Lloyds of London.[23]

The Committee was tasked with 'considering certain questions respecting
the modern types of boilers for naval purposes, and to ascertain practically
and experimentally the relative advantages and disadvantages of the Belleville
boiler for naval purposes as compared with other forms'.[24] In doing this, committee members considered a number of aspects, including the water-tube
boilers in use in British and foreign navies and in mercantile vessels, and this
was done by visiting various ships and taking evidence from a range of people.
These included ship and dockyard officers, Board of Trade officials, design
and other engineers, and representatives from firms that manufactured boilers.
The Committee also considered a whole range of different types of water-
tube boiler and examined the engine rooms of numerous ships fitted with
Belleville and other makes of boiler. They even used two small warships, *Medea*
and *Medusa*, as test platforms.

Interim reports were prepared in 1901 and 1902, with a final version in 1904.
Although there were some slight changes over this period the final report echoed
what had been said in early versions and concluded that:

> the advantages of water tube boilers for naval purposes are so great, chiefly
> from a military point of view that providing a satisfactory type of water-tube
> boiler be adopted, it would be more suitable for use in H.M. Navy than any
> other type of boiler; further, that the Belleville boiler has no such advantages
> over other types of water-tube boilers as to lead members of this Committee to
> recommend it as the best type to be adopted for H.M. Navy.

They further noted that:

The Committee fully recognise that the Belleville boiler, when new and in good condition, is a good steam generator, but its rapid loss of efficiency in ordinary work in commissioned ships, the serious character of the defects which have been developed in it, and the great care required in its manipulation, render it, in the opinion of the Committee, undesirable to fit any more of this type in H.M. Navy.[25]

Ironically by the time the final report had been produced in 1904, Admiral Domvile, who had presided over the Committee as its chairman, was in the Mediterranean flying his flag in the pre-Dreadnought battleship *Bulwark*, a ship that carried twenty Belleville boilers. When sent a copy of the final report for his signature, he noted in his covering letter to the Admiralty that his current experience with Belleville boilers on the Mediterranean station had been very favourable, and it was evident to him that although early boilers of the type might have been defective in a number of ways, as well as being badly used, no serious boiler defects in any of the ships under his command had occurred, and that the working life of these boilers was not so short as he had first imagined. He added that in his view a second commission of the ships in question would be a very good test of the staying power of their boilers.[26]

But by that time, the breakdowns that had occurred in Belleville-boilered ships, together with a widespread perception that these boilers were generally inferior to other water-tube types, meant that they were universally condemned, although the Admiralty was still strongly of the view that water-tube boilers were unquestionably the way forward. As a consequence it chose the Babcock large-tube boiler for capital ships then planned or building, and the small-tube Yarrow, amongst others, for smaller vessels. Where capital ships were concerned this was a good choice and Babcock boilers, though heavy and occupying more space than the Belleville, were reliable in use and gave good service. However the Yarrow and other small-tube boilers that were fitted in cruisers and other craft were for many years highly problematic.[27]

But during this period, when the issue of water-tube boilers, and what would come to be known as the 'battle of the boilers', was raging, the Admiralty was starting to be faced with a number of other fundamental technical and associated issues that heralded further fundamental change, and about which decisions would soon have to be made. These not only included the growing size, power, and cost of warships, but also included many engineering aspects, such as how to cater for changes associated with developing turbine technologies and the possible introduction of oil instead of coal as the main fuel used to generate steam in those ships. Whilst the boiler issue had for the time being been solved, at least where capital warships were concerned, these other issues still needed to be addressed, and although strictly speaking outside the period of the pre-Dreadnoughts, are appropriately, but briefly, described in the final chapter of this book. The next chapter, though, attempts to outline the way in which pre-Dreadnoughts were used and performed under actual battle conditions.

TESTED IN BATTLE

Battleships, although technically sophisticated, and capable of using their large displacement, speed, manoeuvrability, and endurance, together with their powerful ordnance and armour protection to attack an enemy, and in turn defend themselves from attack, were still in essence simply mobile gun platforms. The efficiency of those gun platforms and the effectiveness with which they were capable of exerting superior force was, however, mainly theoretical unless that force could be tested in practice. It was true that fleet manoeuvres were occasionally carried out, but the only real test of both the warships and the crews that operated them, was for fleet, group, or single-ship actions under real conditions of warfare to take place.

Where British pre-Dreadnoughts and their immediate predecessors developed during the period of transition that followed the introduction of steam were concerned, naval actions carried out against enemy forces rarely happened, although later battleship types would of course be involved in numerous twentieth-century naval campaigns. A few late nineteenth-century naval actions involving armoured ships did, however, take place, and although none of these involved British naval forces, many of the warships of the foreign navies that were involved had been designed, and/or built, in British dockyards, or in those of the other great powers.

The armoured batteries used by French and British naval forces in the Crimean War were of course just that, and as these could hardly be classed as warships, their actions have not been included in the paragraphs that follow. By the same token American Civil War monitors, that were used by both Union and Confederate naval forces, and which took part in a number of operations, were used in rivers, estuaries, and lakes, and were never intended as seagoing warships, so actions involving them have been omitted also. It should additionally be noted that in the space available it has not been possible to deal with every nineteenth-century naval action, and as capital ships were in the main designed to operate in squadrons or fleets, only those incidents that involved multi-ship actions have been included.

Many of the nineteenth-century wars and skirmishes resulted from imperialistic ambitions, and during these conflicts naval battles were often so important that they decided the final outcome of the wars in which they occurred.[1] The first of these in which seagoing ironclad fleets took part was the 1866 Battle of

Lissa during the war between Italy and Prussia on the one hand, and Austria on the other. Although Prussia was allied to Italy, the two fleets that took part at Lissa involved Italian and Austrian ships only, as Prussia had little in the way of naval forces, although she did possess a powerful army.

By the 1860s most nations had followed the example of Great Britain and France, and had re-constituted their naval forces.[2] As a result of this, by 1866 Italy had twelve screw-driven broadside ironclads varying in size from 2,000 to 5,800 tons, with an additional thirty-five unarmoured screw-and-paddle ships, whilst the Austrian fleet by comparison was smaller, with seven, broadside screw-powered ironclads of a similar type, and thirty-two unarmoured screw-and-paddle warships. Neither navy was in a high state of efficiency, and the Italian fleet, commanded by Admiral Count Persano, had only been in existence since 1861 and its officers and men had not had the opportunity to train together or become an effective group. In a similar way the Austrian Navy under Rear Admiral Tegetthoff, although having been in existence for some considerable time, was not a coherent fighting force and consisted for the most part of untrained short-service men.

The Italian ironclads had been built in France, Britain, and America, whilst the Austrian ships had for the most part been constructed in their own shipyards. The ships of both navies carried a mixture of smooth-bore and rifled guns, but in practice the Italian rifled ordnance, especially the 10in and 8in shell guns, were significantly heavier than those carried in the Austrian warships. In all cases the guns were protected by 4.5in armour, and ships' vitals were likewise protected by belt and vertical plate of a similar thickness. Irrespective of this, the ships of both navies had large areas, especially towards the bows and sterns, which were completely unprotected.[3]

The Italian fleet under Admiral Persano left the Italian port of Ancona with a number of troop ships and steered for the Island of Lissa, off the Austrian coast. The intention was to silence the gun batteries on the island and to land occupying troops. Initial attacks were unsuccessful, and before the troops could be landed the Austrian fleet was sighted steaming towards them.[4] As they approached, Admiral Tegetthoff formed the Austrian ships into three vee-shaped squadrons for a line-abreast attack, which he led in his flagship *Erzherzog Ferdinand Max*. To counter this Admiral Persano formed his warships into a line in front of the approaching Austrians, with his eleven foreign-built ironclads at the centre. Initially Persano had hoisted his flag in the *Re d'Italia*, but at the last moment switched to the *Affondatore*, but without advising his captains in the other ships what he was doing. This move caused great confusion during the battle, as the wrong ship was consequently looked to for signals. In the event both this, and the confusion that existed concerning Persano's tactics, were of little consequence, as the leading Austrian ships soon broke through the Italian line, closely followed by their consorts in the other squadrons and the battle degenerated into a chaotic melee.[5]

Opposing ships exchanged shots at short range, but as the Austrians had inferior guns and the Italians untrained gun crews, the damage that occurred was not great. However as Tegetthoff had always intended to use ramming as a substitute for his inferior gun power, the confused melee was just what he wanted, and although a number of unsuccessful ramming attempts by Austrian ships took place, at the climax of the four-hour battle *Ferdinand Max* rammed and sank *Re d'Italia*.[6] In addition to this, another Italian ironclad, the *Palestro*, was set on fire and exploded. On the Austrian side only the wooden unarmoured ships suffered, and with the sinking of two of their capital ships and the death of over six hundred crew members, the Italian fleet was forced to withdraw back to Ancona, leaving the Austrians, who had sustained less than sixty casualties and had lost none of their ships, the victors. The Italian ships never ventured out again and not long after peace was declared and hostilities ended.

All the armoured ships from the fleets of both belligerents carried their guns in broadside batteries. In the action the 4.5in armour kept out all shells, even from the heaviest guns, and all the significant hits were in the unprotected parts where damage to steering gear and unprotected guns took place. In addition, numerous fires broke out in the unarmoured wooden ships, although the sole wooden screw line-of-battle ship that took part, the Austrian *Kaiser*, whilst severely damaged from constant attacks by a number of Italian ironclads, remained afloat, firing a broadside that critically damaged the Italian ironclad *Affondatore*. Austrian tactics at the time favoured the ram and the sinking of *Re d'Italia* by *Ferdinand Max* appeared to be a major coup. It should be noted though that the Italian ironclad was lying helpless with a damaged rudder at the time, and that her armour was fixed to a wooden hull, with no watertight flats or compartments that might have saved her from foundering.[7]

In practice most of the many ramming attempts were unsuccessful, and it was only because *Re d'Italia* could not manoeuvre that her fatal ramming by the Austrian flagship was able to take place. Irrespective of this, supporters of the ram judged the incident as proof of the immense power of their favoured weapon. In fact some sceptics were even converted by the action, and in the period after the battle, the hypercritical Edward Reed, not always a ram supporter, wrote that: 'The engagement at Lissa affords more conclusive evidence of the great results that may be achieved by the proper use of this method of attack, especially in actions between seagoing ships.' He further noted: 'With respect to the difficulty of disengaging a ram bow from an enemy's side, I may remark, so far as my information extends, no such difficulty has ever been experienced in actual warfare.'[8]

For the next thirty years or so after Lissa, the ram influenced naval tactics and thought, and affected warship design to a marked degree. In fact the 1871 Committee on Designs saw it as a major element of power, but surprisingly, instead of looking at ways of further developing the ram and ramming tactics, they concentrated in their deliberations on how best to construct ships to resist ram attacks.[9] By doing so they appeared to place defence before offence, and whilst that might have been admirable in some areas, the design of ships of war needed to balance both offensive and defensive capabilities, and this apparent lack of understanding of that principle was perhaps one of the reasons that the Committee's conclusions were slow to affect future British capital ship designs. What was more evident as a result of the Lissa action was that even allowing for the poor marksmanship of the gun crews in both fleets, the defensive power of wrought-iron armour had been well proven, whilst the offensive energy of all the ordnance employed, irrespective of calibre, had been shown to be seriously wanting.

Naval skirmishes and minor wars occasionally occurred in subsequent years but the next important battle as far as naval forces were concerned took place in the estuary of the Yalu River, during the Sino-Japanese War, between the empires of China and Japan, over the domination of Korea. Both China and Japan wanted to make Korea a vassal state, and hostilities broke out in 1894 without the usual formal declaration. Although various land-based skirmishes took place, the main naval action occurred between a Chinese squadron of twelve ships and a similar sized Japanese force.[10] Both Japan and China had used Great Britain as well as France to build some of their warships and both on occasion used naval advisors from Britain and France.

The Chinese fleet under Admiral Ting contained two 7,400-ton armoured battleships of the central-citadel type that had some design similarities to ships of the British Admiral class as well as having their main gun turrets arranged en-echelon, as was the case with the earlier *Inflexible*. The remaining ships were protected cruisers. The Japanese fleet commanded by Admiral Ito mainly consisted of fast, relatively modern, protected cruisers, although it also contained two small ironclads. The two Chinese battleships, *Chen Yuan* and *Ting Yuen*, carried pairs of 12in breech-loading guns in their barbette turrets, as well as smaller weapons in casemates and behind shields. Both of these ships had steel hulls and carried a belt of 14in-thick compound armour, as well as similar armour on the barbettes, and were fitted with 3in-thick armoured decks. The other Chinese ships had ordnance that varied from 4in to 8in in calibre, and carried much lighter armour protection.[11]

The two Japanese capital ships were relatively small and lightly gunned coastal defence ironclads of around 3,000 tons, which carried their armament in central batteries. The protected cruisers in the fleet were, however, more powerful although lightly armoured, and Admiral Ito placed his flag in one of these, *Matsushima*, of 4,217 tons, that carried one 12.6in breech-loading gun in a forward turret and numerous other guns ranging from 5in calibre to smaller 3-pounders, some of which were quick firing. Two further ships of the Matsushima class were also involved in the battle together with other warships that were either categorised as armoured or protected cruisers.[12]

The bulk of the Chinese squadrons were at anchor off the mouth of the Yalu River when the advancing Japanese fleet was sighted. Admiral Ting then signalled for his ships to put to sea to meet the Japanese. The Chinese ships formed into line abreast, with the two battleships at the point of a vee that quickly lost its shape as ships on the wings dropped astern and spacing was not properly maintained. The Japanese ships by contrast steamed in line-ahead formation, although in practice the two squadrons involved tended to act independently.[13] Admiral Ting's decision to attack in line-abreast in the same fashion that Tegetthoff had at Lissa nearly thirty years earlier, reflected the tactical backwardness of the Chinese navy,[14] as although the Austrian tactics had been successful in that earlier conflict, they were by the 1890s generally viewed as being outdated.

The Chinese ships opened fire at around 6,000 yards with little effect, and the Japanese squadrons were then able to advance to 3,000 yards, whereupon they also opened fire. Some of the fast Japanese cruisers then circled the Chinese, and were able to attack from the rear as well, pouring a deadly barrage from their quick-firing guns into the Chinese ships, a number of which were put out of action or sunk. At one stage so many of the Chinese vessels were affected that only the two battleships *Ting Yuen* and *Chen Yuen* were offering any resistance to the circling Japanese ships, and, having superior armour, seemed capable of absorbing the heavy fire directed against them, although their unprotected ends and superstructures were riddled by hits and the air was full of bursting shells. As far as the Japanese ships were concerned many received damage, including Ito's flagship *Matsushima*, which was severely hit and forced to steam out of the action, whereupon Ito transferred his flag to *Hashidate*. Shortly after this, what was left of the Chinese fleet, including the two badly damaged battleships, withdrew to Port Arthur on the Korean peninsula,[15] where after a month's repair work, refitting, and restocking with ammunition, they again ventured out.

By this time, however, the Japanese were too busy escorting troopships to mount a blockade, so that what was left of the Chinese fleet was allowed to escape into the Yellow Sea. The Japanese troops landed on the Korean Liaotung peninsular and soon began an assault on Port Arthur, which was over in a matter of twenty-four hours with the Japanese forces victorious. Japanese advances and associated land-based victories continued, and in 1895, after the siege of Wei-Hai-Wei and with the Chinese capital city Peking now under threat, negotiations were reopened and a peace treaty signed to the effect that Japan gained both Korea and Formosa, as well as enhanced prestige in the eyes of the world,[16] irrespective as it happened of the many atrocities committed by Japanese troops in Port Arthur and elsewhere, that were conveniently forgotten.

The Chinese losses had been relatively heavy with one armoured and one protected cruiser sunk, two protected cruisers disabled and in a sinking condition, and a third one aground. The two battleships, although still just operational, had suffered much damage, and had to contend with numerous fires. The Japanese on the other hand had three ships including the flagship damaged but not lost, with 90 crew members killed and a further 188 wounded. By stark comparison, losses in the Chinese ships amounted to at least 800 killed or wounded.[17]

The Battle of the Yalu River, the first action in which all ships taking part were built of iron or steel, and in which fire caused by shells bursting on board was a regular occurrence, demonstrated that it is not sufficient to only have hulls and upper works of non-inflammable material, but that wood should be eliminated as much as possible in the construction of a warship, unless it can be made fireproof. The compound plates that protected the citadel and turrets of the two Chinese battleships on the other hand, proved once again the power of modern armour to withstand constant attack.[18] The same could not be claimed for the wrought-iron armour of the two Japanese coastal ironclads, supporting the view that obsolete warships had no place in a modern naval battle. Where ordnance was concerned, the Yalu action demonstrated both the firepower of the Chinese big guns, as well as that of the heavy quick-firing weapons of the Japanese cruisers, and clearly vindicated the mixed-battery armament carried by all pre-Dreadnoughts built at that time.[19]

The main action was fought at ranges below 3,000 yards, and the Chinese battleships were each hit by some 200 rounds, many of which struck the unprotected ends of each ship. Whilst these hits caused numerous fires, they did not put either ship out of action, and this fact was noted with some elation in Britain, as all the British central citadel ships had similarly unarmoured ends, and their many critics had always claimed that stability would be lost and capsizing would result if unprotected sections were holed by shellfire. Experience at the Yalu, though, seemed to indicate this view to be erroneous.

The French-designed *Matsushima* and other ships of that class that had not performed well during the fighting were, however, discredited, and as a consequence the Japanese Admiralty refrained from placing any further orders for warships in French shipyards. Although applauding such action, the British Admiralty also had deep concerns about the build-up of Japanese naval power, and this, in conjunction with the subsequent build-up of Russian squadrons in Far-Eastern waters, eventually contributed to the decision to deepen the Suez Canal,[20] so that deeper draught battleships than, say, the shallow-draught Canopus class, could be more readily deployed in Far-Eastern waters if the need ever arose.

The next naval action, the Spanish-American War of 1898, involved two naval battles but, as these were in the main cruiser rather than pre-Dreadnought actions, they have not been described in the context of this book. In 1904, however, the struggle between the Imperial powers of Japan and Russia resulted in two major naval actions in which both powers employed fleets of pre-Dreadnought battleships as well as cruisers, torpedo boats, and torpedo boat destroyers.

Japan and Russia's 1904–1905 conflict was over control of Southern Manchuria and Korea. Some years earlier Russia, France and Germany had forced Japan to return the recently won Liaotung, or Korean peninsula, back to China, the ineffectual Korean Government having no say in the matter. But by 1903 Russia's policies in Manchuria and Korea had become so aggressive that Japan feared for the security of its own islands, and this was brought to a head when Russia began to reinforce her Far Eastern or Pacific fleet.

In view of the Russian build-up and the perceived threat this posed, the Japanese high command began to retrain and organise its personnel and naval resources, and this included the purchase from Britain of a number of modern cruisers, as well as six new pre-Dreadnought battleships that were similar to William White's Royal Sovereign and Majestic classes, although fitted with a more modern main armament. The Russian fleet that was based at both Port Arthur and Vladivostok, Russia's Pacific naval base, was by comparison much less organised, although it did possess a number of large battleships and armoured cruisers that had either been built in Russian dockyards or purchased from France, Germany and even America. Most of these warships were of older designs and there was little conformity within classes. Whilst the two fleets appeared to be about equal in numbers, especially where battleships were concerned, the Russians had an even larger force in European waters that could be sent to the Far Eastern theatre if required. The Japanese commander Admiral Heihachiro Togo, on the other hand, was fully aware that his country had little else in the way of resources to augment his naval forces, and that in the event of any sea battle he would have to succeed with the warships already under his command.[21]

The Japanese initiated action early in 1904, again by pre-emptive strikes on the Port Arthur squadrons, and by landing troops on the Korean mainland. During this period Japanese destroyers were able to torpedo two 13,000-ton battleships, *Retvizan* and *Tsesarevich*, as well as a protected cruiser. The Russians under Admiral Stark were so unprepared that they didn't even return fire, and all the Japanese destroyers escaped. All the three Russian ships that had been attacked were holed below the water line and sank,[22] although the majority of their crew members were subsequently saved.

Further naval skirmishes took place after this action and, although inconclusive, the Japanese had taken the advantage and in the badly organised Russian naval forces morale was badly affected. Later in the year, however, the much-vaunted Admiral Stepan Makarov replaced Admiral Stark as Commander-in-Chief of the Russian squadrons, and this officer, who was considered to be an effective and able commander, arranged for the two damaged battleships to be refloated and repaired, and set about overcoming the morale and other problems prevalent in the Russian ships at Port Arthur. Although Russian fortunes were beginning to turn around as a result of Makarov's leadership, and his naval forces had now become more aggressive when their ships met those of Admiral Togo, the revival was short-lived, as just over a month later, during a sortie by a squadron of six Russian ships that included three battleships, the 11,800-ton pre-Dreadnought *Petropavlovsk*, which carried Makarov's flag, struck a line of floating contact mines, heeled over, suffered an internal explosion, and sank in a matter of minutes. Admiral Makarov and some 550 officers and men perished with their ship.[23]

The Japanese squadrons had by now achieved command of the sea outside Port Arthur and were able to successfully close the harbour, effectively stopping any Russian ships from venturing out. The subsequent inactivity this created in the Russian fleet allowed further Japanese troops to be landed,[24] and after a number of victories against units of the Russian Army, the Japanese laid siege to Port Arthur. Although their capital ships were not able to operate during this period, smaller Russian vessels were sometimes able to lay mines, and as the Japanese Army began its task of securing both Korea and Manchuria, Russian mines were instrumental in sinking two Armstrong-built Japanese pre-Dreadnoughts, the 15,000-ton *Hatsuse* and *Yashima* of 12,300 tons, with a great loss of life, and Vladivostok-based cruisers were also active against Japanese transports and merchant ships, before they too were forced back to port by superior Japanese cruiser squadrons.

With the siege of Port Arthur continuing to have an adverse effect, Admiral Vitgeft, Makarov's successor, was ordered by the Russian high command to attempt a breakout with all the remaining ships of the Pacific squadron, and then steam for Vladivostok. The watching Japanese ships were able to intercept, however, and so the first large naval action during the war, the Battle of the Yellow Sea, began. Competing ships became fully engaged at around 8,000m and at that distance it was only the large calibre guns of both sides that made hits, whilst quick-firing ordnance was less effective in use. Togo constantly used the well-tested tactic of crossing the Tee, concentrating fire on Vitgeft's leading ships, and forcing them to turn away each time the crossing occurred.

The Russians were able to eventually break away, however, and a chase ensued, although the faster Japanese ships were soon gaining on the Russian rear. As the Japanese closed in, a number of shells struck the bridge of the newly repaired Russian flagship, the 13,000-ton *Tsesarevich*, killing Vitgeft and most of his staff. The Russian ships then quickly dispersed, some of them struggling back to Port Arthur whilst others, including the damaged *Tsesarevich*, made for neutral ports, where they were interned for the remainder of the war. Togo, in his 15,200-ton flagship *Mikasa*, chose not to further risk his battleships and armoured cruisers in a bid for complete victory, although his destroyers and torpedo boats continued to harass the fleeing Russian ships, most of which eventually reached Port Arthur, where many of the large-calibre guns and their crews were put ashore to reinforce the land defences, whilst Togo continued his blockade of the port.[25]

Not long after the Yellow Sea battle, Port Arthur fell to the victorious Japanese forces, and although a number of ships in the port had been scuttled or damaged by shellfire, what was left of the Russian Pacific fleet was taken over by Togo's naval forces. Before Port Arthur fell, however, the Russian naval command had decided to send reinforcements, and ships from the Baltic fleet were formed into what was to be called the Second Pacific Squadron, commanded by Admiral Zinovy Petrovich Rozhestvensky, and were sent to the Far East. This hastily formed collection of ships consisted of seven pre-Dreadnought battleships, including four new ones of the Boridino class, seven cruisers, nine destroyers, and fourteen other vessels, including both a hospital ship and a repair vessel.[26] This thirty-seven-ship Armada set off from Libau in October 1904 with the larger ships taking a route round Africa and into the Indian Ocean, whilst the more shallow-draught ships travelled through the Suez Canal, to once again join Rozhestvensky's battleships off Madagascar, some three months later in early 1905. By this date news of the fall of Port Arthur, and the loss of the First Pacific Squadron, had reached both Admiral Rozhestvensky and the naval high command back home in Russia, and consequently Admiral Nokolai Nebogatov and the so-called Third Pacific Squadron, consisting of four small second- and third-class battleships, one cruiser, three destroyers, and six support vessels, was sent to join Rozhestvensky.[27] Being essentially shallow-draught coast-defence vessels, Nebogatov's battleships were able to use the Suez Canal and caught up with the main fleet off the coast of Vietnam. From there the now quite large Russian battle fleet steamed at high speed for the safety of Vladivostok, where they intended to join forces with the cruiser squadrons based there, before seeking action with Admiral Togo's numerically inferior fleet of Japanese ships.

In reality, however, whilst the combined Russian fleet contained some eleven pre-Dreadnought battleships, the *Osliabia* of 12,680 tons and the four powerful 13,520-ton Boridino class ships were the only modern pre-Dreadnoughts in the fleet, whilst three of the four Japanese battleships were significantly larger and more powerful than any of those the Russians possessed. This aside though, Admiral Togo was keenly aware that he still commanded the smaller of the two fleets, and made up for this discrepancy by ensuring that all his captains given the chance would aggressively attack their opponents. In the event this tactic occurred in more than good measure when the Japanese ships intercepted the Russians in the straits of Tsushima, as Rozhestvensky's fleet entered the Sea of Japan and headed for the security of their base at Vladivostok.

The Russian ships had taken all of seven months to travel from the Baltic, and this had given Togo ample time to plan his operational tactics, ensure his ships were in an effective fighting condition, and that his crews were trained and focused on the task ahead. Togo concluded that the Russians would head for the only safe haven they had left now that Port Arthur had fallen. He also rightly deduced that although a number of routes to get there were open to them, the Russian ships, after their long voyage, would be in need of maintenance and supplies, and that the crews would be tired, and given the fate of the First Pacific Squadron might even be demoralised. As a consequence, the Japanese Admiral reasoned, the shortest route would likely be the one that Rozhestvensky would take, and in view of this he stationed his battleships and cruisers off the south coast of Korea, so that interception could be readily made once the Russians were sighted.

When contact was first made, however, high winds and rough seas forced the Japanese destroyers and torpedo boats to shelter and await orders, whilst Togo took his four battleships and cruiser squadrons into the storm to intercept the Russian ships. The Japanese had faster, better armoured ships, but having a greater number of battleships Rozhestvensky had the edge in firepower. The Russian warships though were overloaded with coal, much of which was stored as deck cargo and, in an attempt to increase the speed of his squadrons, Rozhestvensky lightened his vessels by ordering that any excess coal should be thrown overboard.[28]

Clearly the Russians' overriding aim at this stage was to reach Vladivostok with their ships intact, so that they could fight another day and, in view of this, their tactics were for the most part of a defensive nature. The Japanese on the other hand considered offence to be the best approach, and Togo steered his four battleships and eight cruisers from the first and second divisions towards the enemy line, where using similar tactics to those he had employed in the earlier battle, he crossed the path of the Russian fleet in a semicircle some three miles ahead. As the Tee was crossed the battleships in both fleets began to fire with their heavy ordnance, however the Japanese gunnery was generally more effective than that of the Russians, and although Togo's flagship *Mikasa* received a hit on one of her turrets, the leading Russian battleships were soon subjected to an intense barrage. Very quickly Rozhestvensky's flagship, the Borodino class pre-Dreadnought *Kniaz Suvorov* was on fire, and soon after *Osliabia*, another pre-Dreadnought, was so badly damaged that she capsized and sank just twenty minutes after coming under fire[29] from the Japanese guns.

Beset by mechanical breakdowns during her voyage from the Baltic the named ship of the class *Borodino* herself was so badly damaged by Japanese gunfire during the action that she also capsized and sank when her forward magazine exploded. In a like manner *Imperator Alexander III* capsized and sank after being turned into a smoking wreck, taking her complete crew with her. The Russian flagship *Suvorov* still battled on, however, with her alloy-steel armour absorbing a great number of hits from the Japanese guns. Eventually though, her steering gear was so badly damaged that she had to steer using her engines only, becoming an even easier target as a result. Very soon she had become a battered and blazing wreck, and just after the severely wounded Admiral Rozhestvensky had been taken off, she finally sank after being torpedoed by Japanese destroyers. Although swift action by his staff meant that Rozhestvensky was saved, the vast majority of *Suverov*'s crew of 800 perished with their ship.[30]

What was left of the Russian capital and other ships were now in disarray and into the evening and during the night, Japanese armoured cruisers, destroyers and torpedo boats hunted down most of the remaining Russian ships. The next day Admiral Nebogatov surrendered the 13,250-ton *Orel* and the other battleships of the Third Pacific Squadron. As a consequence an armed yacht that somehow managed to escape was the only Russian ship to reach Vladivostok, all others having been sunk, scuttled by their crews, interned, or captured. The Japanese lost a small number of non-capital ships and suffered just over a hundred casualties. In contrast, as well as losing nearly all their ships, the Russians sustained casualties that included 4,830 killed and 5,917 captured. This included Rozhestvensky, who after the war assumed complete responsibility for losing the battle, but was acquitted by a Russian courts martial. On the other hand Admiral Nebogatov, together with captains of the ships that surrendered, received death sentences, although these were later commuted to life imprisonment. Soon after the Battle of Tsushima peace talks between Russia and Japan took place, and, with revolutionary unrest beginning to affect Russia, and Japan running out of money, both belligerents sought an end to the war.[31]

The Russian squadrons under Rozhestvensky's command had performed a difficult feat of navigation in travelling to the Far East, but the ships were badly equipped right from the start, and supply problems were always an issue. In fact because of the lack of coaling stations en-route, most of the ships were forced to carry large volumes of coal on their decks as well as in their bunkers, and this created innumerable problems for working the ships, and ensuring that what should have been essential gunnery practice never took place. In addition, the discontent and revolutionary fervour that was beginning to affect Russian society was rife in the ships of the fleet, and moral and motivation was low amongst the largely uneducated conscript crews that manned them. Together with the poor leadership and superior and non-communicative attitude that many ship's officers displayed, this resulted in a number of near mutinies during the voyage. In view of these factors the Russian Admiral faced an often hopeless task, but in addition his own mistrust of officers and men, an inability to share his plans, and his general lack of direction, meant that in the face of a focused and well-planned Japanese attack, he had little chance of success when battle ensued. It must be said though that the majority of officers and men that crewed the Russian ships fought bravely, using the often inadequate resources at their disposal, although many subsequently perished in the attempt.

The overwhelming nature of the Japanese victory ensured a great amount of post-battle analysis amongst naval professionals worldwide and it was clear that learning from earlier actions, the Japanese had decided to use their superior speed to attack at ranges that would ensure they could achieve decisive results. The Russians, on the other hand, had not met the Japanese ships before, had no experience of fighting against them, and were unable to learn from the experience of their captured colleagues in the first Pacific fleet. Although this for the most part was understood, the consensus amongst naval analysts at the time was that even though Rozhestvensky's ships faced a difficult task, good leadership and better strategic and tactical planning on behalf of the Russian Admiral and his staff would have gone far in making the final contest more evenly matched.[32]

During Tsushima the power of the large guns was impressive, although the main damage to the Russian ships occurred on the superstructure and lightly armoured decks, and neither side was able to fully take advantage of very long firing ranges, due to the inadequate rangefinders and telescopic gun sights then in use.[33] Only a few Japanese ships were put out of action as a result of gunfire, although irrespective of the poor performance of Russian gun crews, some Japanese vessels, including Togo's flagship *Mikasa*, suffered hits. The Japanese lost three torpedo boats at Tsushima, although all their capital ships survived, and their losses up to and including the Yellow Sea battle were also comparatively few. These in fact totalled nineteen and included two battleships, four cruisers, six destroyers and torpedo boats, and seven other vessels. The majority of these, including the battleships, were sunk as a result of striking Russian mines rather than from gunfire. The corresponding losses in the Russian squadrons were, however, very much higher, with fifty-eight ships including seven battleships, some of which were scuttled by their crews prior to the fall of Port Arthur, eight cruisers of all types including armoured ones, twenty-nine destroyers and torpedo boats, and fourteen support and other vessels, perishing prior to the Battle of Tsushima. Total losses in Rozhestvensky's second and third Pacific fleets when they met Togo at Tsushima were somewhat less and included eight battleships, nine cruisers of all types, seven destroyers and torpedo boats, and five other vessels, giving a grand total of twenty-nine. Most of these ships succumbed to gunfire or torpedo attack during the battle, although towards the end of the action at least seven, including two battleships, either surrendered or accepted internment in neutral countries.[34]

A number of the Russian pre-Dreadnoughts, including the four Borodino class ships, capsized before sinking, suggesting that they were unstable at that point. The centre of gravity in these wall-sided ships that had great 'tumblehome', or sides that sloped inwards, diminishing the deck dimensions, was exceptionally high, and the fact that when they went into battle they each still carried around 1,500 tons of coal on their decks, most of which was above their centre of buoyancy, created further stability problems. All these factors, coupled with the ingress of water through shot holes in unprotected ends, and the additional water flowing from hoses used to fight the many fires, probably reduced the metacentric height of these ships to a minus quantity, rapidly hastening their ultimate demise.[35]

Eyewitness accounts from foreign observers in both fleets noted a great difference between the performances of Japanese shells used in the two battles that were fought. At the Yellow Sea, a number of 12in Japanese guns burst as a result of premature explosions of the shells before they exited the barrels, but by the time of Tsushima, this defect had been overcome and redesigned fuses had been fitted.[36] These later shells, however, appear to have had thin walls, large bursting charges of high explosive, and highly sensitive fuses, but did not have adequate armour-piercing capacity. Observers noted that these projectiles often burst on meeting the slightest obstruction, creating showers of fragments that fell over the ships and caused many casualties, as numerous crew members were stationed on deck in unprotected positions. Deck structures, boats, etc. were all badly damaged by these premature explosions, and many of the quick-firing guns were put out of action as a consequence, making it difficult for the larger ships to ward off attacks from torpedo boats.[37]

The propellant contained in the Japanese shells also appeared to be less powerful than it should have been, and the path of individual projectiles as they flew towards their targets could be quite easily seen from the Russian ships, whose crews nicknamed them 'portmanteaus'. A survivor from *Suvorov*, when describing the effect of portmanteau shells, later wrote that they were travelling so slowly that 'the long ones turned complete somersaults and could clearly be seen by the naked eye, curving like so many sticks thrown in the air, but the moment they touched they exploded'.[38]

On the other hand the Russian shells that were filled with wet guncotton rather than Lyddite, as was the case with those used by the Japanese, had slightly better armour-piercing capability,[39] although a large proportion failed to detonate at all and simply rebounded from the armour plate or broke into fragments rather than exploding. It has been suggested that these defects arose as a consequence of the guncotton filling having been provided with more water than normal to allow for tropical conditions, and that this adversely affected their explosive ability.[40] Many torpedoes were fired by both sides but very few hits resulted on any ships, and although Japanese shells were, by and large, quite ineffective in piercing the Russian heavy armour, the numerous violent fires they started, that soon became completely out of control, and the effects of explosions on deck in the lightly protective superstructures, and on steering gear and control areas, was quite catastrophic.

Although it was carefully studied, contemporary British naval authorities tended to view the Russo-Japanese War as either old-fashioned, or one that confirmed many of the ideas and changes they had or intended introducing. It was, however, abundantly shown once more that obsolete and slow ships had no place in modern naval warfare, and that torpedoes without gyros fitted to them were generally ineffective.[41] But the large number of ships sunk as a result of the use of contact mines by both sides came as a surprise, as previous British thinking tended to suggest that a single mine explosion would only be lethal if the ship's magazine exploded as a result.[42] The Japanese problems that had arisen from filling shells with highly sensitive Lyddite, together with the use of armour-piercing fuses that detonated before penetration could take place, applied to shells used by the Royal Navy also, and the British Admiralty's failure to recognise this was a major error.[43]

In Europe by the end of the Russo-Japanese War, the three largest capital ship fleets consisted of Great Britain, with sixty-six pre-Dreadnought or earlier battleships, whilst France, no longer an enemy, had forty, and an expanding Germany ranked third with thirty-seven. Russia, no longer a great naval power as a result of the war, retained ten,[44] but many of these were based on older designs. The Battle of Tsushima was in essence the first complete battle-fleet action that had taken place since Trafalgar, more than a century before, and in addition to its technical lessons, whether acted upon or not, it was viewed as a decisive high seas encounter of fleets, led by large armoured warships, and its actions were seen to validate the vision of naval warfare that was universally popular at the time.

The pre-Dreadnought type of battleship that featured at Tsushima had been improved in Britain quite considerably between 1890 and 1905, and had probably reached its pinnacle in terms of the power it could project. One month after the Russo-Japanese War officially ended, though, a new type of battleship, of unheard-of size and speed, and with a powerful single calibre armament, was laid down by the British naval authorities. The British naval establishment was a prolific warship builder at this time, so this seemingly unimportant act created little immediate interest. However, the building of this particular battleship was pivotal in that it started a further revolution in battleship design, function, and utility, created a new arms race, and was instrumental in rendering the pre-Dreadnought fleets of all the world's navies obsolete at a stroke. The birth of this ship together with some of the further improved versions that came afterwards, are briefly described in the next, and final chapter of this book.

THE COMING OF THE DREADNOUGHT

In 1902, Philip Watts, an ex-Admiralty naval architect who had recently been working as General Manager for Armstrong and Co at their Elswick shipyard, was offered the post of Director of Naval Construction at the Admiralty, a post which had become vacant when William White retired. Watts, who like his predecessor would eventually receive a knighthood, oversaw the completion of White's King Edward VII class of pre-Dreadnoughts, but was of the view that given the state of technology that existed at the time, even more powerful battleships could, and should, be built. In developing such views Watts was likely influenced by the Italian naval architect and Chief Constructor of the Italian Navy Vittorio Cuniberti, who in an article in *Jane's Fighting Ships* for 1903, had built on Clausewitz's military principles concerning the requirement to completely destroy an enemy's forces as well as defeating them, and had proposed a design of what he termed 'the ideal battleship' that had such immense firepower, that it was capable of totally destroying an opposing capital ship[1] irrespective of its size or protective capabilities.

Although the Italian naval authorities, and indeed a number of other European navies, did tentatively support Cuniberti's ideas, the British Admiralty Board did not, and in general appear to have had doubts about the associated views of their new Director of Naval Construction where this matter was concerned. However this attitude was to change, and with support and backing from the influential Admiral John (Jacky) Fisher, already Second Sea Lord, and who in 1904 would become First Sea Lord and professional head of the navy, and who already had his own views on the design of super warships, Watts was allowed to design two 16,500-ton battleships incorporating many of both his own and Cuniberti's ideas. Laid down in 1905 and completed in 1908, both *Lord Nelson* and *Agamemnon* were armoured with Krupp steel up to 14in thick, and carried a main armament of four 12in guns. But importantly in these ships, the secondary armament of 6in guns that had become a standard feature of British pre-Dreadnought battleships was omitted, and a powerful intermediary armament of ten 9.2in weapons all located in turrets and arranged over two decks, was used instead.[2]

Although these two large battleships, that would later collectively become known as semi-Dreadnoughts, were undoubtedly a substantial step forward, their design did in fact become obsolete before the ships were completed, because in

1905 HMS *Dreadnought*, the first all-big-gun-type battleship, that would also be the first capital ship to be powered by steam turbines, was laid down in Portsmouth dockyard. The events leading up to this monumental event are outlined below.

Over a period after he became First Sea Lord, Jacky Fisher carried out a number of far-reaching reforms covering organisation, manning, and material within the British naval service. In doing this he made many enemies but also created a substantial following, and ultimately achieved numerous benefits for the service as a whole. The new First Lord, who was a clear strategic thinker but less so where detail was concerned, believed in swift action, and a mere two months after he had taken office as Head of the Navy, Fisher established a high profile Committee on Designs, which included within its sixteen-strong membership senior naval officers, shipbuilders, scientists, engineers, the then Director of Naval Intelligence Admiral Prince Louis of Battenberg, R.E. Froude of tank-testing fame, and DNC Philip Watts, who, with four other Committee members, Fisher considered to be his 'seven best brains'.

The Committee on Designs, later to be known as the Dreadnought Committee, was to a large extent established because of a perceived threat from an expanding German Navy, which at that time was seen as Britain's main opponent at sea, and which the British Government needed to be able to counter. Under Fisher's chairmanship the Committee was tasked with reviewing the principles on which the different classes of modern warships were constructed, and to examine all the features embodied in them, with a view to establishing what the best form and design of future battleship should be. The existence of this Committee, its membership, and its terms of reference, were made known to a keenly interested public and national press at an early stage, and it soon became evident that where the Committee's work was concerned, something big and important was in the offing.[3]

Perceived naval opinion at the time was that gun power was the most important requirement of a modern battle fleet, but that in addition to this, great operational speed was also a highly desirable asset. The standard battle formation in the days of sail had been single line ahead, but the advent of steam power had made this arrangement appear to be obsolete, as it did not adequately use the advantage of mobility that steam engines had made possible, and so for most of the nineteenth century, fleets were consequently operated by the use of divisions and subdivisions with ships arranged in line abreast. In the early twentieth century, however, new ideas on naval tactics began to emerge and the old single-line-ahead approach was again seen as the most effective formation for ships of the battle fleet when about to engage an enemy. The main reason for this was that such an arrangement ensured that a modern battleship's large and powerful guns could be used with the maximum of unimpeded fire, and that as the distance between opposing fleets, and therefore the range that guns were fired at, was becoming so great as the power of ordnance increased, any other mode of fleet operation was consequently becoming impracticable.[4]

In addition it was evident that with modern high-powered ordnance the firing range of battleships, and thus the distance at which they could engage an enemy, could be even further increased, and that with proper fire control it would still be possible to ensure a large proportion of hits. Even so, accurate range control still depended upon salvo firing, and the exact range could only be determined when the splashes from shells could be observed falling short or beyond the target. Such an assessment could not be accurately carried out, however, if guns of more than one calibre were in use at the same time, and it was soon evident that the difficulties in controlling fire at long ranges increased directly with the number of different gun calibres in a ship's armament.[5]

Fisher's Committee were very well aware of all these issues and within their deliberations took account of the fact that hitting a target at very long range was now possible and might well determine the outcome of an action, but that salvo firing was the only known method of fire control at long ranges. They were also aware that increased battle range was often necessitated by the dangers of medium-range torpedo attack, and that the heaviest guns were associated with the most accurate firing, often with decisive results. When taken together, all these criteria rapidly convinced the Committee of the need for a uniform armament of up to ten heavy calibre guns in each capital ship if maximum effectiveness was to be achieved.

The first of the Dreadnought battleships, the hull of *Dreadnought* herself is shown under construction in a dry dock at Portsmouth dockyard. Laid down towards the end of 1905, *Dreadnought* was completed in fourteen months, setting a record that has never been equalled for a capital ship. (National Museum of the Royal Navy)

Working within their terms of reference Fisher and his colleagues examined a number of draft designs that were presented to them by Watts's constructors, and various combinations of guns and turret arrangements were considered within a displacement restriction of 18,000 tons. Eventually, after prolonged discussion, a final compromise was reached that more than adequately reflected Fisher's own requirement for mainly forward end-on fire, which, as a firm believer in aggressive pursuit action, he had always seen as an important requirement, for in his, what was often dogmatic and fanciful, view, in an action with British battleships, the enemy would always be running away.[6]

The ship specified in the Committee's chosen design was named *Dreadnought* and she was larger and more powerful than any battleship that had ever been constructed before, in fact her design comprised so many novel features that she could properly be described as an experimental ship. In order to obtain trial results and assessments of this new type of battleship as early as possible, and as a prerequisite for building similar vessels, the construction of *Dreadnought* was accelerated to such an extent that it only took eighteen months to build her, and on launching in 1906 she easily met her designed displacement of 17,900 tons.[7]

Dreadnought's armament consisted of ten 12in calibre guns and twenty-four 12-pounder quick-firing anti-torpedo boat weapons, together with five submerged 18in torpedo tubes, four arranged to fire on the beam and one astern. Where the main armament was concerned it became evident that due to the blast effect on gun crews that would likely occur when adjacent guns were fired, ten large calibre weapons was the maximum a battleship of *Dreadnought*'s size should carry. In view of this, and also to give all-round fire, six of *Dreadnought*'s main armament guns were mounted in pairs on the ship's centre line, whilst the remaining four were mounted in pairs on the broadside. By this arrangement it became possible for 80 per cent of the main armament to be fired on either of the ship's broadside, and 60 per cent could be fired simultaneously ahead or astern.

To more effectively counter torpedo-boat attack, and also to guard against a number of quick-firing guns being disabled by particular hits from enemy shells, the quick-firers, all of which were of a new, more powerful design than had hitherto been used, were located at a significant distance from each other, even to the extent that some were placed on the primary gun turret roofs. The main armour belt of Krupp steel was 11in thick, tapering to 4in at bow and stern. Similar thickness plating was used on the barbettes, turret faces, and conning towers, and armoured decks of up to 3in thick were also provided. Special attention was given to safeguard the ship from underwater explosion by extensive compartmentalisation, and most of the transverse bulkheads below the main deck were un-pierced by doorways. Where this occurred lifts were provided to give access to rooms and compartments.[8] In addition *Dreadnought* was provided with the most complete system of torpedo net defence ever fitted to a British ship.[9] It should also be noted that the contour of the stem was modified in this ship as the idea of ramming was finally dropped, and its weaponry confined to the use of gun and torpedo when offensive action was to take place.

Early designs for *Dreadnought* all showed reciprocating engines as the main motive power,[10] however the high speeds obtained by the steam turbine-engined cruiser HMS *Amethyst* had made a deep impression both on Watts's team of naval constructors and on Engineer Rear Admiral John Durston, the British Navy's engineer-in-chief and member of the Dreadnought Committee. As a consequence it was decided to take a leap of faith and install Parsons steam turbines in the new ship, and these were arranged to drive four propeller shafts. Steam was generated in, and fed to, these powerful engines from eighteen Babcock and Wilcox water-tube boilers.

Steam turbines had been in use in merchant ships for some years, but whilst fitted to a few cruisers and smaller ships in more or less an experimental capacity, they had not been utilised in larger naval vessels such as battleships. Turbines, like reciprocating engines, still employed steam in high-pressure, intermediate-pressure and low-pressure capacities to ensure that effective work continued to be generated as steam pressure dropped and its volume increased, but operated on a completely different principle in that reciprocating engines use pressure energy, whilst turbines use velocity energy. In outline this meant that instead of passing steam under pressure, but at little or no velocity, through cylinders connected to a crankshaft, as is the case with a reciprocating engine, the turbine utilises steam of an extremely high velocity, often of the order of 2,000ft per second, that is generated in fixed nozzles and which impinge on the blades of the rotating turbine rotor, forcing it to turn at a high velocity itself as its blades absorb the work energy generated by the dynamic force of the steam.[11] This rotating motion of the turbine rotor is then transmitted via reduction gearing to the shafts that drive the ship's propellers.

The installation of the turbines in *Dreadnought* was such that the two high-pressure units drove the two wing shafts, whilst the intermediate or cruising turbines, together with the low-pressure units, drove the remaining two inner propeller shafts. Each shaft carried an ahead and an astern turbine and the speed achieved by *Dreadnought* in her trials was over 21 knots, some 3 knots faster than any previous battleship was capable of steaming at. As engines went, turbines were also much lighter and less bulky than other forms then available, and this, together with the improved hull lines that the skill of *Dreadnought*'s designers had made possible, enabled a displacement to be achieved that otherwise would have been impossible for a ship of her type. In all probability it was this latter consideration that constituted the real reason that for a period of time the *Dreadnought*'s construction stopped battleship building in other countries, and not the ability of the new ship to carry so many large-calibre guns, which in the scheme of things was probably of secondary importance.[12]

The new concept ship *Dreadnought* rushing through a darkening sea under the power of her turbines and driven by a full head of steam, whilst the two people in the small boat look on in awe. (National Museum of the Royal Navy)

There was for a time, however, a distinct groundswell of opinion within British naval service against *Dreadnought* when she first appeared, and this was based not only on technical grounds, but also because the new ship, and the principles on which she was built, rendered all existing battleships obsolete, and in the minds of numerous naval officers, swept away Britain's overwhelming superiority in pre-Dreadnoughts. This view was forcibly illustrated in correspondence between Fisher's predecessor as First Sea Lord, Admiral Frederick Richards, and Admiral of the Fleet Lord Charles Beresford. Neither of these officers were in any case supporters of Fisher, and in no uncertain terms Richards wrote:

> … the whole British fleet was morally scrapped and labelled obsolete at the moment when it was at the zenith of its efficiency and equal not to two but practically all the navies of the world combined. The Russian fleet had practically ceased to exist, the French in low water, Germany and the United States doing nothing sensational. That was the moment selected by the British Admiralty to start an international competition the end of which no man can foresee.[13]

Concern was also strongly expressed in the national press as well as in Parliament, and a view gained momentum that Fisher's policies would cancel the economies of past naval reforms and destroy many of the gains secured by past expenditure, bring about a period of greater strain in international rivalries, and enable other nations to compete with Britain on more even terms. Fisher for his part never denied that the introduction of the *Dreadnought* was tantamount to starting a new arms race, but believed that the new vessel was equal to any two-and-a-half battleships then existing, and that the all-big-gun warship was inevitable, not only on technical grounds, but also because if Great Britain didn't build them first, other nations undoubtedly would.[14]

Irrespective of the concerns felt in some quarters the lessons of the Russo-Japanese War, where most successful engagements had been at long range using guns of a high calibre, and where medium-sized weapons that had greater rates of fire were less successful, were seen to support Fisher's views, and this, together with the other forthright and convincing technical arguments that Fisher and his colleagues on the Dreadnought Committee put forward to the Admiralty Board, won the day. Once the design and specification for the new warship was finalised, construction work commenced, and in early 1906 the completed vessel, the first of her kind, slid down the ways at Portsmouth dockyard.

Dreadnought performed well in trials, and on entering service was enthusiastically claimed to be the most powerful battleship ever built, whilst the risks involved in fitting turbines as the main power source was more than justified, as vibration was reduced and top speeds could be maintained for long periods. It was evident that the design concepts inherent in *Dreadnought* would form the basis for all subsequent capital ships, and in the aftermath of *Dreadnought*'s commissioning, the first three new battleships to follow were laid down. These three warships to be known as the Bellerophon class were, with some minor amendments, repeats of *Dreadnought*, although at 18,800-tons displacement, they were all slightly bigger ships. The named ship of this class, *Bellerophon* herself, was launched in the summer of 1907, and her two sisters, *Superb* and *Temeraire*, later that year. Some time after commissioning, however, all three ships had their fire control positions altered, and their 12-pounder guns changed for more powerful 4in quick-firers. Later still, anti-aircraft guns were added, and platforms for operating both a biplane fighter and a reconnaissance plane were fitted on the top of two of their turrets.[15]

Irrespective of these developments Fisher's fertile brain had for some time been firmly focused on the question of speed, which he judged as being equal, rather than of secondary importance to, hitting power. He also considered that although *Dreadnought* was faster than any previous battleship, she, like all battleships that had gone before, was over burdened with heavy armour to such an extent that she could not realistically achieve the theoretical speeds that might otherwise be possible. In fact even as early as 1904 Fisher had come to the conclusion that torpedoes launched by fast surface-attack craft or from the rapidly developing submarine boats, would soon make traditional battleships practically obsolete. In accord with this view, and in a paper submitted that year to the then civil head of the Admiralty, Lord Selbourne, Fisher argued that:

> There is good ground for enquiry whether the naval supremacy of a country can any longer be assessed by its battleships. To build battleships merely to fight an enemy's battleships, so long as cheaper craft can destroy them, and prevent them of themselves protecting sea operations, is merely to breed Kilkenny cats, unable to catch rats or mice. For fighting purposes they (the battleships) would be excellent, but for gaining practical results they would be useless.[16]

For more than a decade previously the largest form of cruisers, termed armoured cruisers, had risen in power until in some instances they approached second-class coast defence battleships in both the size of their ordnance and of their hulls, albeit that they were less heavily armoured. In his deliberations as to how great speed could be matched with superior armament, Fisher saw the armoured cruiser as providing the basis for meeting his concerns about the future role of battleships, and as early as 1902 during duty in the Mediterranean, he had, with the assistance of William Gard, the Chief Constructor at Malta dockyard, started to explore various possibilities for using armoured cruisers in more enhanced roles.

On becoming First Sea Lord, Fisher started once more to develop his ideas for a new form of high-speed capital ship that in its design would be a fusion of battleship and armoured cruiser, arguing that such a vessel would in future be necessary to ensure that Britain's control of the sea would be maintained and that whilst still having the capacity for maximum hitting power over great distances, high speed and manoeuvrability would ensure that dangers from torpedo attack whilst under way could be adequately countered. This new type of capital ship would be known as a battle cruiser, and, as such, would be able to outgun any opposing battleship, catch and destroy any armoured cruiser, and by a combination of speed and firepower readily fight off torpedo attacks from both surface craft and submarines, which at that juncture were relatively small, slow, and had quite limited ranges of operation. In fact, Fisher argued, the battle cruiser would be the ideal form of warship.

However, in practice, the battle cruiser had a significant Achilles' heel. To enable a large number of the highest calibre guns with their associated magazines, and hydraulic and other machinery to be accommodated, battle cruiser hulls, like those of Dreadnought battleships, needed to be long and broad. But even with the benefit of steam turbines, to enable their speed potential to be fully utilised, battle cruisers needed to be of lighter displacement than battleships, and the only way that this could be achieved was for the great weight of armour to be drastically reduced. Given the metallurgical knowledge and practice that then existed, the only way of achieving such a requirement was to drastically reduce the extent and thickness of armour plating that would normally have been fitted to such large capital ships, significantly reducing their defensive capabilities as a result.

Fisher, though, considered that a battle cruiser's speed backed up by a uniform battery of powerful guns, together with improved fire-control systems, would be sufficient to ensure that a deficiency in armour would not be too much of a problem and would, in fact, be a price worth paying for the advantages that would accrue. Although there were many in the naval service that disagreed with such views, Fisher's enthusiasm and arguments eventually won the day and the Admiralty Board agreed to include funding for three battle cruisers, to be known as the Invincible class, in the 1905/06 capital ship estimates.

The first of these new battle cruiser types, initially known as battleship cruisers, was laid down just before *Dreadnought* was launched, and all three were completed in 1908. Each ship, *Invincible*, *Inflexible*, and *Indomitable*, displaced 17,200 tons, some 910 tons less than *Dreadnought*, but was in fact around 3ft longer. Armament consisted of eight 12in calibre guns mounted in pairs in four barbette turrets disposed fore and aft and in en-echelon amidships. Additionally sixteen 4in quick-firing guns replaced the smaller calibre 12-pounder weapons that had been fitted to *Dreadnought* and the ships of the Bellerophon class. When launched, however, the lighter armoured protection of these first-generation battle cruisers was inflated in official reports, perhaps because of possible concerns that their reduced armour might generate where the extremely interested public and national press were concerned, but also as misinformation to fool any potential rivals. In reality, however, their very narrow armoured belts of Krupp steel were only 6in thick tapering to 4in at the bows, and this didn't even extend further back than the after turret. The armour on all four turrets was also significantly reduced, having a maximum thickness of only 7in.[17] But these problems apart, the speed of these new warships was impressive; their four-shaft Parsons turbines, the most powerful in the world at the time, fed by thirty-one water-tube boilers could generate a top speed of 28 knots, significantly faster than *Dreadnought*, and nearly 10 knots faster than the most advanced of the pre-Dreadnoughts, such as *King Edward VII* and the other ships in her class.

Speed was one thing, but Fisher was also of the view that *Dreadnought* should in fact be the last British battleship to be built, and that from then on all subsequent capital ships should be battle cruisers. However, although Fisher was an extremely influential and effective organiser, who could quickly understand and take an overview of a problem and was able to rapidly make things happen, he had grave faults as a tactician, and came to believe in his own jargon to such an extent that his favourite saying that 'speed equals protection' became a guiding

The named ship of the Invincible class of three battle cruisers, *Invincible* herself, is shown here at anchor. Her distinctive outline with three funnels and two tripod masts are evident as are two of her four barbette turrets, each housing two 12in guns that were each 45-calibres long. (Author's collection)

Battle cruiser *New Zealand* of 1911, the last of the three ship Indefatigable class, is shown here slowly steaming ahead, showing the typical battle cruiser's sleek lines and great length: *New Zealand* was 137ft longer than the last true pre-Dreadnoughts, and this is evident. (National Museum of the Royal Navy)

framework for him.[18] Consequently he didn't, or couldn't, see that although a battle cruiser squadron might be fast enough to avoid conflict with enemy battleships, given the vagaries of naval warfare they might equally have to stand and fight, and in any case no commander of such a large and powerful ship as a battle cruiser was likely to run away, and would as a result of training and tradition, naturally expect to stand in the line of battle irrespective of the potential dangers to his ship. Added to this, once the secret was out, potential enemies would build both Dreadnoughts and battle cruisers of their own, so that battle cruiser against battle cruiser would also be a likely outcome of any hostilities. In that event speed would give no sure protection against a forcibly driven enemy attack.

In the event, when planning the capital ship building programme for 1906/07, Fisher was unable to gain support for his views, where such a vision was concerned either from within the naval administration or the wider naval service. Apart from what was generally viewed as his particularly radical changes being a step too far, this adverse reaction from Fisher's peers, was also due to the existence at the time of significant diplomatic moves in the European arena, where old enemies were now allies, and all were driven by a common fear of Imperial Germany, and the Kaiser's obvious will to increase its military might and expand Germany's empire to the detriment of its neighbours. As a consequence, the Dreadnought and not the Invincible became the model capital ship and its design was eventually replicated and sometimes even improved in the navies of all the world's major nations.

Although far from having the central function that Fisher had hoped for, the battle cruiser was still perceived as having an important supporting role in the battle fleet, and the major navies all built such ships but in much smaller numbers than their more heavily armoured Dreadnought equivalents. The battle cruiser eventually took over some of the role that heavy, and armoured, cruisers had hitherto carried out, and during both the First and Second World War were used by all the main belligerents. Unfortunately where they assumed the role of battleships during naval actions they suffered great damage, with many casualties amongst their crews, proving that in such large, powerful ships, reducing the protection offered by heavy armour was a major mistake. This apart, certain battle cruisers attained great size; *Lion*, the flagship of Britain's First World War battle cruiser fleet displaced some 26,000 tons, significantly larger than some of her equivalents in the German fleet, as well as being bigger than many contemporary Dreadnought battleships, and the later battle cruiser *Hood* for example, that was sunk in 1941 by the 42,000-ton German super Dreadnought *Bismarck*, had a displacement of nearly 40,000 tons.

Irrespective of its ultimate size and firepower, the battle cruiser type remained a vulnerable and dangerous anomaly, with a confused and doubtful role. Paradoxically though, during both world wars battle cruisers were in action more

The named ship in a proposed class of four, the huge 42,670-ton battle cruiser *Hood*, is seen in the photograph steaming at speed with a reconnaissance biplane on short demountable runway above her fore turret, from which the plane was launched with the aid of a steam-powered catapult. (Author's collection)

often than all the many more numerous battleships, and sank more enemy vessels as a result. Its combination of great size coupled with high speed and the aura of romanticism that surrounded it, made the battle cruiser the most intimidating, yet magnificent, class of warship that ever existed.[19]

Although battle cruisers were not built in any great numbers, the construction of Dreadnought battleships continued unabated, both in British yards and in those of all the other major navies. Where Britain was concerned the next battleships to be laid down were the three vessels that formed the St Vincent class. Displacing some 19,500 tons these ships were similar to the Bellerophons, but had a main armament that consisted of a new model of 12in gun. Laid down in 1907–08, the last of these ships, *Vanguard*, was completed in 1910. The first Dreadnought battleship to be built under the 1908/09 programme was *Neptune*. Of a similar size to the St Vincent class ships, this battleship had its turrets repositioned to try and overcome some of the problems with earlier ships where it was not possible to fire all ten guns on one broadside. In practice this new arrangement was not a success, as the cross-deck firing that resulted tended to excessively stress the hull structure. Two slightly larger ships, the Colossus class, that were half-sisters of *Neptune*, were also laid down within the 1908/09 programme, and this was done in response to what later transpired to be flawed intelligence, that Germany was accelerating her own Dreadnought building with a view to taking the lead from Britain.[20]

By this stage the navies of Great Britain's old enemies were in decline, with the Russian Navy for example still greatly diminished as a consequence of its catastrophic war with Japan, and the once powerful French naval services adversely affected by a change in government that was unsympathetic to naval matters, and which too often listened to hostile public opinion. This had the effect of significantly slowing down France's warship-building programme, just when the naval arms race between Britain and Germany was gaining momentum.[21] Irrespective of what was sometimes unreliable intelligence, the Anglo-German arms race was by now well under way, and by 1909 the apparent pace of German Dreadnought construction was causing great concern in British naval circles, so much so in fact that the naval estimates for 1909–10 allowed for four much larger Dreadnought battleships as well as two additional battle cruisers.

Collectively called the Orion class, these battleships displaced 22,200 tons and, in view of some of the problems that had become apparent with the 12in calibre guns installed in previous classes, were armed with 13.5in weapons in their main armament. This modification gave much greater hitting power and significantly increased the range that these ships were capable of firing at. The new guns were also more accurate in use, and by keeping muzzle velocities down the ordnance designers were able to eliminate much of the tendency for shells to wobble in flight, a problem that was evident with the 12in guns used in earlier classes. Gun layout in previous Dreadnoughts, designed to enable significant numbers of guns to be fired on either broadside, had been cumbersome, and in the Orions gave way to an all centre-line disposition with fore and aft superimposed turrets. The blast effect on crews in the lower turret when these superimposed turrets were in action, however, limited their broadside use.[22] The battle cruisers built at the same time as the Orions were designated the Lion class. Known within the service as 'the Splendid Cats' they saw much action at the Battle of Jutland during the First World War, where the 26,270-ton *Lion* herself led the much vaunted battle cruiser squadron as Admiral David Beatty's flagship.

At the beginning of 1910, Jacky Fisher resigned as First Sea Lord. The Fisher era had pulled what had become a lethargic naval service into the twentieth century, and during his five-year tenure as First Sea Lord, in the face of ultra conservative traditions, he had revolutionised the British Navy and laid firm foundations for the future. There were still problems, however, and by this time Fisher had gained as many enemies as he had friends, and although more efficient as a service, the navy, especially at a senior level, had lost much of its spirit of unity that had long been one of its strengths. This, at least in part, was down to Fisher's methods, and the service now needed a period of rest from internal conflicts and the infighting that had taken place both between naval factions and between the navy and other services. This latter state of affairs had been brought about by Fisher's running feud with the army, and in particular with the War Office and the then War

Minister. It was thus just as well that Fisher, his work as professional head of the navy completed, decided that the time was now ripe for his retirement.[23]

The new First Sea Lord was Admiral Arthur Wilson, who had a distinguished record as a sea officer, although no real experience in the higher echelons of service administration. He was though a follower of Fisher, and it was thought that his appointment would ensure that current policies would continue. However, although Wilson was in general prone to making decisions without much in the way of consultation, other counsels began to prevail within the Admiralty Board and Watts, who still held the post of Director of Naval Construction, was allowed over the next two years to design Dreadnoughts that had a greater emphasis on protection than had been the case when Fisher was in office.

The construction of four slightly larger battleships of the King George V class had, however, already been sanctioned for 1910, and these were in effect similar in design to the previous Orion class ships. It wasn't, therefore, until 1911 that Watts and his team could start designing post-Fisher, or what would become known as second generation Dreadnoughts. In truth though the first of these, the four ships of the 25,000-ton Iron Duke class were little different in design from the Orion and King George V class ships, except that they were somewhat larger again and in planning their secondary ordnance, the Admiralty Board had succumbed to pressure from serving sea officers and reintroduced an upper deck battery of 6in calibre guns, of which there were twelve. The named ship of this class, *Iron Duke* herself, would serve as flagship for Admiral John Jellicoe, Commander in Chief of the British Battle Fleet at the First World War Battle of Jutland.

Last of the so-called first generation of Dreadnoughts, the named ship of the King George V class battleships is shown under way. Completed late in 1912, the last ship of the class to be commissioned, her two tall, flat-sided funnels and superimposed gun turrets are evident in the photograph. (Author's collection)

Iron Duke, Admiral Jellicoe's flagship at the Battle of Jutland, is shown here, possibly in Malta's Grand Harbour at Valletta. The named ship of a class of four and the first to be completed, *Iron Duke*, of 1914, had a distinctive outline that included two narrow funnels. (National Museum of the Royal Navy)

The second of the Iron Duke class to be built, *Marlborough*, also in Grand Harbour. This view of the ship shows her heavy armament to good effect as well as her searchlight towers behind the aftermost funnel and on the mizzenmast top. (National Museum of the Royal Navy)

Although many powerful battleships were built in this period, German Dreadnoughts, although slow in initial developments, soon caught up, and in some cases appeared to overtake, those of the British designers. In the 1912/13 warship-building programme, however, Watts and his naval constructors were able to wipe out the apparent lead German designs had achieved, and produced the greatest all-round class of battleship the Royal Navy had ever possessed. These five ships, together with many of the large battleships that followed, were known as super Dreadnoughts and the first five, built between 1912 and 1916, were collectively named the Queen Elizabeth class.

H.M.S. QUEEN ELIZABETH.

Built in response to claims of large, heavily armed and armoured warships being built by Germany, the super-Dreadnought *Queen Elizabeth* was laid down in 1912 and completed some two years later. The first to be built in a class of five, the 27,500-ton *Queen Elizabeth* is shown here. (Author's collection)

A view taken along the foredeck of *Queen Elizabeth* showing the lower of her two fore turrets in its barbette, and with its two massive 15in guns, each of which was 42 calibres or nearly 53ft long, elevated to around 30 degrees. (Author's collection)

These 27,500-ton ships represented almost as great an advance over their immediate predecessors as had *Dreadnought* over the pre-Dreadnought King Edward VIIs, and their new massive 15in calibre guns, developed in response to rumours that Germany, America, and Japan were arming their Dreadnoughts with 14in weapons, were the first of their kind to be fitted into battleship hulls.[24] Protection in these ships consisted of a belt of Krupp steel armour that at its maximum was 13in thick and this was replicated on the turret faces the main bulk of which was covered with 10in plate. The 15in guns, of which each ship carried eight, proved very accurate in use and had a significantly larger range of fire than that of previous ships. The main engines, consisting of four shaft turbines, were efficient and able to propel each of the five ships at an unheard of 25 knots, only made possible with the onset of oil-fuelled boilers instead of coal, and this provided greater efficiency, economy, and operational range.

Soon after *Malaya*, the last of the Queen Elizabeth class was laid down in 1913, construction of the first of five more 15in calibre gun battleships, the Revenge class, was also instigated. These ships were even larger and set the trend for future construction. By then, however, Philip Watts had retired as Director of Naval Construction to be succeeded by Eustace Tennyson. Super Dreadnoughts continued to be built by all the major naval powers and where Britain and Germany for example were concerned, these ships saw much action during the First World War, where the great battle fleets as well as small groups of ships belonging to each nation, clashed on more than one occasion. This was especially the case at the Battle of Jutland, where many Dreadnought battleships and battle cruisers from both sides were sunk or severely damaged, with a great loss of life. The few remaining pre-Dreadnoughts from both Britain and Germany that were still in commission also saw action during the First World War, and although due to their obsolete nature they were only used in a secondary capacity, a significant number finally succumbed to the rigours of what was then an advanced type of warfare that they had never been designed to take part in.

Super Dreadnought building continued through the Second World War, and America and Japan, for example, built some exceptionally large ships; the Japanese *Yamato*, for example, displacing over 62,000 tons, twice the size of the largest First World War battleships, and nearly four times larger than the last of the pre-Dreadnoughts, had armour up to 16in thick and carried nine huge 18in guns. By then, though, the days of the battleship were numbered, and though America as well as Russia in the guise of the USSR, continued constructing battleships into the 1960s, Aircraft Carriers that displaced up to 50,000 tons and huge missile-carrying submarines, would soon become the new capital ships in the world's navies. The day of the Dreadnought battleship was over, and apart from the very few examples, including the Japanese pre-Dreadnought *Mikasa*, that were saved and retained as museums, these proud ships would, like their pre-Dreadnought sisters before them, be allowed to fall into disuse and decay before being unceremoniously dismantled in whatever breaking yard had been contracted to finally destroy them.

APPENDIX 1

DIAGRAMS SHOWING FORM AND
STRUCTURE OF TYPICAL RAM BOWS

It should be noted that whilst all these diagrams and illustrations may be used for general comparisons, they should not be used for scaling purposes as no attempt has been made to reproduce them to a constant scale.

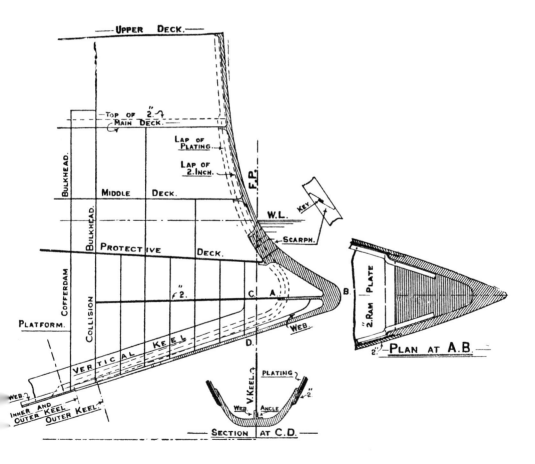

Two piece scarphed cast-steel ram as fitted on Royal Sovereign to Canopus classes. (E.L. Attwood, *Warships*, Longmans & Co., 1908)

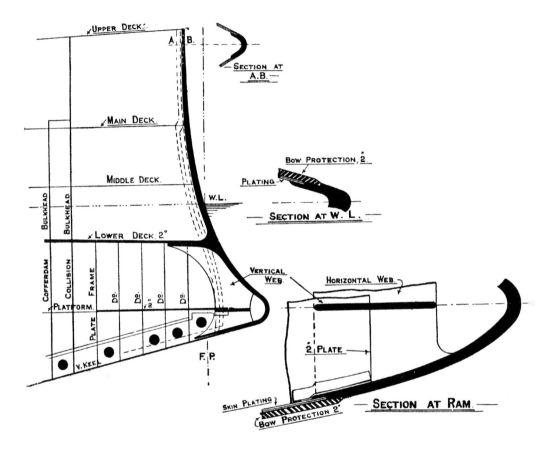

One piece cast-steel ram as fitted to later battleship classes. (Attwood, *Warships*)

APPENDIX 2

SCHEMATIC OF THE 1898 JUBILEE
REVIEW AT SPITHEAD

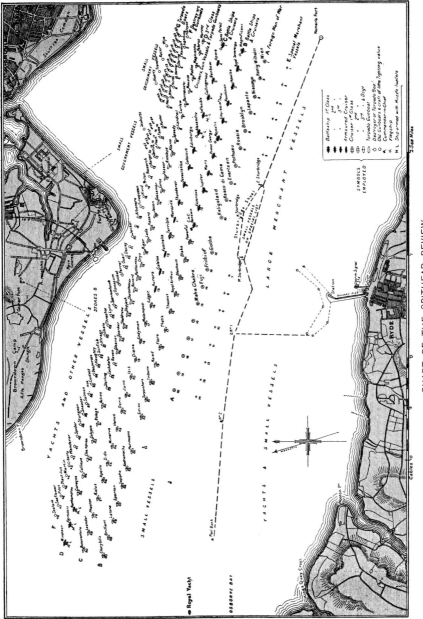

Showing all the ships in the British Home Fleet. (T.A. Brassey, *The Naval Annual*, J. Griffin &
Co. Portsmouth, 1898 edn)

APPENDIX 3

PROFILES AND DECK PLANS SHOWING DISTRIBUTION OF ARMOUR AND GENERAL LAYOUT OF MAIN ARMAMENT

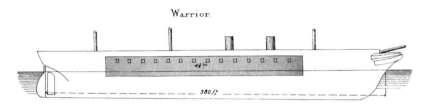

Warrior, broadside ironclad, laid down 1859, completed 1861, displacement 9,137 tons. This was the first British ironclad of a class of two. (T.A. Brassey, *The British Navy, Part I*, Longmans & Co., 1882)

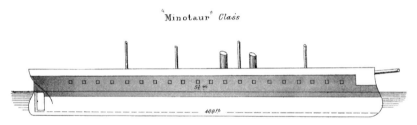

Minotaur, broadside ironclad, laid down 1861, completed 1868, displacement 10,690 tons. This was second to be commissioned of a class of three. (Brassey, *The British Navy*)

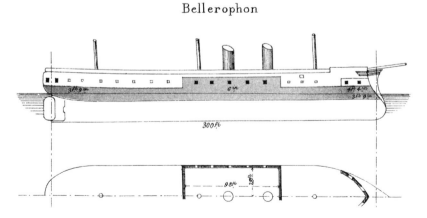

Bellerophon, central battery ironclad, laid down 1863, completed 1866, displacement 7,551 tons, the only ship in this class. (Brassey, *The British Navy*)

Hercules

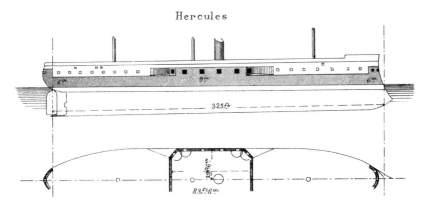

Hercules, central battery ironclad, laid down 1866, completed 1868, displacement 9,492 tons, the only ship in its class. (Brassey, *The British Navy*)

Sultan.

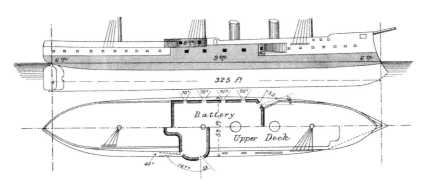

Sultan, central battery ironclad, laid down 1868, completed 1870, displacement 9,290 tons. The only ship in its class, *Sultan* was an improved *Hercules* with a second armoured battery added on the upper deck. (Brassey, *The British Navy*)

Superb.

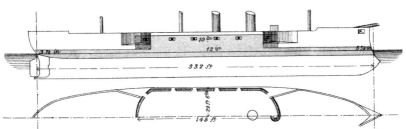

Superb, central battery ironclad, laid down 1873, completed 1880, displacement 9,710 tons. An enlarged *Hercules*, and originally designed by Reed for the Turkish Navy, *Superb* was retained and brought into the British Navy during the Russian war scare. (Brassey, *The British Navy*)

"Audacious" *Class.*

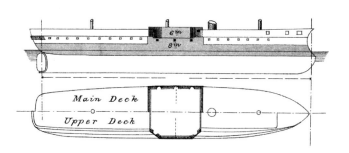

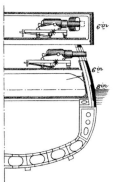

Upper and Main
Batteries,
"Audacious" Class.

Alexandra

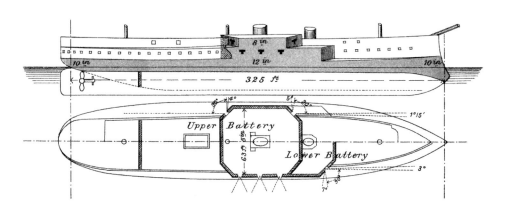

Temeraire.

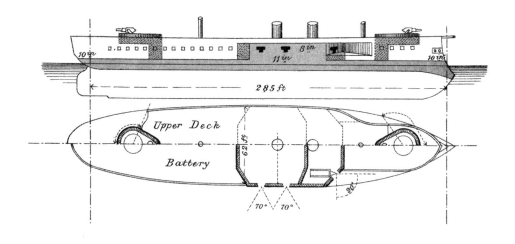

Opposite top: *Audacious*, central battery ironclad, laid down 1867, completed 1870. With a displacement of 5,909 tons, *Audacious* was strictly speaking a second-class ironclad and was designed for use on foreign stations. (Brassey, *The British Navy*)

Opposite middle: *Alexandra*, central battery ironclad, laid down 1873, completed 1877, displacement 9,492 tons. An improved *Sultan* with heavier armament and armour protection and the only ship in her class, *Alexandra* was the ultimate central battery ironclad and highly successful in use. (Brassey, *The British Navy*)

Opposite bottom: *Temeraire*, central battery barbette ship, laid down in 1873, completed in 1877, displacement 8,540 tons. The only ship in the class *Temeraire* was in fact a hybrid as in addition to her central battery ordnance she carried two 11in muzzle-loading guns in barbettes. (Brassey, *The British Navy*)

Monarch.

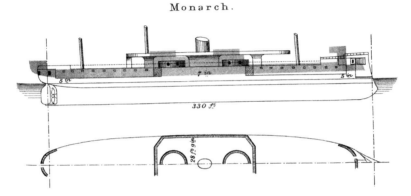

Monarch, masted turret ship, laid down 1866, completed 1869, displacement 8,322 tons. The first masted seagoing turret ship, *Monarch* was the only ship in the class. (Brassey, *The British Navy*)

Captain.

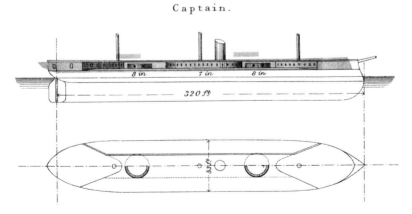

Captain, masted turret ship, laid down 1867, completed 1870, displacement 7,767 tons. Coles's ill-fated low freeboard design was never subsequently repeated, although both Coles and his ship were arguably responsible at the time, at least in part, for keeping the concept of turrets at the forefront of naval thought. (Brassey, *The British Navy*)

Neptune

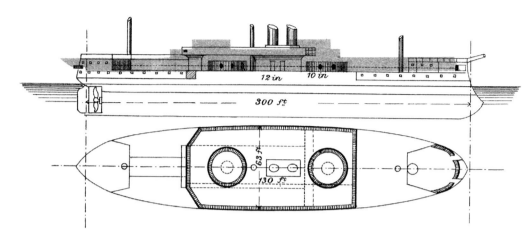

"Devastation" Class

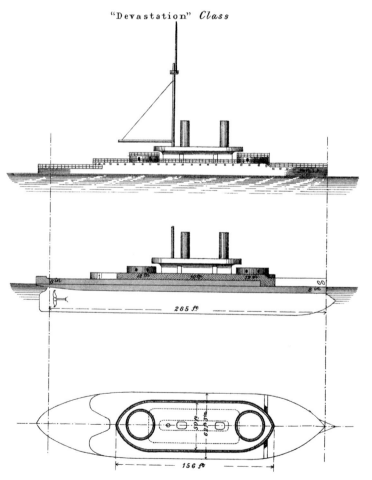

Above: Neptune, masted turret ship, laid down 1873, completed 1881, displacement 9,130 tons. *Neptune* was an improved version of *Monarch*, and was built for the Brazilian Navy but later taken into the British Navy, although by then of an obsolete type. (Brassey, *The British Navy*)

Left: Devastation, turret ship, laid down 1869, completed 1873, displacement 9,330 tons. Named ship of a class of two, *Devastation* was the first seagoing turret ship not to have masts, and as such provided the basic pattern for battleships that would be built in the future. (Brassey, *The British Navy*)

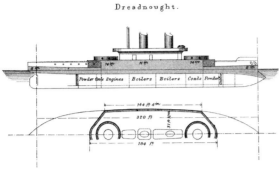

Dreadnought.

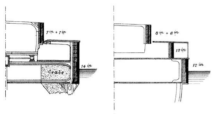

Left: *Dreadnought*, turret ship, laid down 1870, completed 1879, displacement 10,886 tons. *Dreadnought* was an enlarged and more powerful version of *Devastation*, with more extensive armour and heavier ordnance. (Brassey, *The British Navy*)

Below: *Inflexible*, masted turret ship, laid down 1874, completed 1881, displacement 11,880 tons. The only ship in the class, *Inflexible* was heavily armed and armoured and was successful in use although with her masts she was a step backwards from a design point of view. (Brassey, *The British Navy*)

Inflexible

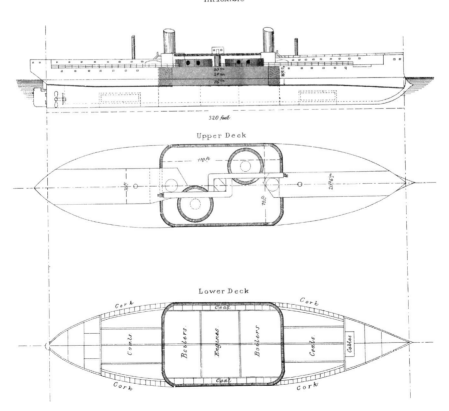

320 feet

Upper Deck

Lower Deck

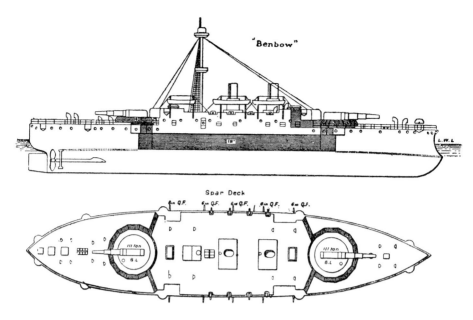

Benbow, barbette ship of the Admiral class, laid down 1882, completed 1888, displacement 10,600 tons. The last of the class to be built. (Brassey, *The Naval Annual*, 1898 edn)

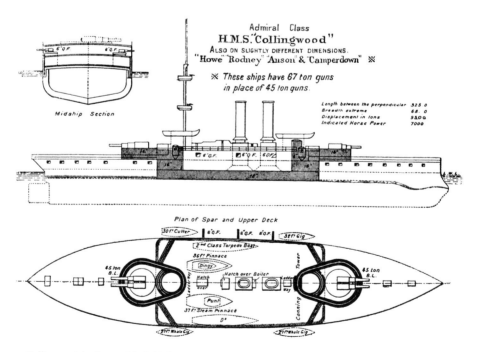

Collingwood, barbette ship, laid down 1882, completed 1887, displacement 9,500 tons. The first of the Admiral class to be built, *Collingwood* was Britain's first true barbette ship. (Brassey, *The Naval Annual*, 1898 edn)

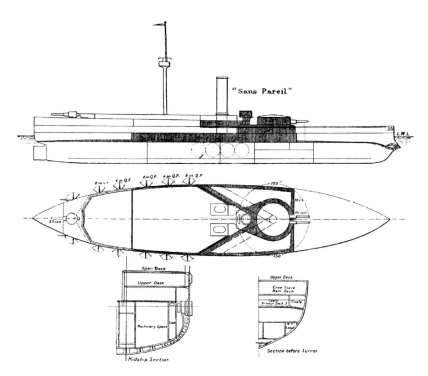

Sans Pareil, turret ship of the Victoria class, laid down 1885, completed 1891, displacement 10,470 tons. The second of a class of two, and with tall funnels fitted side by side, *Sans Pareil* and her sister were the first British capital ships to be fitted with triple-expansion engines. (Brassey, *The Naval Annual*, 1898 edn)

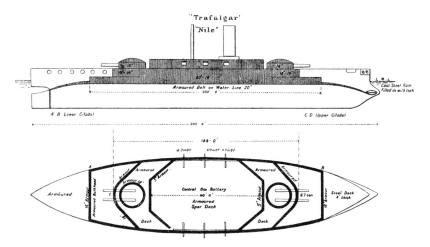

Trafalgar, turret ship laid down 1886, completed 1890, displacement 12,590 tons. Significantly larger than previous capital ships, *Trafalgar* was the first to be built of a class of two which, in addition to their increased size, were better protected than previous ships. (Brassey, *The Naval Annual*, 1898 edn)

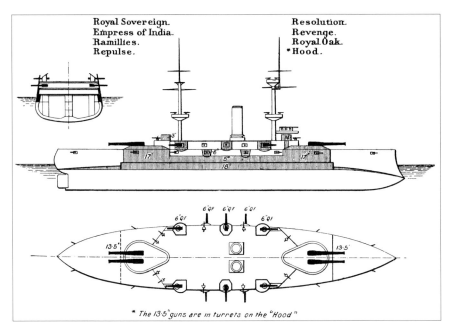

Royal Sovereign, first-class battleship laid down 1889, completed 1892, displacement 14,150 tons. The last of the class of eight ships that formed William White's first designs for a new and improved type of what were now called battleships. (Brassey, *The Naval Annual*, 1904 edn)

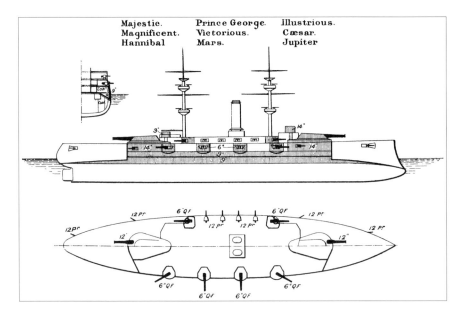

Majestic, first-class battleship, laid down 1894, completed 1895, displacement 14,890 tons. The fifth of what was to be the largest single class of battleships ever built, *Majestic* and her nine sisters were more heavily armed and armoured versions of the Royal Sovereigns. (Brassey, *The Naval Annual*, 1904 edn)

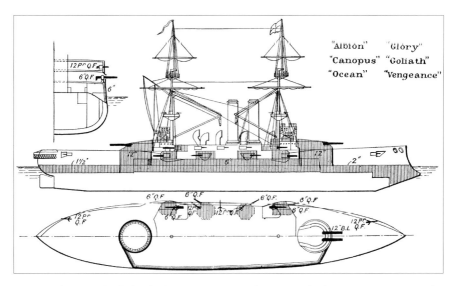

Canopus, first-class battleship, laid down 1897, completed 1899, displacement 13,150 tons. The second of the class to be built, *Canopus* and the other six ships in the class were smaller and faster editions of the Majestics, and were designed for use on the China station. (Brassey, *The Naval Annual*, 1904 edn)

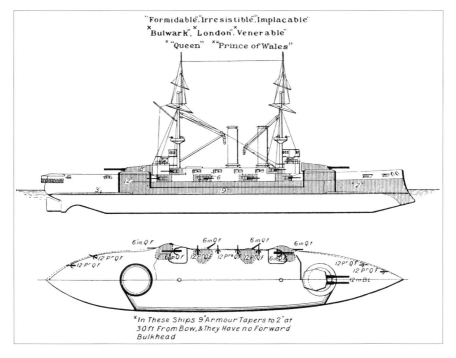

Formidable, first-class battleship, laid down 1898, completed 1901, displacement 14,500 tons. Named ship of a class of three that were in fact enlarged versions of the Canopus class ships, *Formidable* and her sisters were powerful and well protected ships. (Brassey, *The Naval Annual*, 1904 edn)

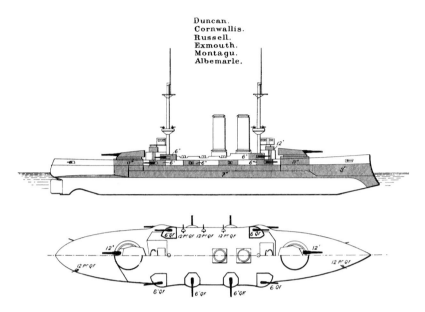

Duncan, first-class battleship, laid down 1899, completed 1903, displacement 13,745 tons. *Duncan* was the third to be built of a class of six ships that were provided as a result of intelligence that both France and Russia were building large quantities of battleships. (Brassey, *The Naval Annual*, 1904 edn)

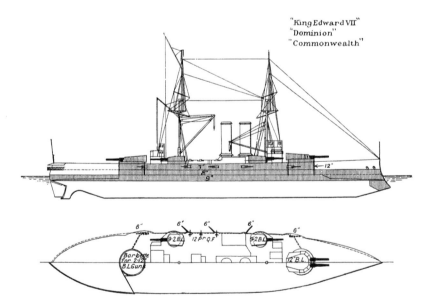

King Edward VII, first-class battleship, laid down 1902, completed 1905, displacement 16,350 tons. Named ship of a class of eight, *King Edward VII* and her sisters were the last of the pre-Dreadnoughts as well as being the last warships designed by William White. (Brassey, *The Naval Annual*, 1904 edn)

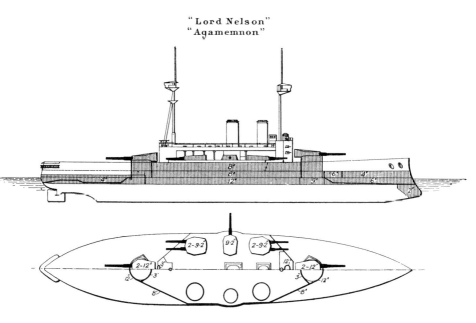

Lord Nelson, first-class battleship, laid down 1905, completed 1908, displacement 16,090 tons. The named ship of a class of two, Lord Nelson and her sister were semi-Dreadnoughts. (Brassey, The Naval Annual, 1907 edn)

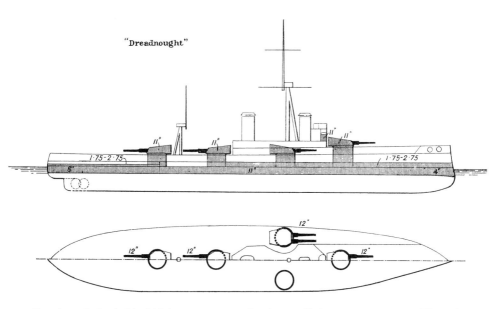

Dreadnought battleship, laid down 1905, completed 1906, displacement 18,110 tons. The only ship in its class, Dreadnought was a new and different concept in battleship design, and would provide the basis for all battleship design in the near and intermediate future. (Brassey, The Naval Annual, 1907 edn)

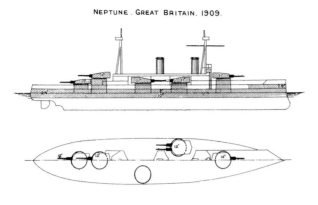

NEPTUNE . GREAT BRITAIN. 1909.

Neptune, battleship, laid down 1909, completed 1911, displacement 19,680 tons. *Neptune*, the only ship in the class, was designed to rationalise and improve the disposition of guns in *Dreadnought* which experience had shown to be problematic. (*Transactions of the Institution of Naval Architects, Part II*, 1911)

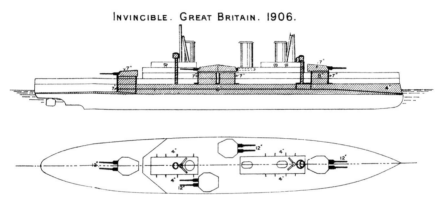

INVINCIBLE. GREAT BRITAIN. 1906.

Invincible, battle cruiser, laid down 1906, completed 1909, displacement 17,373 tons. The third and final ship to be built in the class, *Invincible* was a fast and powerful ship, but like all battle cruisers suffered from the Achilles' heel of being too lightly armoured. (*TINA*, 1911)

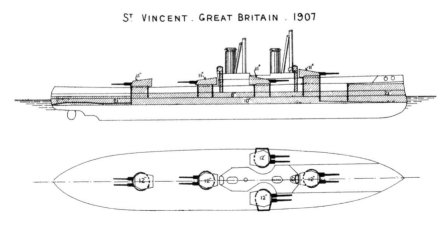

Sᵀ VINCENT . GREAT BRITAIN . 1907

St Vincent, battleship, laid down 1907, completed 1909, displacement 19,560 tons. The named ship of a three-ship class, *St Vincent* was typical of the large Dreadnoughts, being constructed during the early years of the twentieth century. (*TINA*, 1911)

APPENDIX 4

DRAWINGS OF DIFFERENT FORMS OF ORDNANCE INSTALLATION

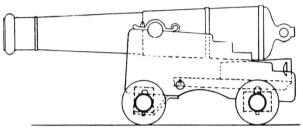

Old **wooden** naval gun-carriage.

Smooth–bore 32lb cannon on wooden carriage. (W. Hovgaard, *Modern History of Warships*, Conway Maritime Press, 1971)

A GUN'S CREW OF H M SHIP "EXCELLENT"(1860)
READY!

Gun crew serving a 32lb cannon that is about to be fired through the gun port. (*TINA*, 1899)

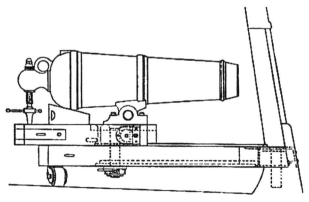

U.S.N. CARRONADE, SLIDE, AND CARRIAGE.

Carronade on its slide positioned at a gun port. (E.J. Reed, *Modern Ships of War*, D.N. Goodchild, 2002)

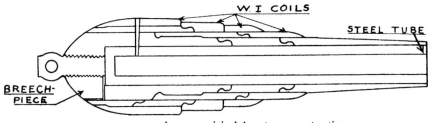

9-in. gun, original Armstrong construction.

Above and below: Heavy-rifled muzzle-loaders showing construction. The drawing indicates the various arrangements of coils that were used. (Hovgaard, *Modern History of Warships*, & Brassey, *The British Navy*)

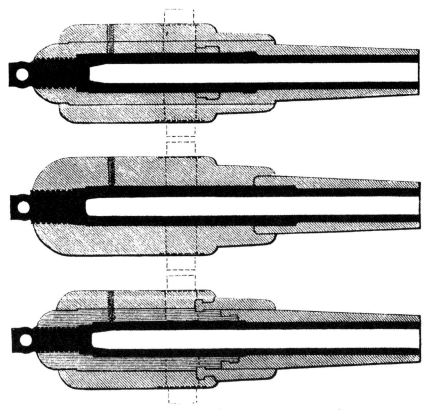

9-IN. WOOLWICH GUNS (FRASER CONSTRUCTION).

Opposite above: Large 100lb muzzle-loading smooth-bore gun on wooden gun carriage and slide that enabled this very large and cumbersome weapon to be more readily moved during operation. (Captain H. Garbett, *Naval Gunnery*, S.R. Publishers Ltd, 1897)

Opposite below: Armstrong muzzle-loader on iron carriage and slide. Because of the violent recoil created when wrought-iron rifled guns were fired, various braking systems using compressor plates had to be developed and fitted as indicated in the drawing. (Hovgaard, *Modern History of Warships*)

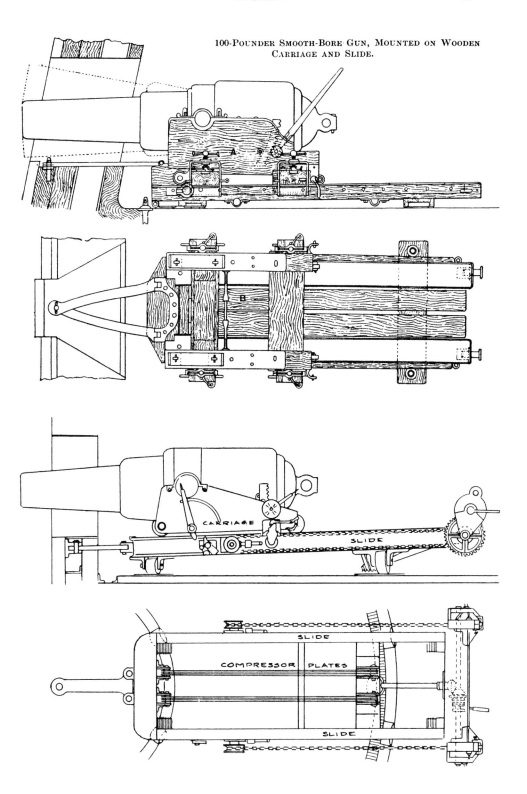

100-Pounder Smooth-Bore Gun, Mounted on Wooden Carriage and Slide.

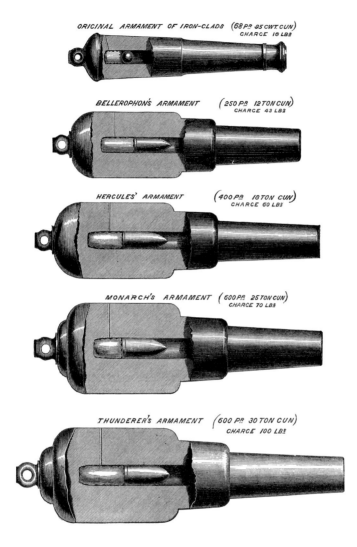

Diagram indicating the steady increase in size of muzzle-loading rifled guns that occurred in the twelve-year period between the completion of *Warrior* and *Thunderer*. (E.J. Reed, *Our Iron-Clad Ships*, John Murray, 1869)

Opposite top: The early form of barbette that was used in *Temeraire* to house two of her 11in muzzle-loading rifles. Within the barbettes the guns were mounted on Moncrieff disappearing mountings that enabled the guns to be lowered and loaded behind the barbette rim. (Brassey, *The British Navy*)

Opposite middle: Coles's turret as used in *Captain* shown with a muzzle-loading rifle in the firing position. (Hovgaard, *Modern History of Warships*)

Opposite bottom: One of *Thunderer*'s turrets housing a 12in muzzle-loading rifled gun and indicating various details of the equipment used for loading and operating this heavy weapon. (*Manual of Hydraulics*, 1883, in E.C. Smith, *A Short History of Naval and Marine Engineering*, Cambridge University Press, 1937)

Téméraire's Gun,
loading position.

Téméraire's Gun,
firing position.

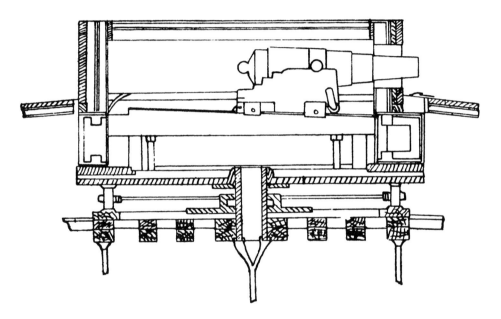

" Artillery, its Progress and Present Position."

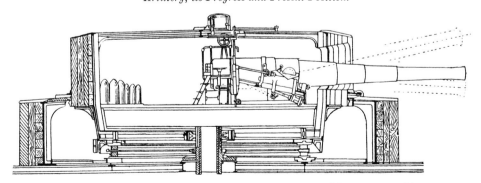

TURRET OF H.M.S. "THUNDERER," SHOWING MOUNTING OF 10-INCH
BREECH-LOADING GUN.

TURRET

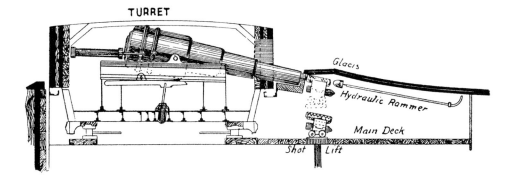

H. M. S. "THUNDERER"

**SECTION OF TURRET SHEWING SYSTEM OF MOUNTING AND
HYDRAULIC ARRANGEMENT FOR WORKING THE GUNS.**

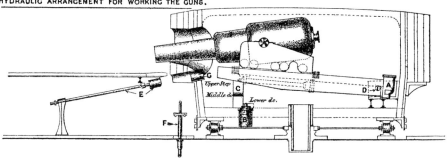

REFERENCE.

A — RECOIL PRESS.	**D** — PIVOT OF SLIDE.
B — ELEVATING CYLINDER.	**E** — RAMMER.
C — CHOCK WITH STEPS	**F** — SHOT HOIST.
FOR SLIDE TO REST ON.	**G** — LOADING TUBE.

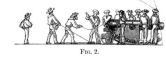

FIG. 2.

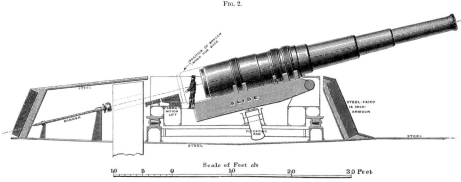

FIG. 3

FIG. 2. LARGEST SHIP'S GUN IN YEAR 1837.   FIG. 3. 111-TON GUN OF BENBOW.   BOTH GUNS DRAWN TO SCALE.

Opposite top: Loading arrangements for the 80-ton muzzle-loading rifled guns used in *Inflexible*. The guns were depressed after firing and the muzzle positioned next to an armoured glacis, where it was loaded under cover. (Hovgaard, *Modern History of Warships*)

Opposite middle: One of *Thunderer*'s turrets at a later date, when 10in breech-loading guns and their associated hydraulic mountings had been installed, the first time such an arrangement was used in a British capital ship. (Garbett, *Naval Gunnery*)

Opposite bottom: Comparison of the largest ship's gun in 1837 with the 111-ton, 16.25in, breech-loading gun of *Benbow* shown in its barbette with associated hydraulic mounting and loading equipment. (Brassey, *The Naval Annual*, 1887 edn)

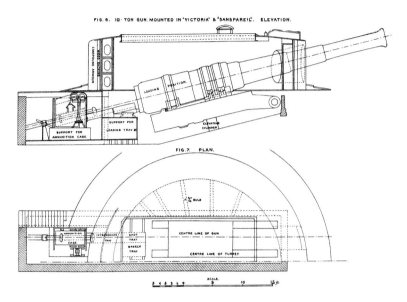

Elevation and plan of large 16.25in breech-loading gun in the main turret of *Victoria* and *Sans Pareil*, showing detail of hydraulic loading arrangements. (Brassey, *The Naval Annual*, 1887 edn)

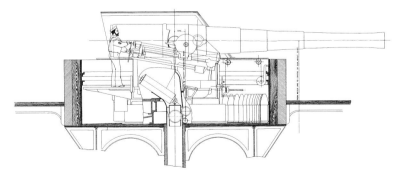

Part of a pre-Dreadnought's secondary armament showing a 9.2in breech-loading gun in a circular barbette and with manual operating arrangements. (*TINA*, 1888)

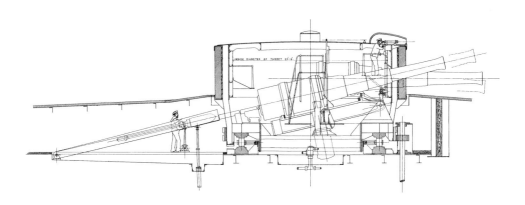

H.M.Ss "FORMIDABLE" & "IMPLACABLE"

GENERAL ARRANGEMENT OF TURRET AND MOUNTING FOR A PAIR OF 12 INCH 49 TON GUNS.

SCALE

SECTIONAL ELEVATION

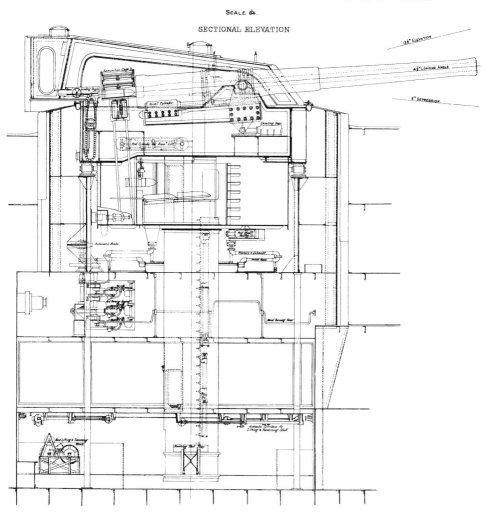

Opposite above: Part of a pre-Dreadnought's secondary armament showing a pair of 43-ton breech-loading guns in a turret with its associated hydraulic operating arrangements. (*TINA*, 1888)

Opposite below: Sectional elevation of one of *Formidable*'s barbette turrets housing a pair of 12in breech-loading guns, and showing the general arrangements within the turret and mounting. (*TINA*, 1899)

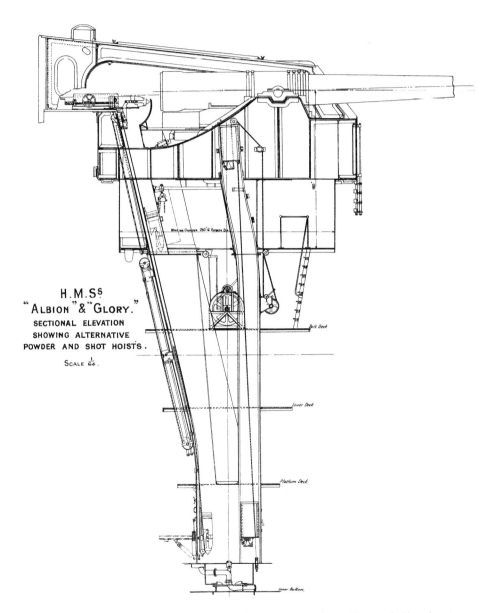

Sectional elevation of 12in barbette turret of Canopus class ships *Albion* and *Glory* showing arrangements of powder and shot hoists within the turret installation. (*TINA*, 1899)

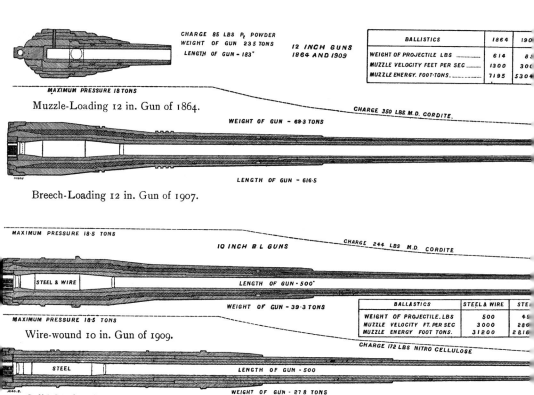

CHARGE 85 LBS P₂ POWDER
WEIGHT OF GUN 235 TONS
LENGTH OF GUN - 183"

12 INCH GUNS
1864 AND 1909

BALLISTICS	1864	190
WEIGHT OF PROJECTILE LBS	614	8 5
MUZZLE VELOCITY FEET PER SEC	1300	30 0
MUZZLE ENERGY. FOOT-TONS.	7195	5 3 0 4

MAXIMUM PRESSURE 18 TONS

Muzzle-Loading 12 in. Gun of 1864.

CHARGE 350 LBS. M.D. CORDITE.

WEIGHT OF GUN - 69·3 TONS

LENGTH OF GUN - 616·5

Breech-Loading 12 in. Gun of 1907.

MAXIMUM PRESSURE 18·5 TONS

IO INCH B L GUNS

CHARGE 244 LBS M.D. CORDITE

STEEL & WIRE

LENGTH OF GUN - 500"

WEIGHT OF GUN - 39·3 TONS

MAXIMUM PRESSURE 18·5 TONS

Wire-wound 10 in. Gun of 1909.

BALLISTICS	STEEL & WIRE	STE
WEIGHT OF PROJECTILE. LBS	500	4 9
MUZZLE VELOCITY FT. PER SEC	3000	28 9
MUZZLE ENERGY FOOT TONS	31200	2 8 1 6

CHARGE 172 LBS NITRO CELLULOSE

STEEL

LENGTH OF GUN - 500

WEIGHT OF GUN - 27·8 TONS

Solid Steel 10 in. Gun of 1909.

6 INCH Q F GUN (1899)

Opposite above: Comparison of different naval guns over a forty-five-year period from the Crimean War to the onset of the Dreadnought era, showing their development and ballistics details from an iron muzzle-loading 12in gun of 1864 to a breech-loading solid steel 10in gun of 1909. (A.T. Dawson, *The Engineering of Ordnance*, Percival Marshall & Co., 1909)

Opposite below: A 6in quick-firing gun of 1899 with its four-man gun crew. (*TINA*, 1899)

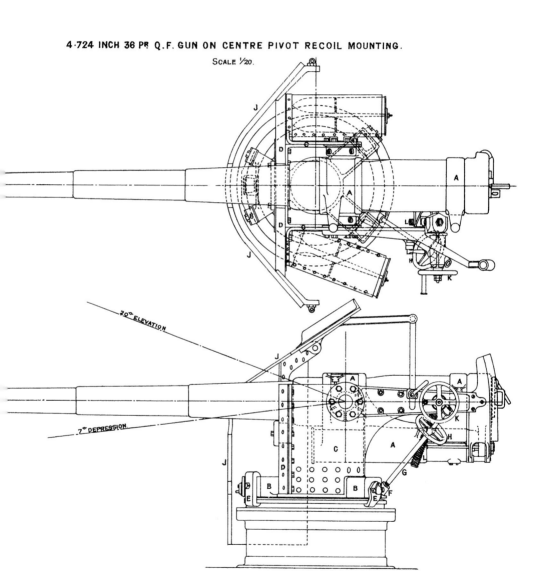

Armstrong pattern centre-pivot 4.7in quick-firing gun of 1887. (*TINA*, 1899)

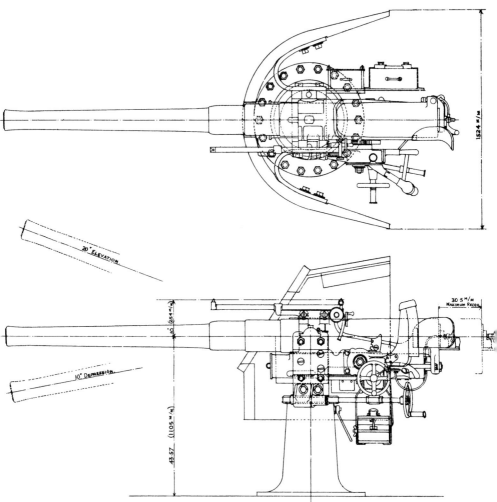

Armstrong pattern pedestal-mount 3in quick-firing gun of 1890. (*TINA*, 1899)

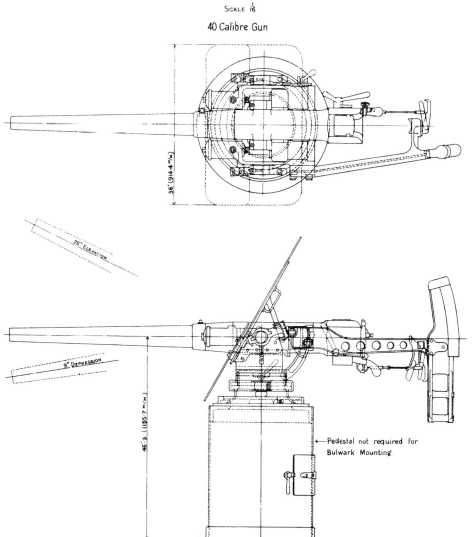

47 M/M 3 PR. QUICK FIRING GUN ON ELSWICK PEDESTAL RECOIL MOUNTING.

SCALE $\frac{1}{16}$

40 Calibre Gun

Detail plan and elevation of Armstrong 3-pounder quick-firing gun on Elswick pedestal recoil mounting. (*TINA*, 1899)

APPENDIX 5

DRAWINGS OF TYPICAL ENGINES
AND BOILERS

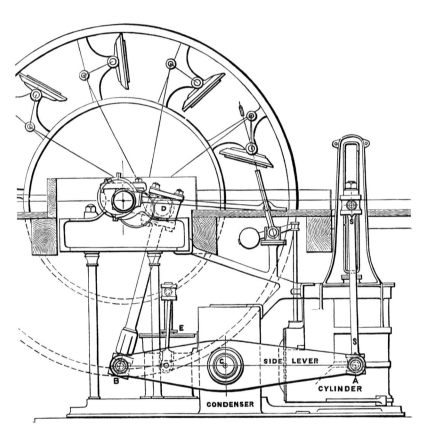

Side lever form of beam engine of the type fitted to early paddle warships. The outline of one paddle wheel is shown in the drawing. (R. Sennett & H.J. Oram, *The Marine Steam Engine*, Longmans & Co., 1898)

Opposite above: Cross section of double–cylinder engine used at a later date to drive the paddle wheels of warships. Engines of this type enabled space saving in the cramped engine rooms of such ships, as the cumbersome beams were not now required. (Sennett & Oram, *The Marine Steam Engine*)

Opposite below: Section of a warship's hull showing a two-cylinder, oscillating engine built by John Rennie, and with one paddle wheel shown. The small cylinder shown between the two larger ones is the air pump. (J. Bourne, *A Catechism of the Steam-Engine*, Longmans & Co., 1861)

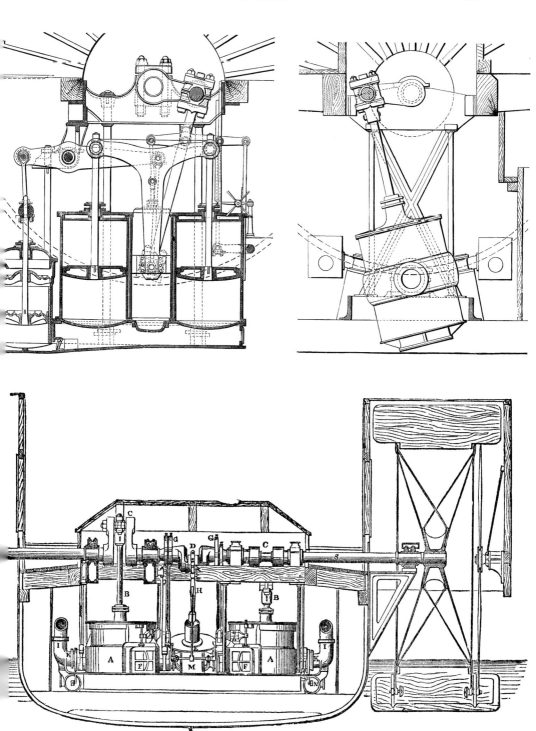

OSCILLATING MARINE ENGINES. By Messrs. Rennie.

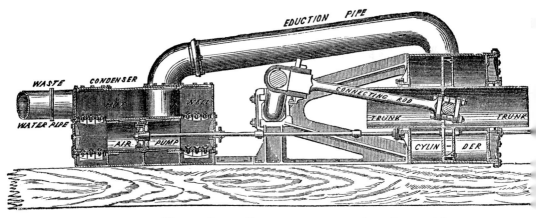

DIRECT ACTING MARINE SCREW ENGINES. By Messrs. John Penn and Son.

Longitudinal Section.

Longitudinal section of a direct acting trunk engine type built by John Penn. This type of engine was used to drive a screw propeller and whilst it took up greater engine-room floor space, its low profile meant that it could be readily fitted between decks. (Bourne, *A Catechism*)

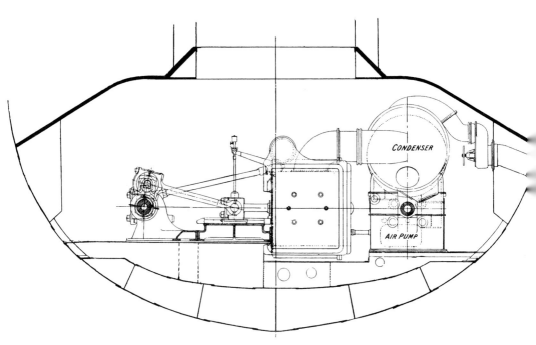

Another low-profile engine that was often used was the non-trunk type direct-acting engine. The one shown here located within a ship's hull is of the sort built by Humphrys and Tennant. (Sennett & Oram, *The Marine Steam Engine*)

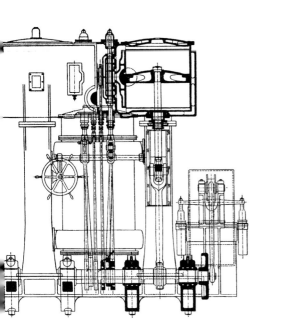
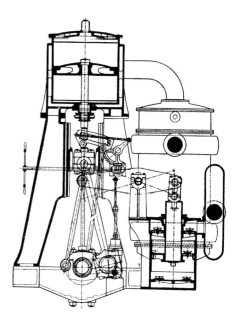

Sectional elevations of a two-cylinder vertical compound engine. With the onset of iron, then steel hulls, improvements in warship design, and the use of armour protection and extensive coalbunkers adjacent to the ship's sides, it became possible to use more efficient vertical engines to drive the screw propellers. (Sennett & Oram, *The Marine Steam Engine*)

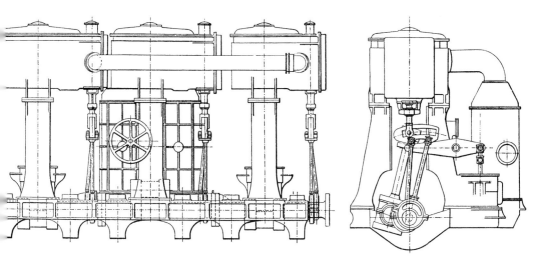

With the increase in power of compound engines, that required corresponding increases in the diameters of low-pressure cylinders, that then took up a great deal of engine-room space and were additionally difficult to manufacture, it became necessary to fit two low-pressure cylinders instead of one. This arrangement is shown via the two sectional views in the diagram. (Sennett & Oram, *The Marine Steam Engine*)

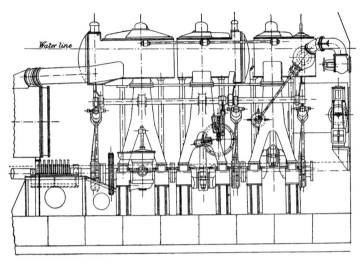

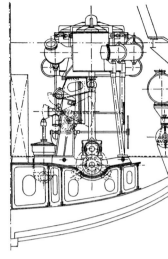

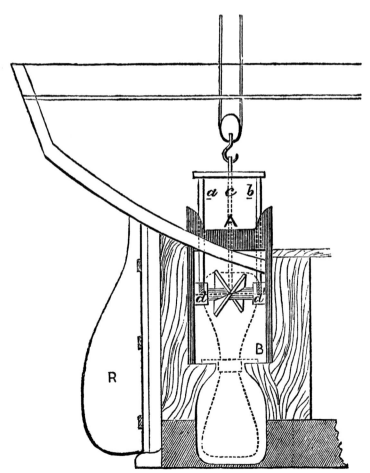

Above: When steam pressures increased to over 100lb/sq. in, it became possible, as well as necessary, to extend the compounding system and divide the steam expansion into three stages. Triple-expansion engines of the type shown were then introduced. (Sennett & Oram, *The Marine Steam Engine*)

Left: Sectional elevation showing the way the screw propeller was lifted when the sails of early steam ships were being used as the main motive power. (H. Evers, *Steam and the Steam Engine*, Collins' Advanced Series, 1872)

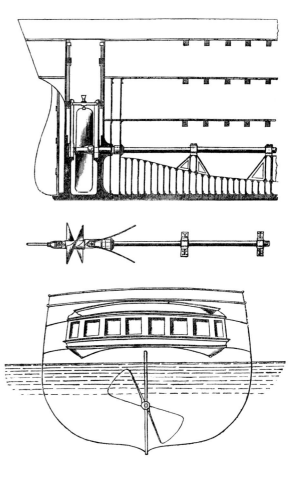

Right: Screw lifting arrangements, and location of propeller shaft in a wooden three-decked steam-powered ship of the line. (R. Murray, *Rudimentary Treatise on the Marine Engine*, John Weale, 1858)

Below: Longitudinal sectional elevation of a paddle warship's hull showing an early flue boiler providing low-pressure steam to a side-lever engine. The outline of the paddle wheel is also shown. (Bourne, *A Catechism*)

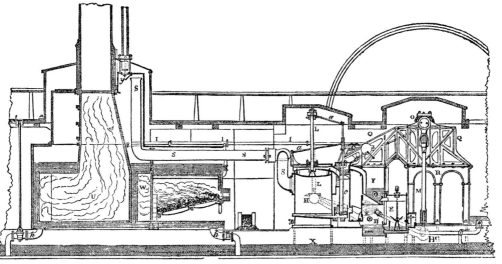

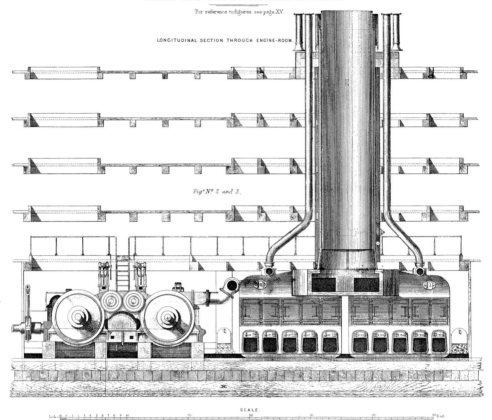

H. M. SCREW STEAM SHIP "DUKE OF WELLINGTON," MACHINERY CONSTRUCTED BY ROBERT NAPIER ESQ^{RE}, GLASGO

TONNAGE 3826¼ TONS._ 131 GUNS._ NOMINAL POWER 780 H.P.

For reference to figures see page XV.

LONGITUDINAL SECTION THROUGH ENGINE-ROOM.

Fig.^{d} N° 2 and 3.

SCALE.

Longitudinal sectional elevation of 131-gun steam line-of-battle ship *Duke of Wellington* showing her horizontal two-cylinder direct-acting engine and box boilers. The various gun decks are also shown as are her flue and lifting funnel. (Murray, *Rudimentary Treatise*)

Opposite above: A further section of *Duke of Wellington*'s engines, this time looking forward, and showing the location of decks, hatches, and position of engine-room ladder. (Murray, *Rudimentary Treatise*)

Opposite below: A further transverse view of *Duke of Wellington*'s engine room showing the stokehold, and more details of the lifting funnel, including the position of the two hand winches used for lifting and lowering operations. (Murray, *Rudimentary Treatise*)

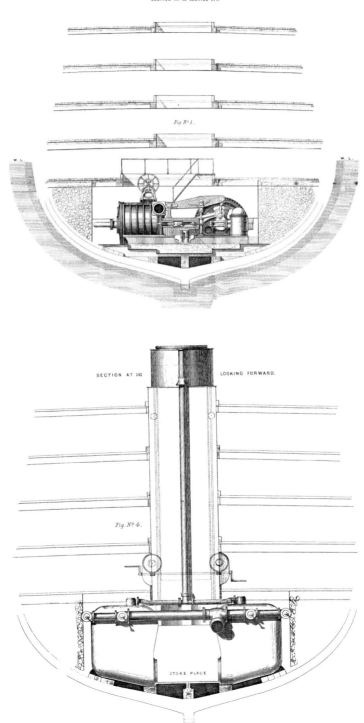

SECTION AT ⅗ LOOKING AFT.

Fig. Nº 1.

W. L.   W. L.

SECTION AT ⅗   LOOKING FORWARD.

Fig. Nº 4.

STOKE PLACE

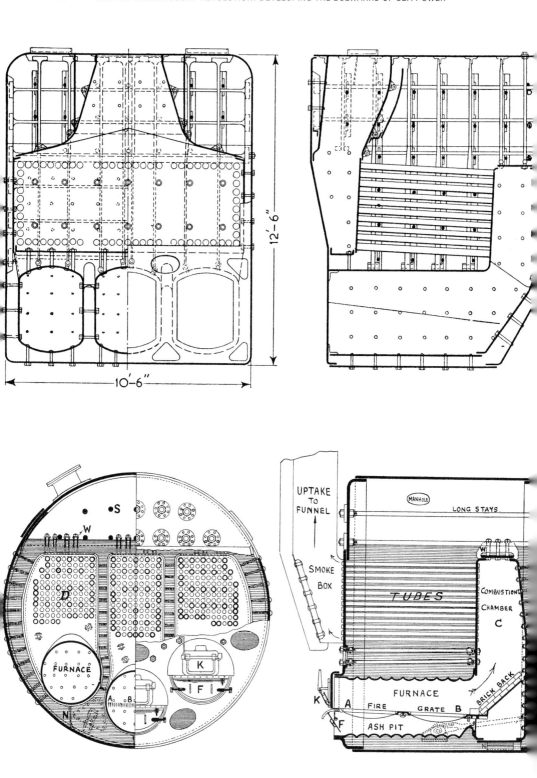

Opposite above: Sectional elevations of early low-pressure box boiler showing the fire tubes, furnace, and furnace doors at the front. As can be seen from the dimensions these boilers were very small in size. (J.H. Milton, *Newnes Marine Engineering*, Vol. I, George Newnes Ltd, 1954)

Opposite below: Sectional elevations of cylindrical return-tube boiler, the next stage in evolution. These elevations show the tubes and furnace arrangements in somewhat more detail. (A.E. Tompkins, *Marine Engineering*, MacMillan & Co., 1921)

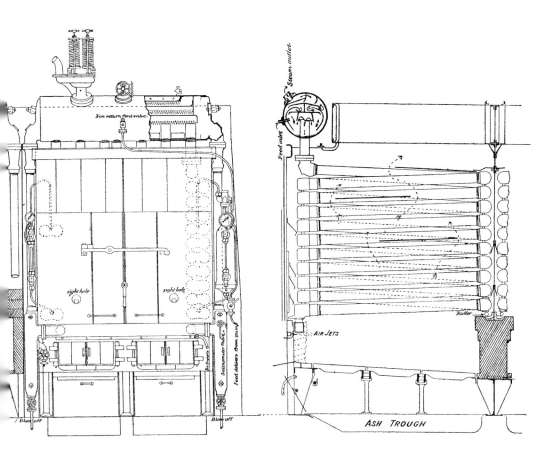

One of the first water-tube boilers to be used by the British Navy, the much maligned Belleville type. (Sennett & Oram, *The Marine Steam Engine*)

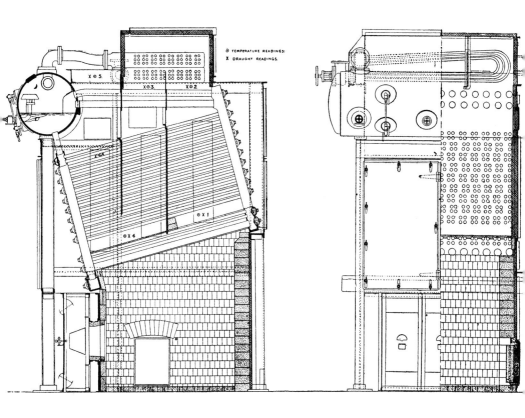

One of the first of its type to be used in Britain's capital ships, the Babcock and Wilcox water–tube boiler was oil rather than coal fired and was widely introduced into HM ships once decisions to discontinue with the use of Bellevilles had been made. (Tompkins, *Marine Engineering*)

REFERENCES

CHAPTER 1 – SAILING SHIPS AND SEA POWER

1   Busk, H., *The Navies of the World: Their Present State and Future Capabilities*, London (1859), p. 75. The numbers vary somewhat depending on source, and if ships being built are included.
2   Roskill, S.W., *The Strategy of Sea Power*, Aylesbury (1986), p. 89.
3   Kennedy P.M., *The Rise and Fall of British Naval Mastery*, New York (1976), p. 156.
4   Humble, R., *Before the Dreadnought*, London (1976), p. 3.
5   Dodds, J., and Moore, J., *Building the Wooden Fighting Ship*, London (1984).
6   Peake, J.P., *Rudiments of Naval Architecture*, London (1884), p. 244.
7   Lavery, B., *Nelson's Navy*, London (1989), p. 255.
8   Graviere, Jurien de la., *Guerres Maritime, vol. 2*, pp. 175–6, quoted in Douglas, H., *Naval Gunnery*, London (1855), p. 314, and Padfield, P., *The Battleship Era*, London (1972), p. 8.
9   Watts, A.J., *The Royal Navy: An Illustrated History*, London (1974), p. 8.
10 Graham, G.S., *The Politics of Naval Supremacy*, Cambridge (1965), pp. 118–19.
11 Rodger, N.A.M., *The Command of the Ocean*, London (2004), pp. 582–3.
12 Lavery, B., *Nelson's Navy 1793–1815*, London (1989), p. 25.
13 Kennedy, P.M., op. cit., p. 157.
14 Kennedy, P.M., ibid.
15 Graham, G.S., op. cit., pp. 120–1.
16 Albion, R.G., *Forests and Sea Power*, Harvard (1926), p. 412.
17 Dodds, J. and Moore, J., *Building the Wooden Fighting Ship*, London (1984), p. 13.
18 Brown, D.K., 'The Structural Improvements to Wooden Ships Instigated by Sir Robert Seppings', *The Naval Architect*, London (1979), pp. 103–4. Quoted in Lambert, A., *Battleships in Transition*, London (1984), p. 13.
19 Fincham, J., *A History of Naval Architecture*, London (1851), p. 197.
20 Brown, D.K., *Before the Ironclad*, London (1990), p. 16.
21 Brown, D.K., *A Century of Naval Construction*, London (1983), p. 27.
22 Brown, D.K., ibid., p. 29.

CHAPTER 2 – FROM SAIL TO STEAM ASSIST

1   Ropp, T., *The Development of a Modern Navy*, Annapolis (1987), p. 5.
2   Kennedy, P.M., *The Rise and Fall of British Naval Mastery*, New York (1976), p. 171.
3   Ropp, T., op. cit., p. 8.
4   Graham, G.S., *The Politics of Naval Supremacy*, Cambridge (1965), p. 108.
5   Smith, E.C., *A Short History of Marine Engineering*, Cambridge (1937), p. 3.
6   Sennett, R. and Oram, H.J., *The Marine Steam Engine*, London (1898), p. 3.
7   Smith, E.C., 'The Centenary of Naval Engineering', *Transactions of the Institute of Marine Engineers*, London (1922), p. 88.

8   Smith, E.C., ibid., tables on pp. 106–13.

9   Brown, D.K., *Paddle Warships*, London (1993), p. 64.

10 Smith, E.C., op. cit., notes to tables on pp. 106–13.

11 Brown, D.K., op. cit., p. 78.

12 Peake, J.P., *Naval Architecture*, London (1884), pp. 279–80.

13 Evans, D., *Building the Steam Navy*, London (2004), p. 62.

14 Sennett, R. and Oram, H.J., op. cit., p. 4.

15 Lambert, A., *Battleships in Transition*, London (1984), p. 19.

16 Bourne, J., *A Treatise on the Screw Propeller*, London (1852), pp. 11–76.

17 Bourne, J., ibid., pp. 21–3, 87.

18 Brown, D.K., *A Century of Naval Construction*, London (1983), pp. 32–3.

19 Brown, D.K., ibid., p. 35.

20 Fincham, J., *A History of Naval Architecture*, London (1851), p. 411.

21 Brown, D.K., *Before the Ironclad*, London (1990), p. 130.

22 Brown, D.K., ibid., p. 130.

23 Brown, D.K., *A Century of Naval Construction*, London (1983), p. 35.

24 Evers, H., *Steam and the Steam Engine*, London (1872), p. 90.

25 Murray, R., Rudimentary Treatise on the Steam Engine, London (1858), p. 150.

26 Evers, H., op. cit., pp. 106–197.

27 Garbett, H., *Naval Gunnery*, London (1897), p. 18.

28 Brown, D.K., *Before the Ironclad*, London (1990), pp. 132–3.

29 Fletcher, I. and Ishchenko, N., *The Crimean War*, Staplehurst (2004), p. 3.

30 Brown, D.K., op. cit., p. 137.

31 Baxter, J.P., *The Introduction of the Ironclad Warship*, Cambridge (1933), pp. 69–70.

32 Baxter, J.P., ibid., pp. 70–2.

33 Baxter, J.P., ibid., pp. 78–80.

34 Sondhaus, L., *Naval Warfare*, London (2001), p. 64.

35 Robertson, F.L., *The Evolution of Naval Armament*, London (1968), p. 244.

CHAPTER 3 – THE BLACK BATTLE FLEET

1   Barnaby, N., On Ships of War, *Transactions of the Institute of Naval Architects*, London (1876), p. 1.

2   Parkes, O., *British Battleships 1860–1950*, London (1957), p. 2.

3   Baxter, J.P., *The Introduction of the Ironclad Warship*, Cambridge Mass (1933), p. 110.

4   Gardiner, R. Editor, *All The World's Fighting Ships 1860–1905*, London (1979), p. 286.

5   Eardley Wilmot, S., *Our Fleet Today*, London (1900), p. 48.

6   Baxter, J.P., op. cit., pp. 112–13.

7   Gardiner, R. Editor, op. cit., p. 7.

8   Oram, H.J., 'Fifty Years' Changes in British Warships Machinery', *Transactions of the Institution of Naval Architects*, London (1911), p. 97.

9   Hovgaard, W., *Modern History of Warships*, London (1920), pp. 8–9.

10 Gardiner, R., op. cit., p. 7.

11 Lambert, A., *Warrior: Restoring the World's First Ironclad*, London (1987) p. 82.

12 Noble, A., 'The Rise and Progress of Rifled Naval Artillery', *Transactions of the Institution of Naval Architects*, London (1899), p. 236.

13 Garbett, H., *Naval Gunnery*, London (1897), pp. 40–41.

14 Lambert, A., op. cit., p. 82.

15 Oram, H.J., 'Fifty Years' Changes in British Warship Machinery', *Transactions of the Institution of Naval Architects*, London (1911), p. 96.

16 Oram, H.J., ibid., pp. 97–8.

17 Barnaby, N., *Naval Developments of the Century*, London (1904), pp. 68–9.

18 Gardiner, R., Editor, *All the World's Fighting Ships 1860–1905*, London (1979), p. 9.
19 Eardley-Wilmot, S., *Our Fleet Today*, London (1900), p. 60.
20 Gardiner, R., Editor, op. cit., p. 10.
21 Oram, H.J., op. cit., p. 98.
22 Ballard, G.A., *The Black Battle Fleet*, London (1980), pp. 25–6.
23 Eardley-Wilmot, S., op. cit., p. 59.
24 Brown, D.K., *Warrior to Dreadnought*, London (1997), p. 16.
25 Fuller, H.J., 'Portsmouth Record Series, Portsmouth Dockyard Papers 1852–1869', *From Wood to Iron*, Portsmouth (1869), p. 30.
26 Sandler, S., *The Emergence of the Modern Capital Ship*, London (1937), p. 20.
27 Jane, F.T., *The British Battle Fleet, vol. 1*, London (1915), p. 264.
28 Sandler, S., op. cit., pp. 31–2.
29 Brown, D.K., op. cit., p. 26.
30 Hovgaard, W., op. cit., pp. 13–14.
31 Hovgaard, W., ibid., pp. 15–17.
32 Ballard, G A., op. cit., pp. 20–1.

CHAPTER 4 – OF RAMS AND TURRETS

1   Reed, E.J., *Our Ironclad Ships*, London (1869), p. 256.
2   Barnaby, N., *Naval Developments of the Century*, London (1904), p. 163.
3   Eardley-Wilmot, S., *Our Fleet Today*, London (1900), p. 130.
4   Jaques, W.H., 'The Detachable Ram or the Submarine Gun as a Substitute for the Ram', *Transactions of the Institution of Naval Architects*, London (1894), p. 243.
5   Parkes, O., *British Battleships 1860–1950*, London (1957), p. 177.
6   Wilson, H.W., *Ironclads in Action, vol. 1*, London (1896), pp. 291–7.
7   Brown, D.K. and Pugh, P., Ramming, *Warship*, London (1990), p. 25.
8   Attwood, E.L., *War Ships*, London (1908), pp. 78–80.
9   Brown, D.K. and Pugh, P., op. cit., p. 25.
10 White, W. H., *Manual of Naval Architecture*, London (1877), pp. 33–4.
11 Brown, D.K. and Pugh., op. cit., pp. 29–30.
12 Brown, D.K. and Pugh., ibid., pp. 29–34.
13 Berry, R.W., 'Technical Change and the Development of the Pre-Dreadnought Battleship', unpublished MA dissertation, University of Exeter (2002).
14 Hovgaard, W., *Modern History of Warships*, London (1929), p. 20.
15 Eardley-Wilmot, S., *Our Fleet Today*, London (1900), pp. 71–2.
16 Eardley-Wilmot, S., ibid., p. 79.
17 Beeler, J.F., *British Naval Policy in the Gladstone Disraeli Era: 1866–1880*, Stanford (1997), p. 110.
18 Reed, E.J., op. cit., pp. 224–6.
19 Spencer Robinson to Admiralty, March 1868, PRO; ADM12/818//91.1., quoted in Beeler, J.F., *British Naval Policy*, p. 110.
20 Beeler, J.F., ibid., pp. 110–11.
21 Gardiner, R., Editor, *All the World's Fighting Ships 1860–1905*, London (1979), p. 20.
22 Reed, E.J., op. cit., p. 227.
23 Brown, D.K., *Warrior to Dreadnought*, London (1997), pp. 47–8.
24 Gardiner, R., op. cit., p. 21.
25 Hawkey, A., *HMS Captain*, London (1963), pp. 79–89.
26 Brown, D.K., op. cit., p. 51.
27 Jane, F.T., *The British Battle Fleet, vol. 1*, London (1915), p. 291.
28 Hovgaard, W., op. cit., pp. 29–30.
29 Jane, F.T., op. cit., p. 307.

30 Brown, D.K. op. cit., p. 58.

31 Ballard, G.A., *The Black Battle Fleet*, London (1980), p. 224.

32 Gardiner, R., op. cit., p. 23.

33 Ballard, G.A., op. cit., p. 225.

34 Jane, F.T., op. cit., pp. 316–17.

35 Garbett, H., *Naval Gunnery*, London (1897), pp. 76–7.

36 Rippon, P.M., *Evolution of Engineering in the Royal Navy*, Tunbridge Wells (1988), p. 69.

37 Garbett, H. op. cit., pp. 64–5.

38 Brown, D.K., op. cit., p. 78.

39 Hovgaard, W., op. cit., p. 32.

40 White, W.H., 'Warship Building 1863–1870', *Proceedings of the Chartered Institute of Civil Engineers*, London (1904).

41 Sandler, S., *The Emergence of the Modern Capital Ship*, London (1979), p. 32.

42 Brown, D.K., op. cit., p. 48.

CHAPTER 5 – BEYOND THE FLEET OF SAMPLES

1   Beeler, J., *The Birth of the Battleship*, London (2001), p. 211.

2   Beeler, J., *British Naval Policy in the Gladstone–Disraeli Era*, Stanford (1997), pp. 125–9.

3   Beeler, J., *The Birth of the Battleship*, London (2001), p. 211.

4   Parkes, O., *British Battleships*, London (1957), p. 191.

5   'Report of the Committee on Designs of Ships of War', *Parliamentary Papers*, hereafter referenced as the '1872 Committee', London (1872), p. vii.

6   Sandler, S., *The Emergence of the Modern Capital Ship*, London (1979), p. 246.

7   'Report of the 1872 Committee on Designs', op. cit., pp. vii–xix.

8   'Report of the 1872 Committee on Designs', ibid., p. xix.

9   Sandler, S., op. cit., p. 247.

10 Beeler, J., op. cit., p. 215.

11 Gardiner, R., *Steam, Steel, and Shellfire*, London (1992), p. 83.

12 Parkes, O., *British Battleships*, London (1957), p. 230.

13 Rodger, N.A.M., *The Mariners Mirror, vol. 62, no. 1*, 'The Dark Ages of the Admiralty', London (1976), p. 33.

14 Rodger, N.A.M., ibid., pp. 34–6.

15 Rodger, N.A.M., ibid., pp. 37–41.

16 Rodger, N.A.M., ibid., p. 43.

17 Parkes, O., op. cit., p. 204.

18 Barnaby, N., 'On Ships of War', *Transactions of the Institution of Naval Architects vol. 17*, London (1876), p. 2.

19 Brown, D.K., *Warrior to Dreadnought*, London (1997), p. 68.

20 Ballard, G.A., *The Black Battle Fleet*, London (1980), pp. 234–5.

21 Gardiner, R., Editor, *All the World's Fighting Ships 1860–1905*, London (1979), p. 17.

22 Parkes, O., op. cit., pp. 216–17.

23 Gardiner, R., Editor, op. cit., p. 18.

24 Parkes, O., op. cit., p. 230.

25 Parkes, O., ibid., p. 230.

26 Rodger, N.A.M., op. cit., p. 45.

27 Gardiner, R., op. cit., p. 26.

28 Hovgaard, W., *Modern History of Warships*, London, (1920), p. 62.

29 White, W.H., *Manual of Naval Architecture*, London, (1882), pp. 426–7.

30 Parkes, O., op. cit., p. 316.

31 Parkes, O., ibid., p. 331.

32 Brown, D.K., op. cit., p. 100.
33 Reed, E.J. and Simpson, E., *Modern Ships of War*, New York, (1882), pp. 75–6.
34 Colomb, P.H., Letter, *The Times Newspaper*, London (22 March 1889).
35 Gardiner, R., Editor, *Steam, Steel, and Shellfire*, London (1992), p. 95.
36 Parkes, O., op. cit., p. 230.
37 Gardiner, R., Editor, op. cit., p. 95.

CHAPTER 6 – THE PRE-DREADNOUGHT EMERGES

1   Padfield, P., *The Battleship Era*, London (1972), p. 12.
2   Parkes, O., *British Battleships*, London (1957), p. 340.
3   Parkes, O., ibid., p. 340.
4   Brown, D.K., *Warrior to Dreadnought*, London (1997), p. 123.
5   Quoted in Manning, F., *The Life of Sir William White*, London (1923), p. 188.
6   Quoted in Manning, F., ibid., p. 188.
7   Manning, F., *The Life of Sir William White*, London (1923), p. 189.
8   Manning, F., ibid., p. 190.
9   Brown, D. K., *A Century of Naval Construction*, London (1983), pp. 62–3.
10 Manning, F., op. cit., p. 195.
11 Manning, F., ibid., p. 204.
12 Brown, D.K., *Warrior to Dreadnought*, London (1997), pp. 123–4.
13 Sumida, J.T., *In Defence of Naval Supremacy*, London (1989), p. 13.
14 Parkes, O., op. cit., p. 352.
15 Sumida, J.T., op. cit., p. 11.
16 Brown, D.K., *Warrior to Dreadnought*, London (1997), pp. 124–5.
17 White, W.H., Presidential Address, *Minutes of the Proceedings of the Institution of Civil Engineers*, volume CLV, London (1904), pp. 151–2.
18 Gardiner, R., Editor, *Steam, Steel, and Shellfire*, London (1992). p. 112.
19 White, W.H., 'On the Designs for the New Battleships', *Transactions of the Institution of Naval Architects*, London (1889), p. 150.
20 Manning, F., op. cit., p. 262.
21 Parkes, O., op. cit., p. 356.
22 Attwood, E.L., *Warships*, London (1908), pp. 148–9.
23 Eardley-Wilmot, S., *Our Fleet Today*, London (1900), pp. 116–7.
24 Gardiner, R. Editor, *All the World's Fighting Ships 1860–1905*, London (1079), p. 32.
25 Jane, F.T., *The British Battle Fleet, vol. 1*, London (1914), pp. 64–7.
26 Rippon, P.M., *Evolution of Engineering in the Royal Navy, vol. 1*, Tunbridge Wells (1988), p. 51.
27 Jane, F.T., op. cit., p. 68.
28 Sumida, J.T., *In Defence of Naval Supremacy*, London (1989), p. 16.
29 Manning, F., op. cit., p. 314.
30 Watts, P., 'Warship Building 1860–1910', *Transactions of the Institution of Naval Architects, Part 2*, London (1911), p. 302.
31 Hovgaard, W., *Modern History of Warships*, London (1920), p. 410.
32 Gardiner, R., op. cit., p. 34.
33 Jane, F.T., op. cit., p. 88.
34 Parkes, O., op. cit., pp. 181–2.

CHAPTER 7 – THE GREAT ARMS RACE

1   Marder, A.J., *The Anatomy of British Sea Power*, London (1940), pp. 238–9.
2   Marder, A.J., ibid., pp. 236–7.

3   Manning, F., *The Life of Sir William White*, London (1923), p. 345.

4   Atwood, E.L., *Warships: A Text Book*, London (1908), pp. 259–64.

5   Atwood, E.L., ibid., pp. 134–5.

6   Jane, F.T., *The British Battle Fleet, vol. 1*, London (1914), p. 99.

7   Jane, F.T., ibid., p. 98.

8   Brassey, T.A., Editor, *The Naval Annual*, Portsmouth (1898), p. 18.

9   Marder, A.J., op. cit., p. 282.

10 Custance, R., quoted in Marder, A.J., ibid., p. 351.

11 Kennedy, P.M., *The Rise and Fall of British Naval Mastery*, New York (1976), pp. 208–9.

12 Marder, A.J., op. cit., p. 351.

13 Brassey, T.A., Editor, op. cit., pp. 235–7.

14 Brassey, T.A., Editor, ibid., pp. 64–5.

15 Jane, F.T., op. cit., pp. 100–01.

16 Narbeth, J.H., 'Three Steps in Naval Construction', *Transactions of the Institution of Naval Architects*, London (1922), p. 28.

17 Parkes, O., *British Battleships*, London (1957), pp. 404–5.

18 Narbeth, J.H., op. cit., pp. 28–9.

19 Parkes, O., op. cit., p. 409.

20 Narbeth, J.A., op. cit., p. 30.

21 Brown, D.K., *Warrior to Dreadnought*, London (1997), p. 146.

22 Narbeth, J.A., op. cit., p. 31.

23 Jane, F.T., op. cit., pp. 108–9.

24 Narbeth, J.A., op. cit., p. 33.

25 Manning, F., op. cit., p. 428.

CHAPTER 8 – FORTRESSES OF STEEL

1   Atwood, E.L., *War Ships*, London (1908), p. 142.

2   White, W.H., 'The Principles and Methods of Armour Protection in Modern War Ships', *The Naval Annual*, Portsmouth (1904), pp. 108–9.

3   Manning, F., *The Life of Sir William White*, London (1923), pp. 49–50.

4   Barnaby, N., 'The Protection of Buoyancy and Stability in Ships', *Transactions of the Institution of Naval Architects*, London (1889), pp. 225–7.

5   Ellis, C.E., 'Armour for Ships 1860–1910', *Transactions of the Institution of Naval Architects, Part 2*, London (1911), p. 340.

6   Ellis, C.E., ibid., p. 341.

7   Hovgaard, W., *Modern History of Warships*, London (1920), p. 459.

8   Ellis, C.E., 'Recent Experiments in Armour', *Transactions of the Institution of Naval Architects*, London (1894), pp. 215–18.

9   Atwood, E.L., op. cit., p. 147.

10 Ellis, C.E., 'Armour for Ships 1860–1910', *Transactions of the Institution of Naval Architects, Part 2*, London (1911), p. 342.

11 Ellis, C.E., ibid., p. 342.

12 Hovgaard, W., op. cit., pp. 464–5.

13 Roberts, J., 'The Pre-Dreadnought Age 1890–1905', in Gardiner, R., Editor, *Steam, Steel, and Shellfire*, London (1992), p. 113.

14 Ellis, C.E., 'Recent Experiments in Armour', *Transactions of the Institution of Naval Architects*, London (1894), p. 222.

15 Ellis C.E., 'Armour for Ships 1866–1910', *Transactions of the Institution of Naval Architects, Part 2*, London (1911) p. 343.

16 Roberts, J., op. cit., p. 113.

17 Ellis, C.E., op. cit., p. 347.

18 Ellis, C.E., 'Recent Experiments in Armour', *Transactions of the Institution of Naval Architects*, London (1894), pp. 222–3.

19 Hovgaard, W., op. cit., p. 467.

20 Brown, D.K., *Warrior to Dreadnought*, London (1997), p. 151.

21 Hovgaard, W., op. cit., p. 468.

22 Brassey, T.A., Editor, 'Armour and Ordnance', *The Naval Annual*, London (1905), p. 338.

23 Hovgaard, W., op. cit., p. 468.

24 Brodie, B., *Sea Power in the Machine Age*, Princetown (1943), p. 213

CHAPTER 9 – THUNDER OF THE GUNS

1 Brodie, B., *Sea Power in the Machine Age*, Princetown (1943), pp. 212–13

2 Orde-Brown, C., 'The Attack of Ships By Artillery Fire', *Brassey's Naval Annual*, Portsmouth (1897), pp. 109–10.

3 Noble, A., 'Notes on Progress in Naval Artillery: 1860–1910', *Transactions of the Institution of Naval Architects, Part 2*, London (1911), pp. 279–80.

4 Hogg, I., and Batchelor, J., *Naval Gun*, Poole (1978), pp. 21–4.

5 Garbett, H., *Naval Gunnery*, London (1897), p. 31.

6 Garbett, H., ibid., p. 47.

7 Noble, A., 'The Rise and Progress of Rifled Naval Artillery', *Transactions of the Institution of Naval Architects*, London (1899), p. 236.

8 Clowes, W.L., *The Royal Navy: A History from the Earliest Times to 1900, vol. 7*, London (1903), pp. 43–5.

9 Hovgaard, W., *Modern History of Warships*, London (1920), p. 388.

10 Ropp, T., *The Development of a Modern Navy, French Naval Policy 1871–1904*, Annapolis (1987), pp. 94–5.

11 Ropp, T., ibid., p. 389.

12 Garbett H., op. cit., p. 79.

13 Garbett, H., ibid., p. 53.

14 Garbett, H., ibid., p. 57.

15 Noble, A., op. cit., p. 237.

16 Robertson, F.L., *The Evolution of Naval Armament*, London (1968), p. 208.

17 Hovgaard, W., op. cit., p. 390.

18 Hovgaard, W., ibid., p. 391.

19 Campbell, N.J.M., 'British Naval Armaments, Royal Armouries Conference Proceedings One', *The Development of Naval Guns 1850–1900*, London (1989), pp. 68–9.

20 Hovgaard, W., op. cit., pp. 391–2.

21 Garbett, H., op. cit., pp. 109–110.

22 Armstrong, W., and Vavasseur, J., 'The Application of Hydraulic Power to Naval Gunnery', *Transactions of the Institution of Naval Architects*, London (1888), p. 8.

23 Armstrong, W., and Vavasseur, J., ibid., p. 9.

24 Hovgaard, W., op. cit., pp. 401–16.

25 Hogg, J., and Batchelor, J., op. cit., p. 92.

26 Hodges, P., *The Big Gun, Battleship Main Armament 1860–1945*, London (1981), p. 18.

27 Armstrong, W., and Vavasseur, J., op. cit., p. 10.

28 Padfield, P., *Guns at Sea*, London (1973), pp. 197–201.

29 Lautenshlager, K., 'A Majestic Revolution', *Warship no. 25*, London (1983), p. 98.

30 Grenfell, H., 'The Development of Modern Weapons Considered in Relation to the Design of Warships', *Transactions of the Institution of Naval Architects*, London (1888), pp. 182–3.

31 Armstrong, W., and Vavasseur, J., op. cit., pp. 10–11.

32 Armstrong, W., and Vavasseur, J., ibid., pp. 11–14.

33 Gardiner, R., Editor, *Steam, Steel, and Shellfire*, London (1992), p. 163.

34 Grenfell, H., op. cit., p. 181.

35 Noble, A., op. cit., pp. 421–2.

36 Hovgaard, W., op. cit., p. 423.

37 White, W., Presidential Address, *Minutes of the Proceedings of the Institution of Civil Engineers, vol. CLV*, London (1904), p. 148.

38 White, W., ibid., p. 148.

CHAPTER 10 – TO PIERCE THE ARMOURED WALLS

1   Gardiner, R., Editor, 'Naval Armaments and Armour', *Steam, Steel, and Shellfire*, London (1992), p. 158.

2   Garbett, H., *Naval Gunnery*, London (1897), p. 219.

3   Garbett, H., ibid., pp. 219–221.

4   Brown, D.K., *Warrior to Dreadnought*, London (1997), p. 78.

5   Noble, A., 'The Rise and Progress of Rifled Naval Artillery', *Transactions of the Institution of Naval Architects*, London (1899), p. 237.

6   Dawson, A.T., *The Engineering of Ordnance*, London (1909), p. 14.

7   Dawson, A.T., ibid., p. 15.

8   Tressidder, T.J., 'Modern Armour and its Attack', *Transactions of the Institution of Naval Architects*, London (1908), pp. 28–9.

9   Padfield, P., *Guns at Sea*, London (1973), p. 201.

10 Padfield, P., ibid., p. 201.

11 Brassey, T.A., Editor, Ordnance, *The Naval Annual*, London (1887), p. 445.

12 Hovgaard, W., *Modern History of Warships*, London (1920), p. 436.

13 Eardley-Wilmot, S., *Our Fleet Today*, London (1900), pp. 197–8.

14 Barnaby, N., *Naval Development of the Century*, London (1904), pp. 164–5.

15 Robinson, C., *The British Fleet*, London (1894), p. 281.

16 Clowes, W.L., *The Royal Navy, Volume 7*, London (1903), pp. 60–6

17 Richards, F., minute February 11th 1897, quoted in Cowpe, A., The Royal Navy and the Whitehead Torpedo, in Ranft, B., Editor, *Technical Change and British Naval Policy, 1860–1939*, London (1977), p. 23.

18 Torpedo Committee notes, quoted in Cowpe, A., ibid., pp. 24–5.

CHAPTER 11 – OF BOILERS, ENGINES, AND STEAM

1   Fox, W.J., and McBirnie, S.C., *Marine Steam Engines and Turbines*, London (1952), p. 56.

2   Sennett, R., and Oram, H.J., *The Marine Steam Engine*, London (1898), pp. 1–2.

3   Evers, H., *Steam and the Steam Engine*, Plymouth (1872), p. 78.

4   Sennett, R., and Oram, H.J., op. cit., p. 3.

5   Evers, H., op. cit., pp. 79–80.

6   Murray, R., *Elementary Treatise on The Marine Engine*, London (1858), pp. 36–8.

7   Tompkins, A.E., *Marine Engineering*, London (1896), p. 75.

8   Sennett, R., and Oram, H.J., op. cit., p. 4.

9   Murray, R., op. cit., p. 143.

10 Sennett, R., and Oram, H.J., op. cit., p. 6.

11 Sennett, R., and Oram, H.J., ibid., p. 7.

12 Murray, R., op. cit., pp. 14–15.

13 Oram, H.J., 'Fifty Years Changes in British Warship Machinery', *Transactions of the Institution of Naval Architects*, London (1911), p. 100.

14 Tompkins, A.E., op. cit., p. 9.
15 Tompkins, A.E. ibid., p. 74.
16 Sennett, R. and Oram, H.J., op. cit., pp. 100–2.
17 Sennett, R. and Oram, H.J., ibid., p. 17.
18 Smith, E.C., *A Short History of Marine Engineering*, Cambridge (1937), p. 198.
19 Smith, E.C., ibid., pp. 198–201.
20 Hovgaard, W., *Modern History of Warships*, London (1920), p. 369.
21 Hill, S., 'Battle of the Boilers', *Journal of Naval Engineering no. 3*, London (1955), p. 351.
22 Hill, S., ibid., p. 352.
23 Hill, S., ibid., p. 353.
24 *Report of the 1902 Committee on Modern Types of Boilers for Naval Purposes*, London (1902), p. 6.
25 *Report of the 1902 Committee*, ibid., p. 6.
26 Domvile, C., letter to Admiralty, quoted in Hill, S., op. cit., p. 353.
27 Hill, S., ibid., pp. 350–60.

CHAPTER 12 – TESTED IN BATTLE

1 Tucker, S.C., *Handbook of 19th Century Naval Warfare*, Stroud (2000), p. 238.
2 Eardley-Wilmot, S., *Our Fleet Today*, London (1900), p. 94.
3 Custance, R., *The Ship of the Line in Battle*, London (1912), pp. 47–9.
4 Eardley-Wilmot, S., op. cit., pp. 96–8.
5 Sondhaus, L., *Naval Warfare 1815–1914*, London (2001), pp. 95–6.
6 Sondhaus, L. ibid., p. 96.
7 Hovgaard, W. *Modern History of Warships*, London (1920), p. 15.
8 Reed, E.J., *Our Ironclad Ships*, London (1869), pp. 258 and 273.
9 Custance, R., op. cit., p. 76.
10 Brown, D.K., *Warrior to Dreadnought*, London (1997), p. 167.
11 Gardiner, R., *All the World's Fighting Ships 1860–1905*, London (1979), p. 395.
12 Gardiner, R., ibid., pp. 223–7.
13 Eardley-Wilmot, S., op. cit., pp. 282–3.
14 Sondhaus, L., op. cit., p. 171.
15 Wilson, H.W., *Ironclads in Action*, London (1896), pp. 88–92.
16 Wilson, H.W., ibid., pp. 92–3.
17 Wright, R.N.J., *The Chinese Steam Navy 1862–1945*, London (2000), pp. 95–6 and 105.
18 Eardley-Wilmot, op. cit., p. 286.
19 Sondhaus, L., op. cit., p. 172.
20 Fairbanks, C.H., *The Origins of the Dreadnought Revolution, International History Review 13*, London (1991), p. 35. Quoted in Sondhaus, L., p. 172.
21 Sondhaus, L., op. cit., p. 188.
22 Jukes, G., *The Russo-Japanese War 1904–1905*, Oxford (2002), pp. 25–6.
23 Brassey, T.A., Editor, *The Russo-Japanese Naval campaign of 1904, Naval Annual*, London (1905), pp. 133–7.
24 Brassey, T.A., ibid., p. 140.
25 Sondhaus, L., op. cit., pp. 189–90.
26 Brassey, T.A., op. cit., p. 166.
27 Brassey, T.A., ibid.
28 Jukes, G., op. cit., p. 71.
29 Jukes, G., ibid., p. 73.
30 Watts, A.J., *The Imperial Russian Navy*, London (1990), p. 55.
31 Sondhaus, L., op. cit., pp. 191–2.
32 Mitchell, D.W., *A History of Russian and Soviet Sea Power*, London (1974), p. 265.

33 Watts, A.J., op. cit., p. 23.

34 Corbett, J.S., *Maritime Operations in the Russo-Japanese War 1904–1905, vol. 2*, London (1915), pp. 443–6.

35 White, R.D., 'With the Baltic Fleet at Tsushima', *Proceedings of the U.S. Naval Institute*, Annapolis (1907), p. 616.

36 Brown, D.K., *Warrior to Dreadnought*, London (1997), p. 171.

37 Hovgaard, W., op. cit., p. 126.

38 Semenoff, V., *The Battle of Tsushima*, London (1906), pp. 56–7.

39 Brown, D.K., op. cit., p. 171.

40 Novikoff-Priboy, A., *Tsushima*, London (1936), p. 172.

41 Brown, D.K., *The Russo-Japanese War, Warship 1996*, London (1996), p.76.

42 Brown, D.K., *Warrior to Dreadnought*, London (1997), p. 171.

43 Brown, D.K., *The Russo-Japanese War, Warship 1996*, London (1996), p. 76.

44 Sondhaus, L., op. cit., p. 192.

CHAPTER 13 – THE COMING OF THE DREADNOUGHT

1   Hovgaard, W., *Modern History of Warships*, London (1920), pp. 136–7.

2   Watts, P., 'Warship Building 1860–1910', *Institution of Naval Architects Part 2*, London (1911), p. 307.

3   Hough, R., *Dreadnought*, London (1965), pp. 17–18.

4   Marder, A.J., *The Anatomy of British Sea Power*, London (1940), pp. 516–17.

5   Parkes, O., *British Battleships*, London (1957), p. 466.

6   Hough, R., op. cit., p. 18.

7   Hovgaard, W., op. cit., p. 139.

8   Watts, P., op. cit., p. 308.

9   Narbeth, J.H., 'Three Steps in Naval Construction', *Institution of Naval Architects*, London (1922), p. 41.

10 Brown, D.K., *A Century of Naval Construction*, London (1983), p. 86.

11 Fox, W.J., McBirnie, and Milton, J.H., *Newnes Marine Engineering vol. 1*, London (1954), p. 249.

12 Narbeth, J.H., op. cit., p. 40.

13 Richards, F., quoted in Marder, A.J., *From the Dreadnought to Scapa Flow, vol. 1, 1904–1914*, London (1961), p. 56.

14 Marder, A.J., *From the Dreadnought to Scapa Flow, vol. 1, 1904–1914*, London (1961), pp. 56–7.

15 Gardiner, R., (ed.), *All the World's Fighting Ships 1906–1921*, London (1985), pp. 22–3.

16 Fisher Papers, volume 1, p. 41. Quoted in Sumida, J.T., *In Defence of Naval Supremacy*, London (1989), p. 52.

17 Hough, R., op. cit., pp. 83–4.

18 Hough, R., ibid., p. 85.

19 Hough, R., ibid., p. 81.

20 Gardiner, R., Editor, op. cit., pp. 23–6.

21 Ropp, T., *The Development of a Modern Navy*, Annapolis (1987), p. 358.

22 Gardiner, R., Editor, op. cit., p. 28.

23 Marder, A.J., op. cit., pp. 204–5.

24 Hough, R., op. cit., p. 124.

BIBLIOGRAPHY

PRIMARY SOURCES

BOOKS

Attwood, E.L., *Warships*, London: Longmans & Co. (1908)
Barnaby, N., *Naval Developments of the Century*, London (1904)
Bourne, J., *A Treatise on the Screw Propeller: With Various Suggestions of Improvement*, London (1852)
——, *A Catechism of the Steam Engine*, London: Longmans & Co. (1861)
Brassey, T.A., *The British Navy, Part I*, London: Longmans & Co. (1882)
——, *The Naval Annual*, J. Griffin & Co. Portsmouth (1887, 1898, 1904 & 1907 edns)
Busk, H., *The Navies of the World – Their Present State and Power*, London (1859)
Clowes, W.L., *The Royal Navy: A History from the Earliest Times to 1900*, vol. 7, London (1903)
Corbett, J.S., *Maritime Operations in the Russo-Japanese War*, vol. 2, London (1915)
Custance, R., *The Ship of the Line in Battle*, London (1912)
Dawson, A.T., *The Engineering of Ordnance*, London: Percival Marshall & Co. (1909)
Douglas, H., *Naval Gunnery*, London (1855)
Eardley-Wilmot, S., *Our Fleet Today*, London (1900).
Evers, H., *Steam and the Steam-Engine*, Collins' Advanced Series, London (1872)
Fincham, J., *A History of Naval Architecture*, London (1851)
Garbett, H., *Naval Gunnery*, London: S.R. Publishers Ltd (1897)
Murray, R., *Rudimentary Treatise on the Marine Engine*, London: John Weale (1858)
Peake, J.P., *Rudiments of Naval Architecture*, London (1884)
Reed, E.J., *Our Iron-Clad Ships*, London: John Murray (1869)
Reed, E.J. and Simpson, E., *Modern Ships of War*, New York: D.N. Goodchild (2002)
Robinson, C., *The British Fleet*, London (1894)
Semenoff, V., *The Battle of Tsushima*, London (1906)
Sennett, R. and Oram, H.J., *The Marine Steam Engine*, London: Longmans & Co. (1898)
Tompkins, A.E., *Marine Engineering*, London: MacMillan & Co. (1921)
White, W.H., *Manual of Naval Architecture*, London (1897)
Wilson, H.W., *Ironclads in Action*, Vol. I, London (1896)

JOURNALS, ARTICLES, LETTERS & REPORTS

Armstrong, W. and Vavasseur, J., 'The Application of Hydraulic Power to Naval Gunnery' in *Transactions of the Institution of Naval Architects*, London (1888, 1899)
Barnaby, N., 'On Ships of War' in *Transactions of the Institution of Naval Architects*, London (1876)
——, 'The Protection of Buoyancy and Stability in Ships' in *Transactions of the Institution of Naval Architects*, London (1889)
Brassey, T.A. (ed.), 'Ordnance' in *The Naval Annual*, London (1887)
—— (ed.), 'Armour and Ordnance' in *The Naval Annual*, London (1904)

—— (ed.), 'The Russo-Japanese Naval Campaign of 1904' in *The Naval Annual*, London (1904)

Colomb, P.H., Letter to *The Times* newspaper, London, 22 March 1889

Domvile, C., *Report of the 1902 Committee on Modern Types of Boilers for Naval Purposes*, London (1902)

Ellis, C.E., 'Recent Experiments in Armour' in *Transactions of the Institution of Naval Architects*, London (1894)

——, 'Armour for Ships 1860–1910' in *Transactions of the Institution of Naval Architects*, London (1911)

Fuller, H.J., 'From Wood to Iron' in *Portsmouth Record Series, Portsmouth Dockyard Papers 1852–1869*, Portsmouth (1869)

Grenfell, H., 'The Development of Modern Weapons Considered in Relation to the Design of Warships' in *Transactions of the Institution of Naval Architects*, London (1888)

Jaques, W.H., 'The Detachable Ram or the Submarine Gun as a Substitute for the Ram' in *Transactions of the Institution of Naval Architects*, London (1894)

Narbeth, J.H., 'Three Steps in Naval Construction' in *Transactions of the Institution of Naval Architects*, London (1922)

Noble, A., 'The Rise and Progress of Rifled Naval Artillery' in *Transactions of the Institution of Naval Architects*, London (1899)

——, 'Notes on Progress in Naval Artillery 1860–1910' in *Transactions of the Institution of Naval Architects*, London (1911)

Oram, H.J., 'Fifty Years' Changes in British Warships Machinery' in *Transactions of the Institution of Naval Architects*, London (1911)

Orde-Brown, C., 'The Attack of Ships by Artillery Fire' in *The Naval Annual*, Portsmouth (1897)

Parliamentary Papers, Report of the Committee on Designs of Ships of War, London (1872)

Robinson, S., Letter to the Admiralty, March 1868, PRO ADM12/818/91.1

Tressidder, T.J., 'Modern Armour and its Attack' in *Transactions of the Institution of Naval Architects*, London (1908)

Watts, P., 'Warship Building 1860–1910' in *Transactions of the Institution of Naval Architects*, London (1911)

White, R.D., 'With the Baltic Fleet at Tsushima' in *Proceedings of the U.S. Naval Institute*, Annapolis (1907)

White, W.H., 'On the Designs for the New Battleships' in *Transactions of the Institution of Naval Architects*, London (1989)

——, 'Warship Building 1863–1870' in *Proceedings of the Institution of Civil Engineers*, London (1904)

——, Presidential Address, *Minutes of the Proceedings of the Institution of Civil Engineers*, Vol. CLV, London (1904)

——, 'The Principles and Methods of Armour Protection in Modern Warships' in *The Naval Annual*, Portsmouth (1904)

SECONDARY SOURCES & FURTHER READING

BOOKS

Albion, R.G., *Forests and Sea Power*, Harvard (1926)

Ballard, G.A., *The Black Battlefleet*, London (1980)

Baxter, J.P., *The Introduction of the Ironclad Warship*, Cambridge (1933)

Beeler, J.F., *British Naval Policy in the Gladstone–Disraeli Era 1866–1880*, Stanford (1997)

——, *The Birth of the Battleship*, London (2001)

Brodie, B., *Sea Power in the Machine Age*, Princetown (1943)

Brown, D.K., *A Century of Naval Construction – The History of the Royal Corps of Naval Constructors*, London (1983)

——, *Before the Ironclad – Development of Ship Design, Propulsion, and Armament in the Royal Navy 1815–1860*, London (1990)

——, *Paddle Warships – The Earliest Steam Powered Fighting Ships 1815–1850*, London (1993)

——, *Warrior to Dreadnought – Warship Development 1860–1905*, London (1997)

Dodds, J. and Moore, J., *Building the Wooden Fighting Ship*, London (1984)

Evans, D., *Building the Steam Navy – Dockyard Technology and the Creation of the Victorian Battle Fleet 1830–1906*, London (2004)

Fletcher, I. and Ishchenko, N., *The Crimean War – A Clash of Empires*, Staplehurst (2004)

Fox, W.J. and McBirnie, S.C., *Marine Steam Engines and Turbines*, London (1952)

Fox, W.J., McBirnie, S.C. and Milton, J.H., *Newnes Marine Engineering*, Vol. I, London: George Newnes Ltd (1954)

Gardener, R. (ed.), *All the World's Fighting Ships 1860–1905*, London (1979)

——, *Steam, Steel, and Shellfire, the Steam Warship 1815–1905*, London (1992)

Graham, G.S., *The Politics of Naval Supremacy*, Cambridge (1965)

Hawkey, A., *H.M.S. Captain*, London (1963)

Hodges, P., *The Big Gun: Battleship Main Armament 1860–1945*, London (1981)

Hogg, I. and Batchelor, J., *Naval Gun*, Poole (1978)

Hough, R., *Dreadnought*, London (1965)

Hovgaard, W., *Modern History of Warships*, London: Conway Maritime Press (1971)

Humble, R., *Before the Dreadnoughts*, London (1976)

Jane, F.T., *The British Battlefleet*, Vol. I, London (1915)

Jukes, G., *The Russo-Japanese War 1904–1905*, Oxford (2002)

Kennedy, P.M., *The Rise and Fall of British Naval Mastery*, New York (1976)

Lambert, A., *Battleships in Transition – The Creation of the Steam Battlefleet 1815–1860*, London (1984)

——, '*Warrior': Restoring the World's First Ironclad*, London (1987)

Lavery, B., *Nelson's Navy – The Ships, Men, and Organisation 1793–1815*, London (1989)

Manning, F., *The Life of Sir William White*, London (1923)

Marder, A.J., *The Anatomy of British Sea Power*, London (1940)

——, *From the Dreadnought to Scapa Flow*, Vol. I, *1904–1914*, London (1961)

Mitchell, D.W., *A History of Russian and Soviet Sea Power*, London (1974)

Novikoff-Priboy, A., *Tsushima*, London (1936)

Padfield, P., *The Battleship Era*, London (1972)

——, *Guns at Sea*, London (1973)

Parkes, O., *British Battleships – A History of Design, Construction and Armaments*, London (1957)

Rippon, P.M., *Evolution of Engineering in the Royal Navy*, Vol. I, Tunbridge Wells (1988)

Ranft, B. (ed.), *Technical Change and British Naval Policy 1860–1939*, London (1937)

Robertson, F.L., *The Evolution of Naval Armament*, London (1968)

Rodger, N.A.M., *The Command of the Ocean – A Naval History of Britain 1649–1815*, London (1984)

Ropp, T., *The Development of a Modern Navy – French Naval Policy 1871–1904*, Annapolis (1987)

Roskill, S.W., *The Strategy of Sea Power*, Aylesbury (1986)

Sandler, S., *The Emergence of the Modern Capital Ship*, London (1937)

Smith, E.C., *A Short History of Naval and Marine Engineering*, Cambridge University Press (1937)

Sondhaus, I., *Naval Warfare, 1815–1914*, London (2001)

Sumida, J.T., *In Defence of Naval Supremacy*, London (1989)

Tucker, S.C., *Handbook of Nineteenth Century Naval Warfare*, Stroud (2000)

Watts, A.J., *The Royal Navy – An Illustrated History*, London (1974)

——, *The Imperial Russian Navy*, London (1990)

Watts, A.J. and Gordon, B.G., *The Imperial Japanese Navy*, London (1971)

Wright, R.N.J., *The Chinese Steam Navy 1862–1945*, London (2000)

JOURNALS, ARTICLES & REPORTS

Berry, R.W., 'Technical Change and the Development of the Pre-Dreadnought Battleship', unpublished MA dissertation, University of Exeter (2002)

Brown, D.K., 'Structural Improvements in Wooden Ships Instigated by Sir Robert Seppings' in *The Naval Architect*, London (1979)

——, 'The Russo-Japanese War' in *Warship*, London (1996)

Brown, D.K. and Pugh, P., 'Ramming' in *Warship*, London (1990)

Campbell, N.J.M., 'The Development of Naval Guns 1850–1900' in *British Naval Armaments, Royal Armouries Conference Proceedings One*, London (1989)

Fairbanks, C.H., 'The Origins of the Dreadnought Revolution' in *International History Review 13*, London (1991)

Hill, S., 'Battle of the Boilers' in *Journal of Naval Engineering*, no, 3, London (1955)

Rodger, N.A.M., 'The Dark Ages of the Admiralty' in *The Mariner's Mirror*, vol. 62, no. 1, London (1976)

Lautenshlager, K., 'A Majestic Revolution' in *Warship*, no. 25, London (1983)

Smith, E.C., 'The Centenary of Naval Engineering' in *Transactions of the Institution of Marine Engineers*, London (1922)

INDEX